IMAGES
*of Rail*

# BUFFALO RAILROADS

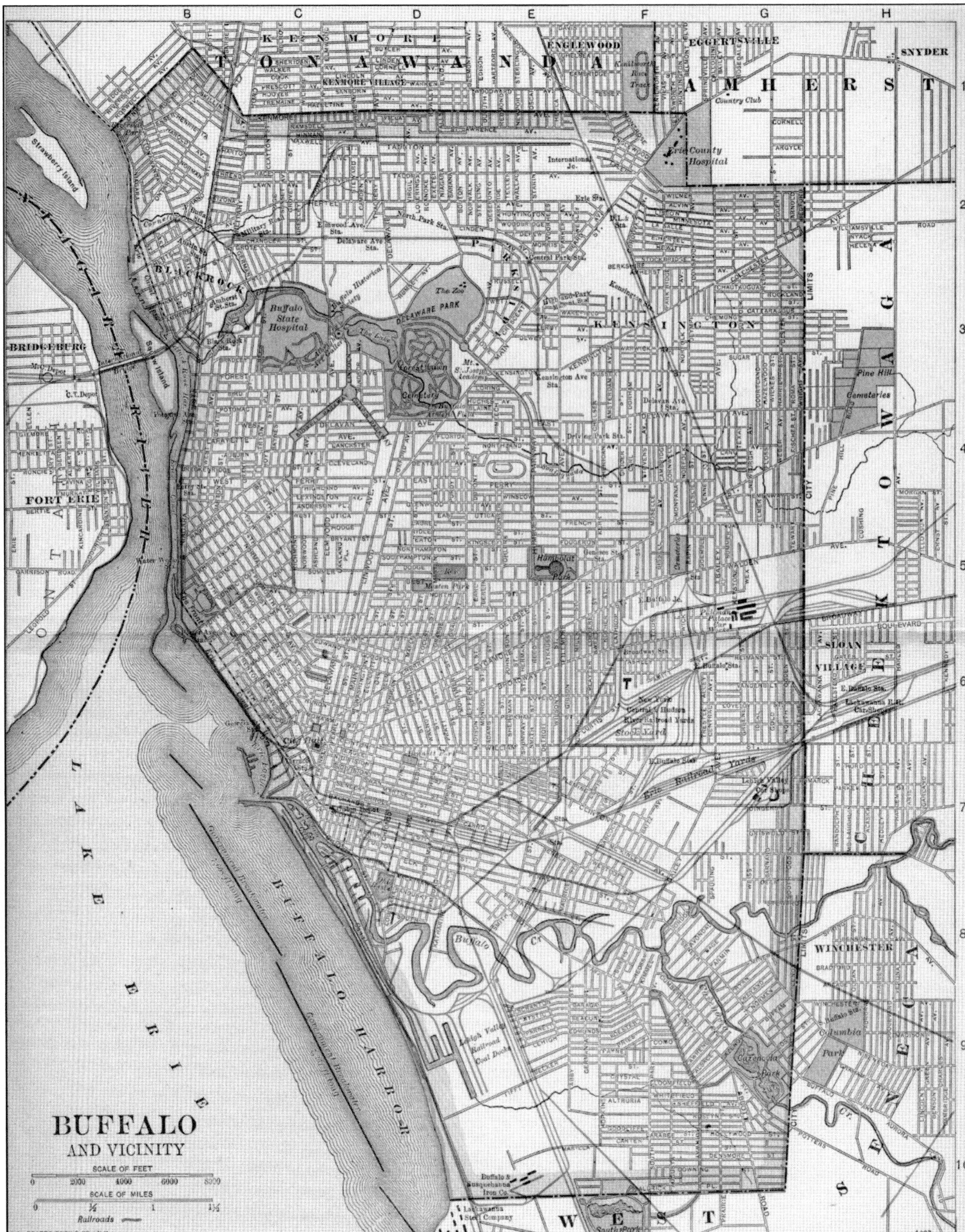


In this 1907 map, Buffalo was a proud and growing city. European immigrants were finding work in the many mills and factories. Meanwhile, Buffalo was the first American city to have electricity available for most residents. Life was improving for many and with the improvements came the vast railroad lines intertwining the city. These ribbons of steel provided dependable transportation and good jobs for many Buffalo residents. (Stephen G. Myers collection.)

**On the Cover:** A New York Central freight train makes its way past the Buffalo City Hall. (Lower Lakes Marine Historical Society.)

IMAGES
*of Rail*

# BUFFALO RAILROADS

Stephen G. Myers
and Michael J. Connor

ARCADIA
PUBLISHING

ISBN 978-0-7385-7371-7

Published by Arcadia Publishing
Charleston, South Carolina

Printed in the United States of America

Library of Congress Control Number: 2010925883

For all general information, please contact Arcadia Publishing:
Telephone 843-853-2070
Fax 843-853-0044
E-mail sales@arcadiapublishing.com
For customer service and orders:
Toll-Free 1-888-313-2665

Visit us on the Internet at www.arcadiapublishing.com

*This book is dedicated to Clifton Sipley, Patsy Delory, and Eldo Butera, three fine men who took an interest in a boy without a dad.*

# Contents

# ACKNOWLEDGMENTS

We would like to thank Marty Phelps of the Medina Railroad Museum, village of Depew historian Arthur J. Domino, Mike Malyak of the Steel Plant Museum, the Iron Island Museum, the Central Terminal Restoration Corporation, the Lower Lakes Marine Historical Society, the Western New York Railway Historical Society, Erie Lackawanna Historical Society, New York Central System Historical Society, Western New York Heritage Press, John C. Dahl, Ron Dukarm, Steve Koenig, Phil Soyring, Patrick Connors, Dave Eagen, Roy O. Davis, Paul Hoffman, Paul Pietrak, Jane Schyver, Joseph Schveder, Jeremy Taylor, James A. Van Brocklin, Robert I. Warrick, the late William C. Kessel, and Gino DiCarlo for their time, knowledge, and photographs. We would also like to thank Margaret Stiffler Dick for an encyclopedic knowledge and photographs of Buffalo's urban landscape. I would also like to thank my wife, Marianne, and my loving children, Stephen, Leslie, and Joshua, for all of their time sitting in a car at a train yard through the years. To all of the above we owe what success and interest this book generates.

# INTRODUCTION

When most people hear the name of Buffalo, they think of long, cold winters and snow—lots of snow—but the history of Buffalo in the building of our nation has so much more to tell than just a look at one of the four seasons. Buffalo, the second largest city in the great state of New York, is known as the Queen City, second only to New York City. Buffalo was a natural location for a city, being at the west end of the state of New York, at the international border with Canada, and on the banks of Lake Erie with waterway shipping access to four of the Great Lakes. Lake Erie and surrounding rivers and streams could provide plenty of fresh water for drinking, farming, and industry. Buffalo also had the advantage of the Niagara River and nearby Niagara Falls as a vast source of inexpensive electricity. With the arrival of the Erie Canal in 1825, Buffalo became a transportation and industrial hub with the incoming midwestern grain and northern lumber being transferred from Great Lakes ships to canal boats.

The year 1832 brought a new idea for transportation with the incorporation of the Buffalo and Erie Railroad. While no one dreamed that such an idea could ever compete with the ships of the Great Lakes, or the pack boats of the Erie Canal, the railway industry had begun in the Buffalo region. With the opening of the Erie Canal, Buffalo became home to the largest grain milling in the United States; Joseph Dart invented the grain elevator here in 1842. All of these goods hitting the shores at Buffalo would have to be shipped, moved rapidly, inexpensively, and year-round. Canals and lakes were seasonal due to the long winters, but the railroad could overcome those obstacles. The idea of railroads was off and running and Buffalo was situated to be at the forefront of the new industry.

With the immigration boom of Europeans through Ellis Island and the never-ending stream of humanity to the new western frontier, Buffalo became a gateway. By 1900, the Queen City became the eighth largest city in the United States. In the same year, construction began in Buffalo on what was destined to become the largest steel maker in the world. It was transportation that brought these industries to the eastern shore of Lake Erie and it was the railroad that made it happen. With the growth of railroads in the Buffalo region came railroad supply and manufacturing companies like the Gould Coupler works in nearby Depew, New York, the Wagner Palace Car Works, The Buffalo Brass Company, and The American Car and Foundry. Great American industries began to develop in Buffalo such as the Lackawanna Steel Mill, Republic Steel, Donner-Hanna, Symington-Gould, Ford Motor, Chevrolet, and Curtiss-Wright Aircraft, and all would need a reliable, year round transportation system to bring in the raw materials and send out the finished products to the rest of the country and the world.

As time progressed, Buffalo became the interchange point of the greatest railroads, such as the New York Central System, Pennsylvania, Baltimore & Ohio, Lehigh Valley, Erie, Delaware, Lackawanna & Western, Delaware & Hudson, Wabash, Canadian National, Canadian Pacific, Chesapeake & Ohio, Nickel Plate, Toronto, Hamilton & Buffalo, Grand Trunk, Pere Marquette, and the Lake Shore & Michigan Southern, to name just some. With the great names in American railroading and the title of Queen City, it would be only fitting for Buffalo to have some of the most beautiful train stations in the country. The grand Lehigh Valley terminal located on Washington Street graced Buffalo. The DL&W terminal was located on the waterfront by Main Street and South Park, served by the Delaware, Lackawanna, & Western, Nickel Plate, and Baltimore & Ohio Railroads. However, the gem of them all would have to be the Buffalo Central Terminal, which was built by the New York Central Railroad in 1929.

The development of the Queen City was facilitated by the movement of people and goods across her borders, from the Great Lakes ships, and from her tremendous factories by the steel ribbons known as railroads, that made their way to and through Buffalo. As Buffalo grew in stature, presidents, who traveled by rail, visited her. In 1861, President Abraham Lincoln visited Buffalo by rail on his triumphant ride to Washington, and in little more than four years, his funeral train, the "saddest train" as it was called, arrived in Buffalo on April 27, 1865. The Pan-American Exposition was held in Buffalo in 1901; a forerunner of modern world's fairs. On September 6, 1901, President William McKinley was shot while visiting the Expo and died eight days later. Theodore Roosevelt was inaugurated as president at the Wilcox House on September 14, 1901. The "Queen of Speed," the New York Central & Hudson River Railroads' *Empire State Express*, pulled by locomotive No. 999, traveled at 112.5 miles per hour between Batavia, New York, and Buffalo on May 10, 1893, which made her the fastest man-made machine on record at that time. The 999 was built by the New York Central at their own West Albany, New York, shops.

Railroads have been a part of the fabric of Buffalo for the last 176 years, and although the world and economies have changed, Buffalo still remains a hub of railroad activities. Trains still stop in this great city to be reclassified and made up into new trains; others glide past on their journeys to faraway places in North America. Passenger trains still serve the traveling public in and through Buffalo. Amtrak's *Empire Service Corridor* extends from Buffalo to New York City with eight trains daily, while NFTA's light rail vehicles move thousands of commuters to and from downtown daily. Turning the pages in this book allows readers take a trip back in time to see what parents and grandparents observed, rode, or even worked on as a part of Buffalo railroads.

# One

# The Beginning

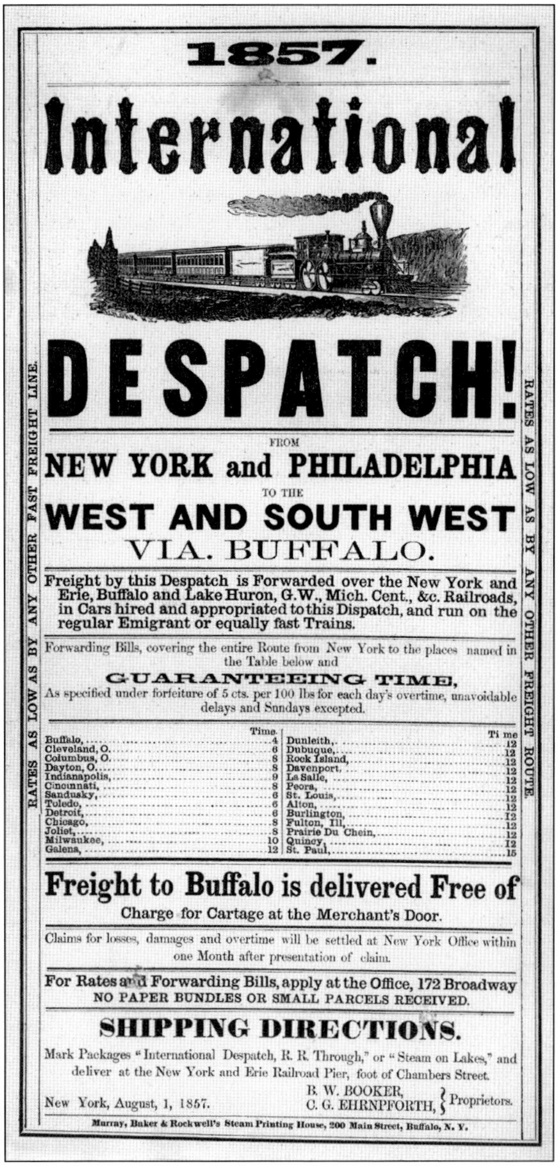


With the opening of the Erie Canal in 1825 came the first transportation route to the west other than wagons pulled over rough and uneven terrain by horse or oxen. Buffalo was located at the end of the canal on the shore of Lake Erie where people and goods could transfer from canal boats to the ships of the Great Lakes. (Library of Congress.)

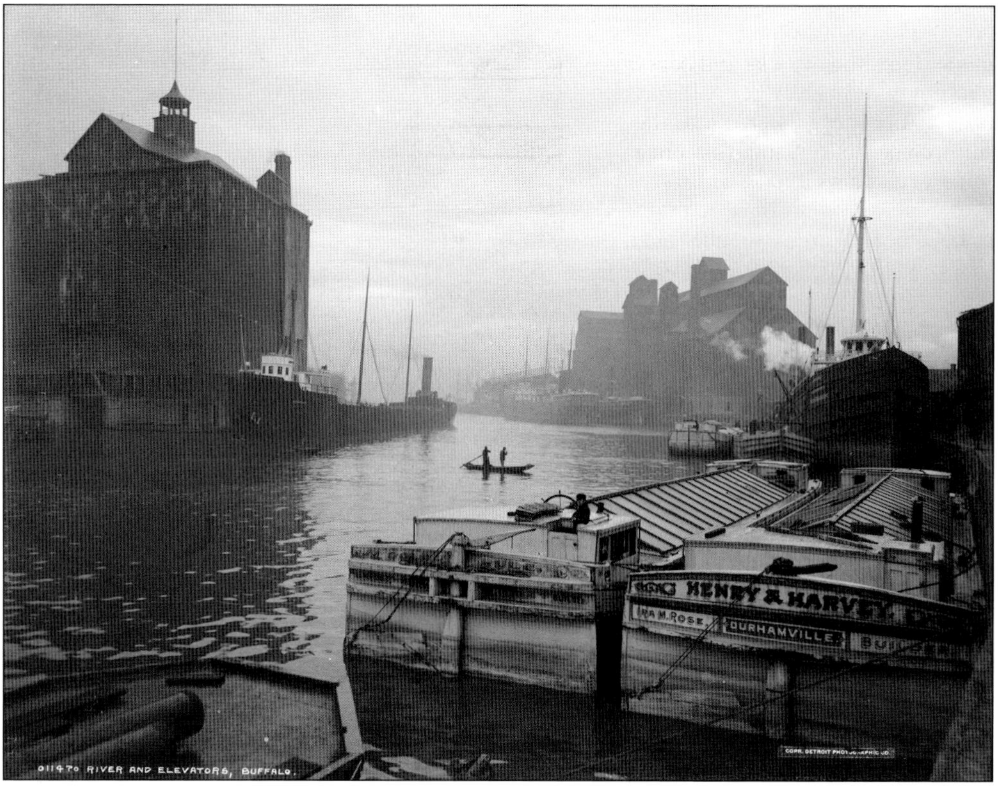


The canal was a great success and a boon for the area, but it was hindered by slow speeds and long winters that would cease all transportation. Men were already developing both the railroad and the steam locomotive; by 1832, the charter for the first railroad to serve the Buffalo area was created. Railroads rapidly grew to prominence first to augment the waterway, and then to overtake it. (Library of Congress.)

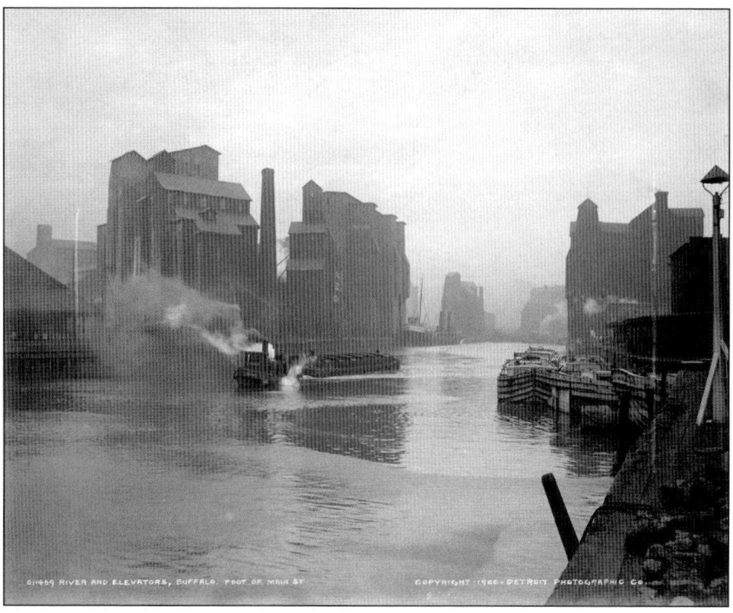


The first railroad in Buffalo, which used horses as a mode of power, was completed in 1834. By 1836 Buffalo had its first railroad operating by steam locomotive. As the area grew to be a transportation hub, new innovations to help in the transferring of goods from rail to ship were developed. In 1842, Joseph Dart, a Buffalo merchant, invented the grain elevator. (Library of Congress.)

Joseph Dart's invention replaced the manual loading of sacks and bags of grain by using a conveyor belt and buckets that were lowered into the ship's cargo hold. A ship that once took several days to unload could now be completed in just one. Buffalo was to become the largest supplier of grain in the world. (Library of Congress.)

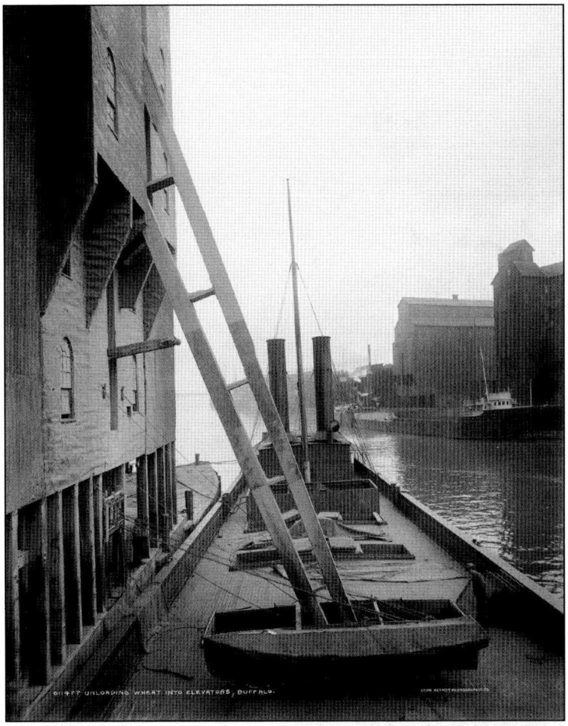


A close examination of the bottom right of this photograph reveals that these huge grain legs used to unload ships were mounted on railroad wheels and moved back and forth on railroad tracks. To the left is an ingenious method to push railroad cars up to the top of the Lackawanna coal chutes almost looking like a roller coaster. (Library of Congress.)

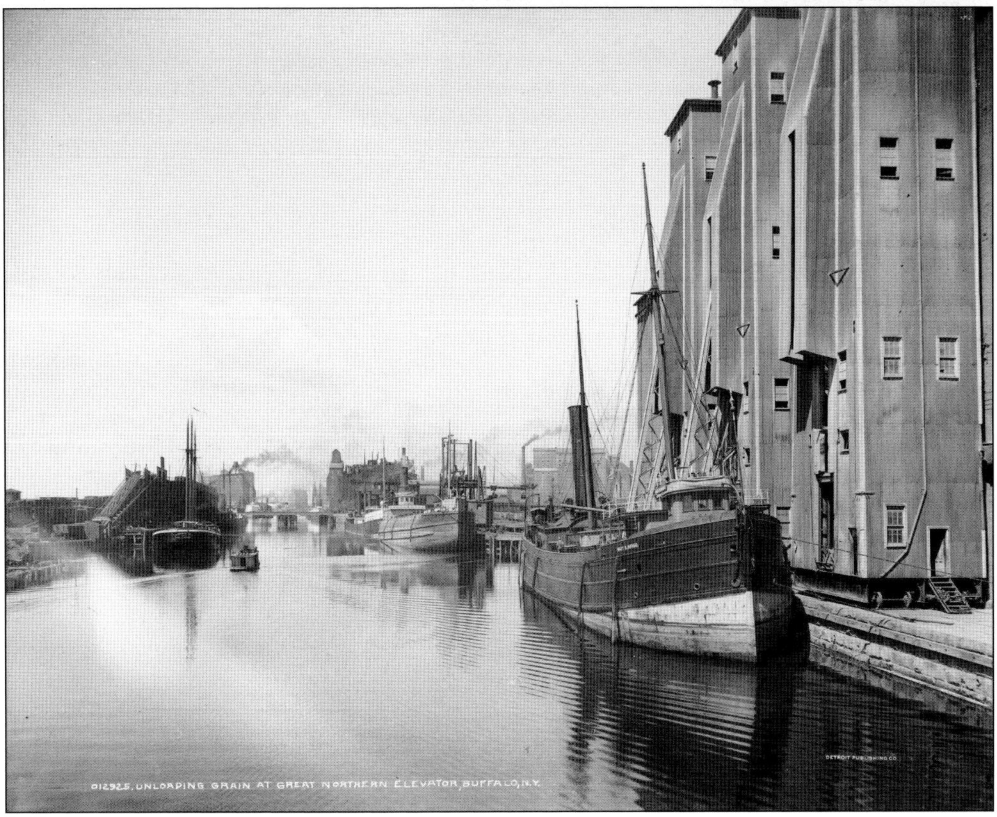

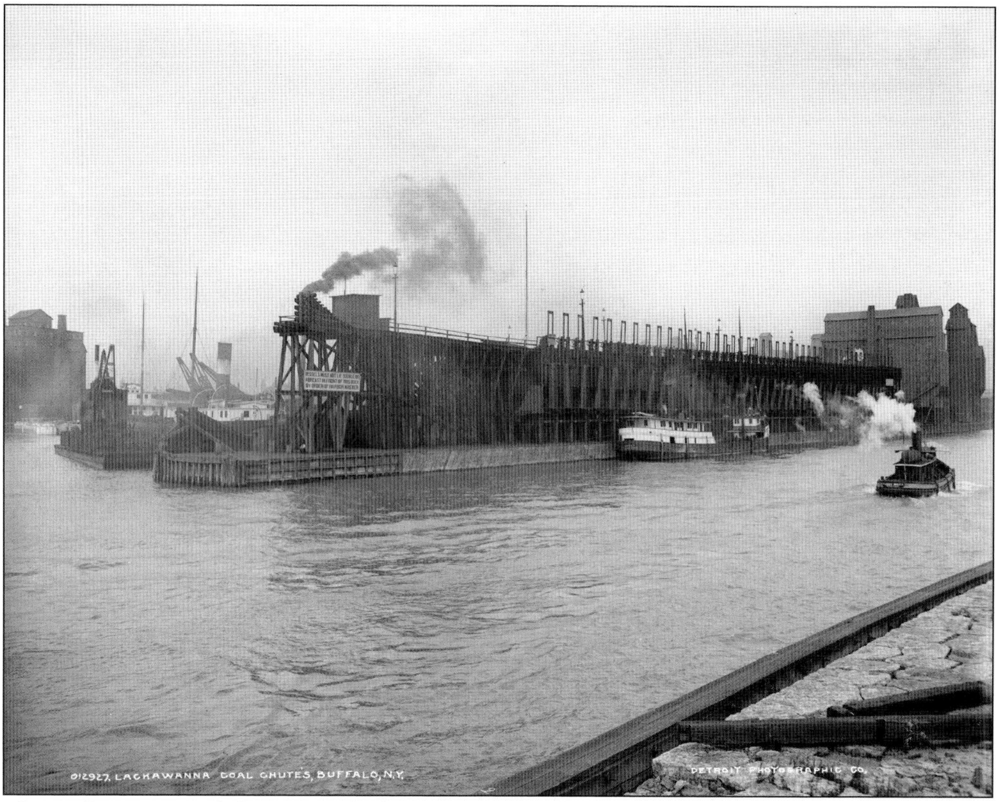


The Lackawanna coal chutes were built in 1879 by the Delaware, Lackawanna & Western (DL&W) Railroad. During the construction, it seems that the DL&W forgot where their land was when a unit of American soldiers arrived and put a halt to all construction, claiming that the new coal chutes were on U.S. military land. (Library of Congress.)

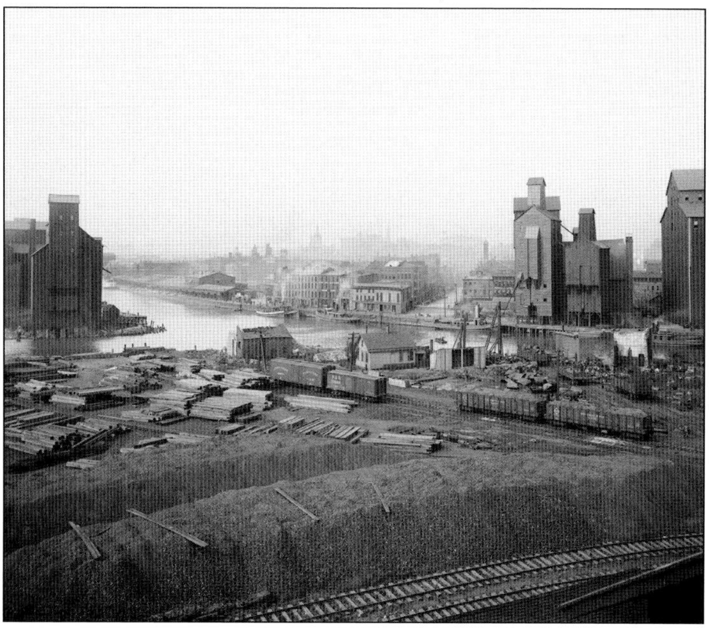

The city of Buffalo and its harbor continued to change as it prepared for new ways to move the freight of a growing nation. People in search of freedom, affordable land, and a better life were arriving in Buffalo where many decided to stay while others continued on their westward journey. As the nation expanded, agricultural products, lumber, and manufactured goods followed. (Library of Congress.)

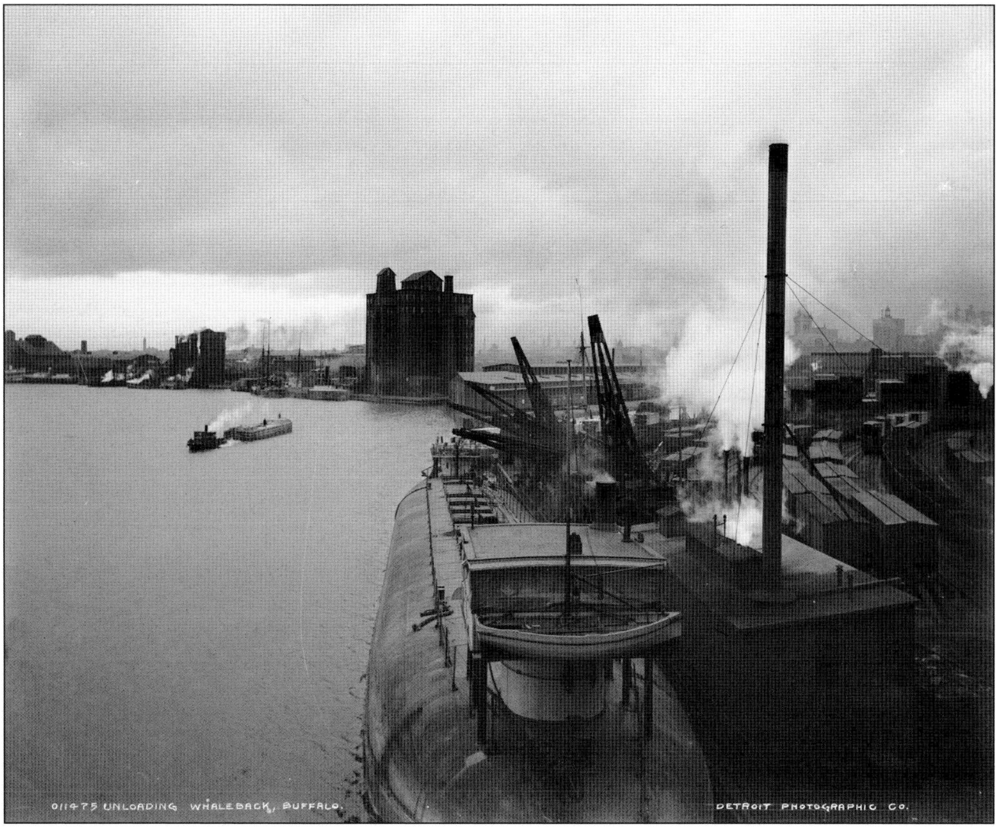


A whaleback ship is unloading her ore into railcars at the waterfront while just beyond is the New York Central and Hudson River Railroad warehouse, built in 1895. Buffalo had grown from a small trading center to the eighth largest city in the United States and the second largest rail hub. (Library of Congress.)

DL&W gondolas cars are loaded with ore from the whaleback ship in the Buffalo harbor. The odd machine scoops iron ore from the ship's hold and with an upright swing moves it to the railcars. The Buffalo lighthouse can be seen in this photo; it was built in 1833 to replace the original 1818 lighthouse and is the oldest building left on the waterfront. (Library of Congress.)

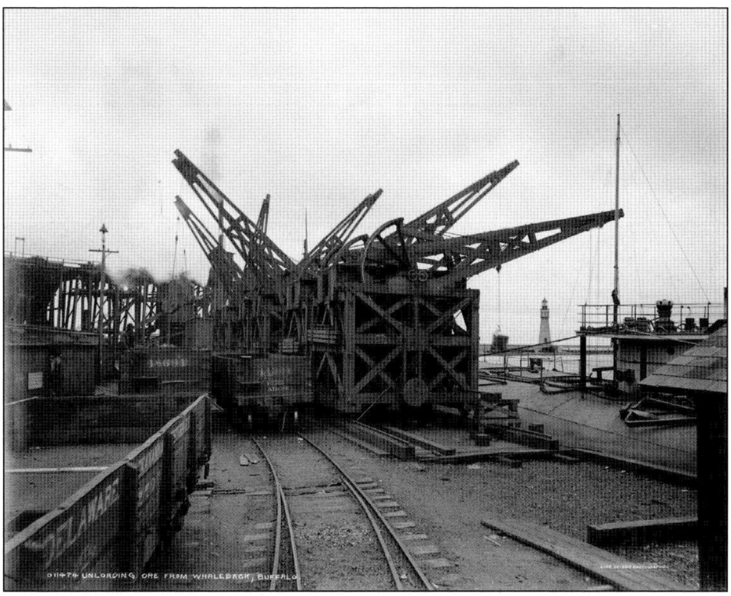

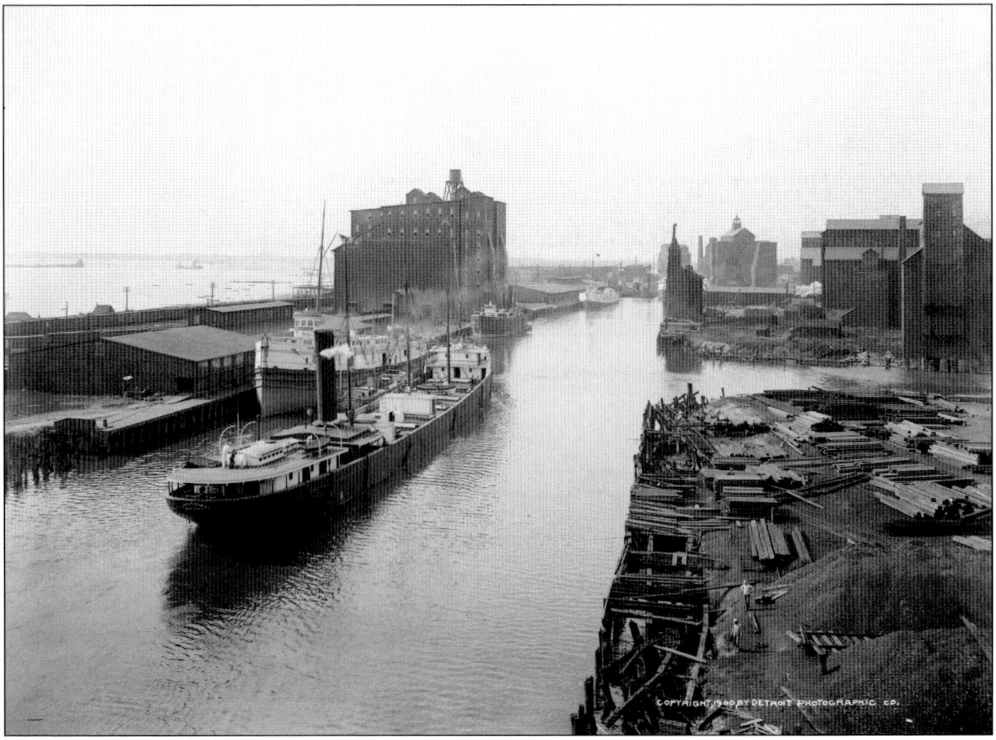


At the left of this photograph is the Cleveland & Toledo (C&T) Railroad freight house. In 1868, the Lake Shore Railway absorbed the C&T, and a year later, it became the Lake Shore and Michigan Southern Railway. In 1877, Cornelius Vanderbilt gained control, and in 1914, it was merged with the New York Central and Hudson River Railroad to become the New York Central Railroad. (Library of Congress.)

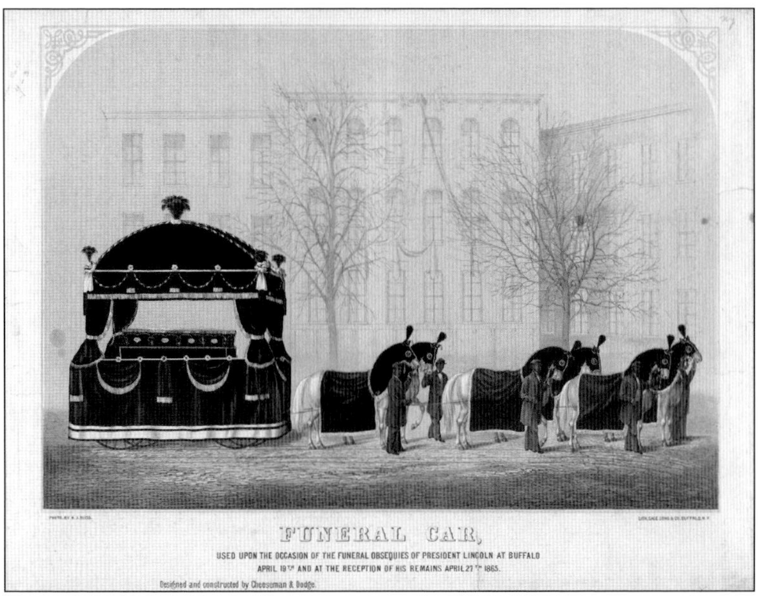


On February 18, 1861, president-elect Abraham Lincoln stopped at Buffalo while approximately 75,000 people crowded the train station to see and hear him. Four short years later, on April 27, 1865, the saddest train in America brought the president's lifeless body back to Buffalo on its way to Springfield. (Library of Congress.)

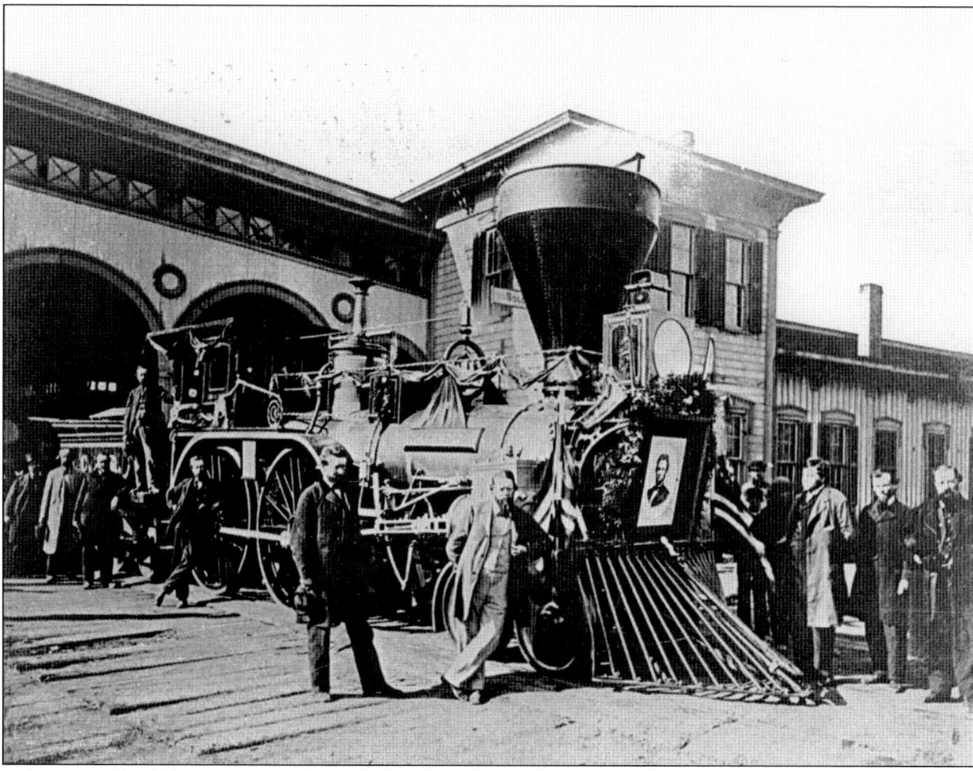

A beautifully decorated funeral train retraced the route of President Lincoln's inauguration train and arrived at Buffalo at 7:00 a.m. on April 27, 1865. The president's body was put onto a carriage drawn by six white horses covered in black and brought to Saint James Hall for public display. (Stephen G. Myers collection.)

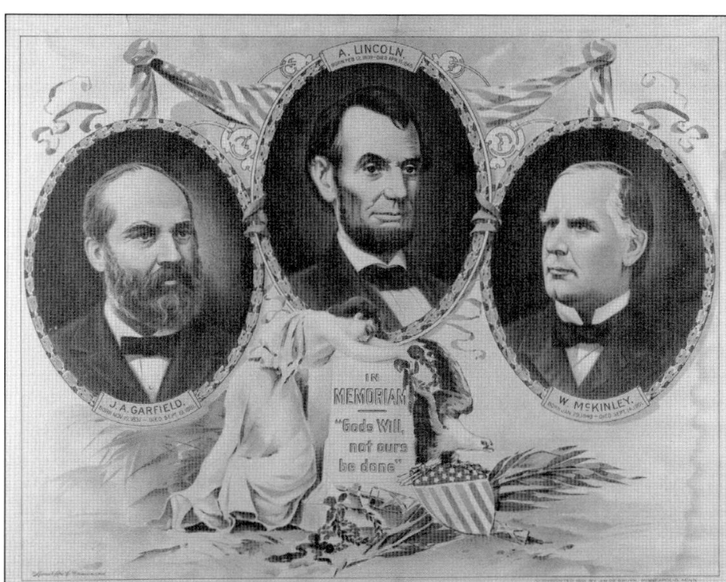


Again on September 6, 1901, tragedy hit Buffalo when President William McKinley was shot while attending the Pan-American Exposition. On September 14, the president died from his wound and Vice President Teddy Roosevelt was rushed by train from North Creek, New York, to Buffalo, where he was sworn in as the 26th president. (Library of Congress.)

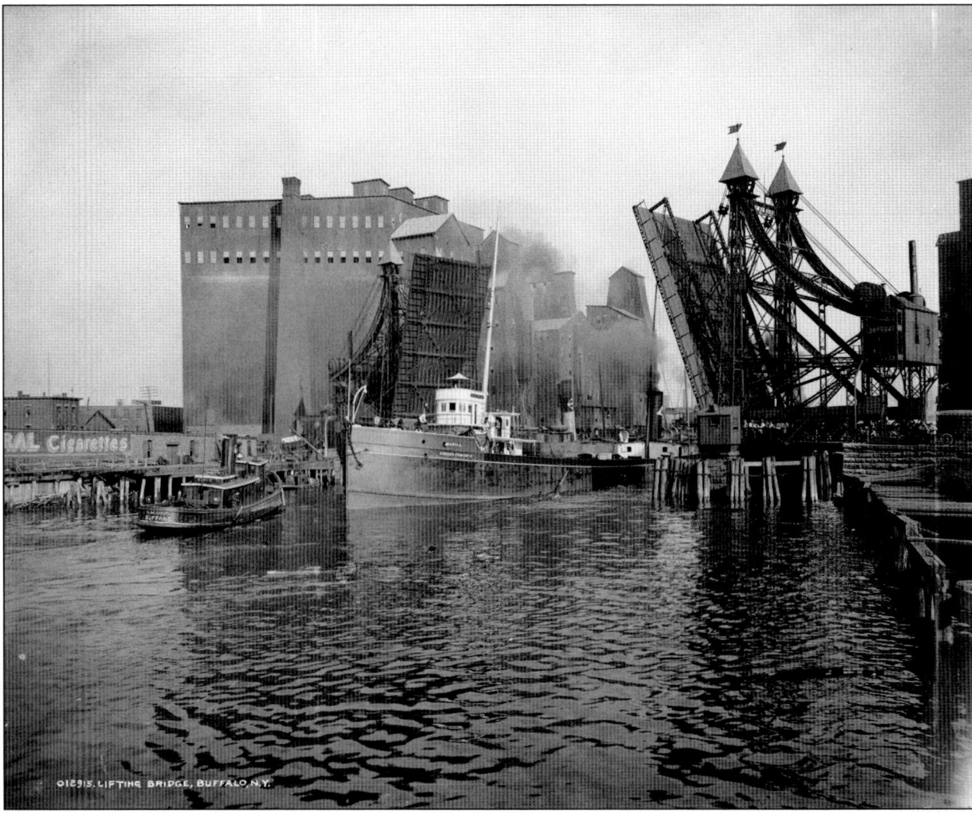


Railroads were eager to gain access to the harbor, where grain, coal, and ore could be loaded from ships to railcars. Railroads also invested in ships and tugboats until 1914, when the Panama Canal Act called for separate ownership between water carriers and railway carriers. Note the ship with the Erie logo in the background. (Library of Congress.)

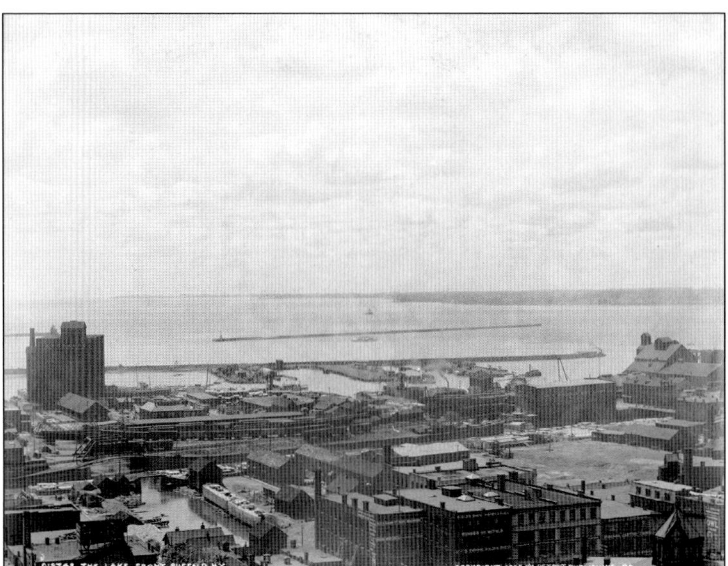

Buffalo's strategic location was quickly establishing her as a great American city, and since railroads had proven their worth as a primary transportation system, the battle was on for them to reach Buffalo. With the consolidation of small railroads into major trunk lines, these new giants of railroading had a common goal to enter the markets of Buffalo. (Library of Congress.)

# *Two*

# The New York Central System

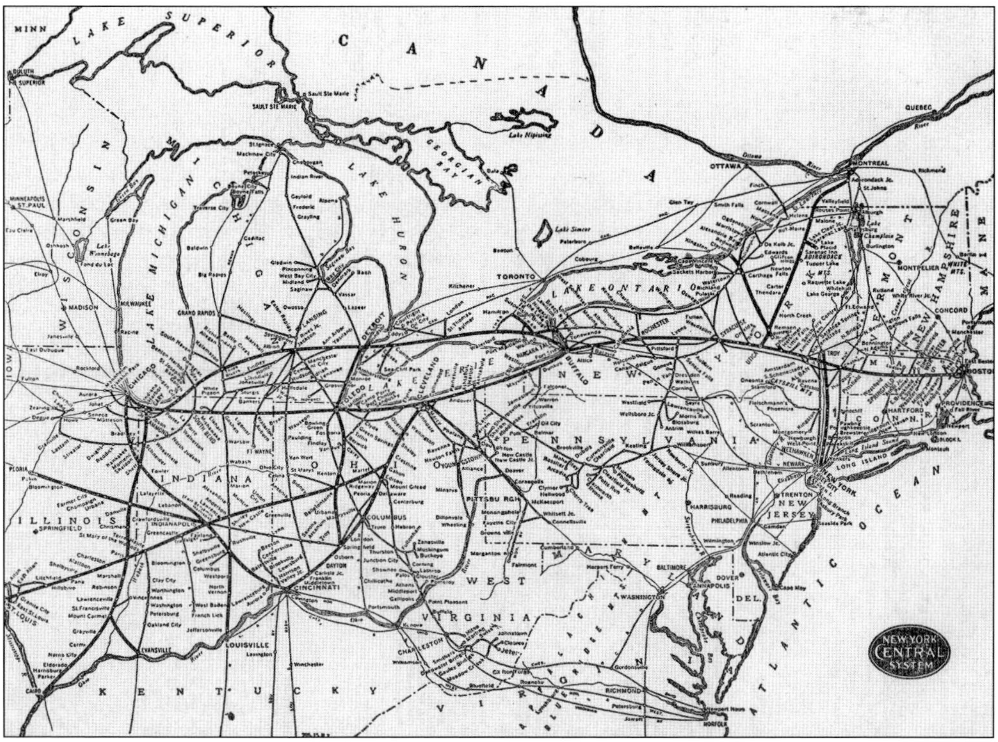


The New York Central System (NYC) was Buffalo's largest railroad and Buffalo was its heart. Here three affiliates converged, the New York Central and Hudson River, the Lake Shore and Michigan Southern, and the Michigan Central. Nearly two-thirds of Buffalo's rail passengers and freight used the NYC, which employed nearly 10,000 people in the area to do that transportation job. (Michael J. Connor collection.)

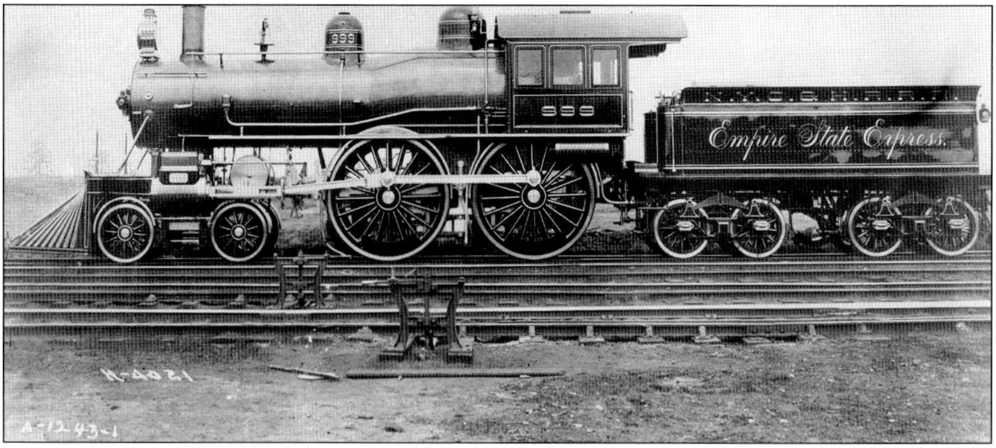

A hallmark of the New York Central was a well-earned reputation for speed. A speed zenith was reached on May 10, 1893, by locomotive engineer Charlie Hogan on NYC&HR 999, an American-type 4-4-0 wheel arrangement locomotive. Hogan and 999 pulled the *Empire State Express* at 112.5 m.p.h. east of Buffalo, setting a long-standing world land speed record. (Michael J. Connor collection.)

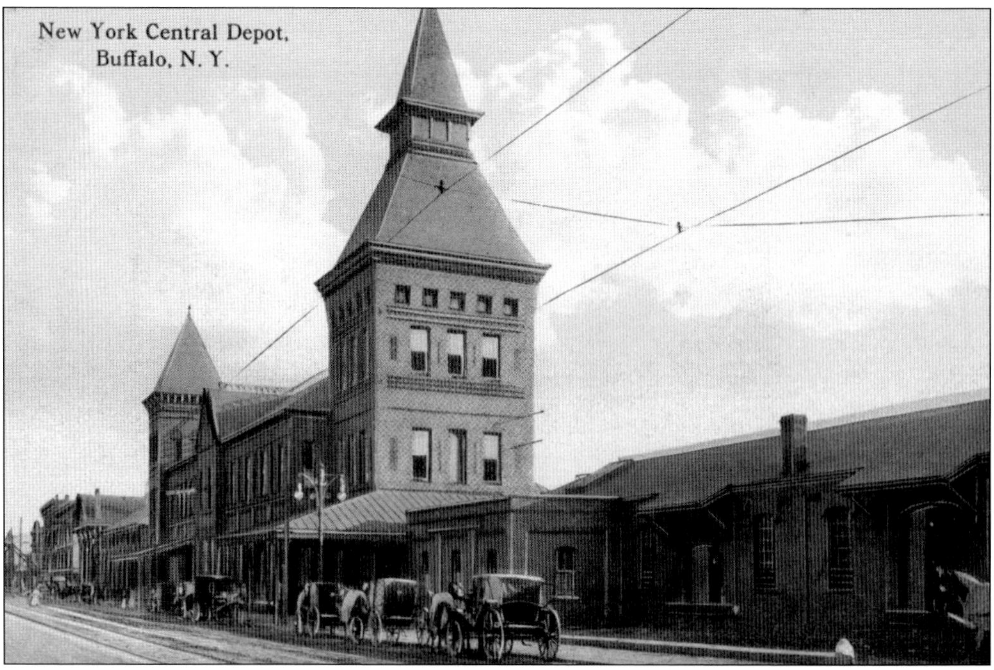


Prior to the 1929 opening of Central Terminal, the New York Central's principal Buffalo passenger station was this rambling structure paralleling Exchange Street between Washington and Michigan Streets. Almost from the time its original section was built in 1855–1856, growing traffic overwhelmed it, but it soldiered on while railroad and city officials argued the details of a never-built downtown Union Station. (Stephen G. Myers collection.)

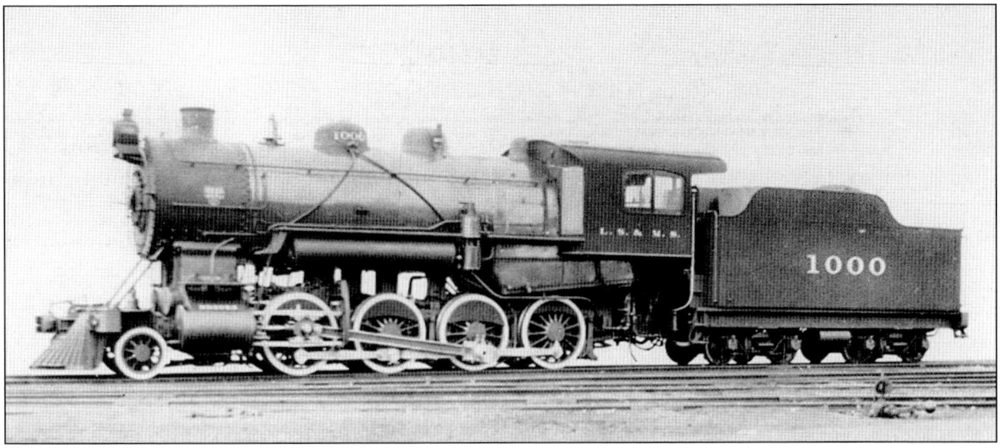


The New York Central's major artery to the west was the Lake Shore & Michigan Southern Railway, whose nearly water-level route connected Buffalo with Chicago via Cleveland. Controlled by the NYC since 1869, the Lake Shore was, from an engineering perspective, almost inarguably one of Buffalo's best railroads. LS&MS Engine 1000, a Consolidation-type, was designed to best use its light grades and easy curves. (Michael J. Connor collection.)

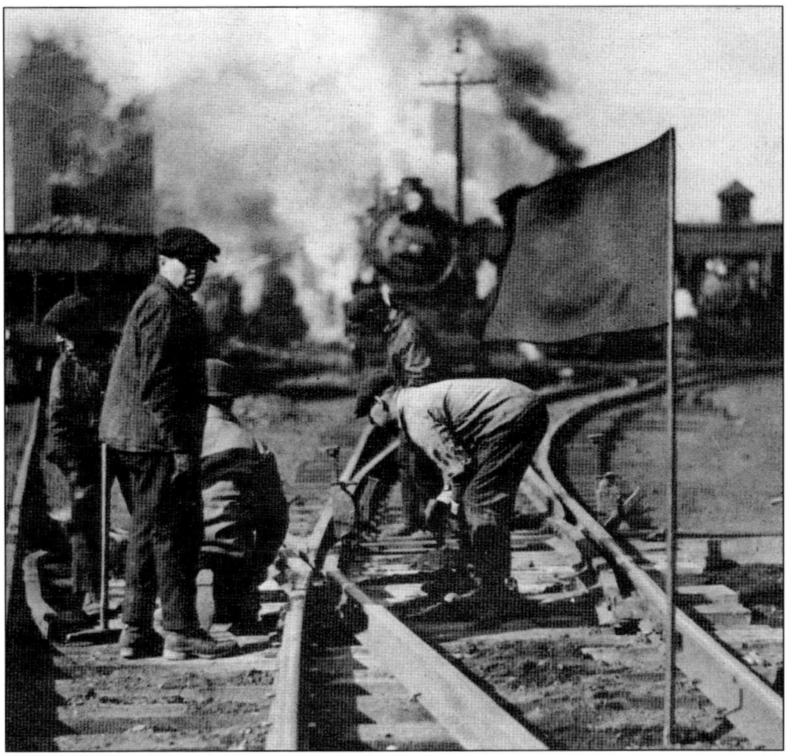

The track gang was ever ready to maintain the numerous yard tracks and main lines through Buffalo. Here a gang works on a frog near the roundhouse in the early 1900s. Missing are the hard hats and safety glasses that modern track workers would be wearing. (Western New York Heritage Press, Inc. Used with permission.)

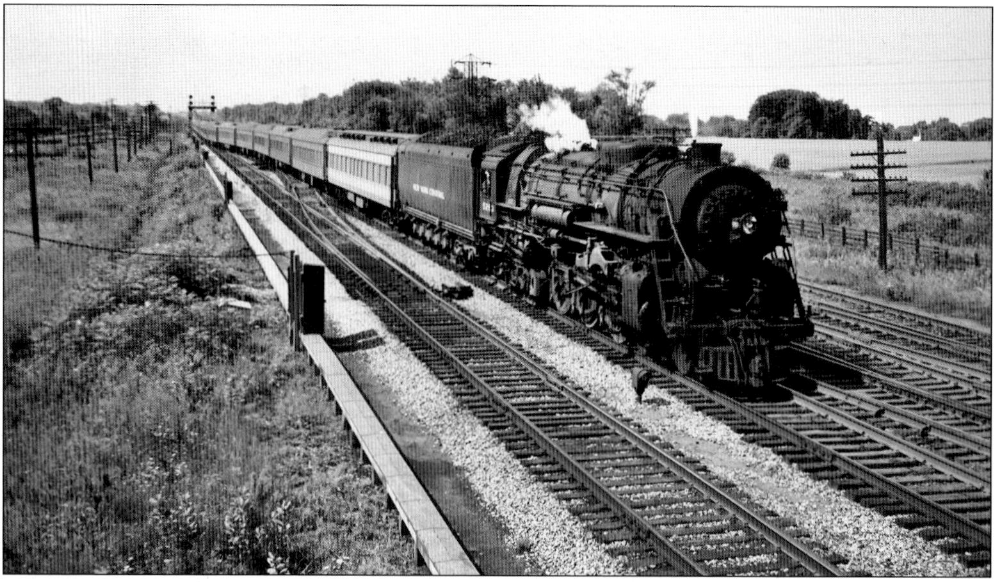

Many students of the steam locomotive would argue that the New York Central brought the steam locomotive to near perfection. It is hard to dispute them when looking at Hudson type No. 5263 near Depew in 1953, pulling a train of empty passenger equipment. The 5263 was near the end of her career, being scrapped in 1956. (Photograph by Jeremy Taylor; courtesy New York Central System Historical Society.)

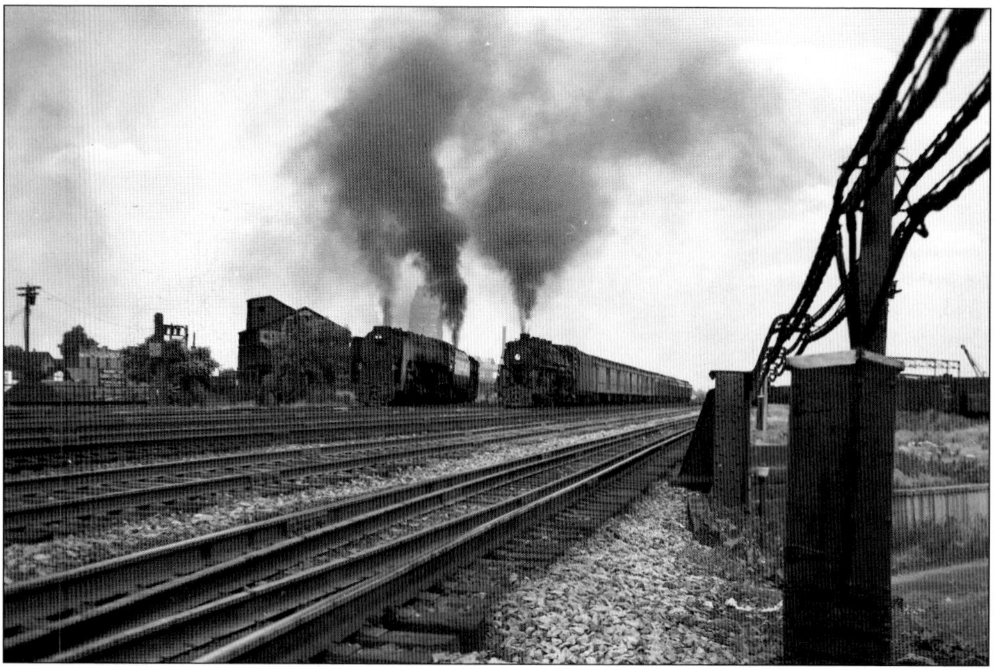

Near Fillmore Avenue in 1953, Toronto, Hamilton & Buffalo Railway train 379, pulled by TH&B No. 502, a near clone of the New York Central's iconic Hudson type J-class locomotives, is beginning its 2-hour-and-25-minute sprint from Buffalo Central Terminal to Hamilton. NYC 6003, a Niagara-type S-class, pulls mail train X-35 on a parallel track. (Photograph by Jeremy Taylor; courtesy New York Central System Historical Society.)

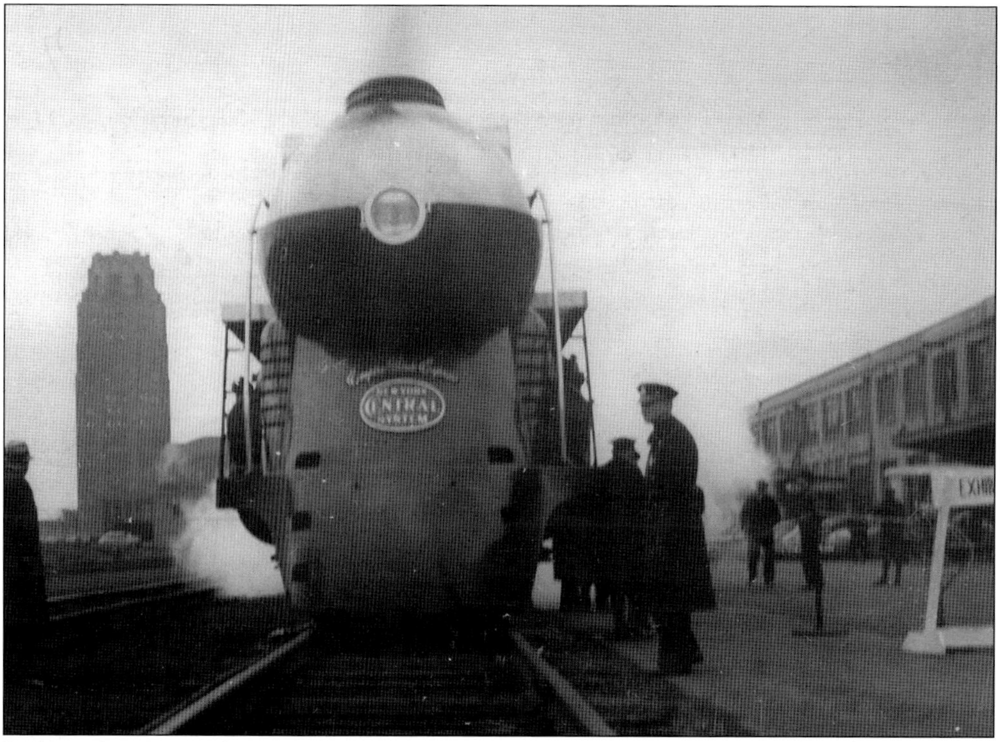

In 1941 the New York Central reequipped the *Empire State Express* with new, streamlined cars and locomotives. On December 6, 1941, the new train was displayed near the Central terminal while local residents were given a chance to look her over. The next day she would begin her runs between New York and Cleveland via Buffalo. (Mark Pempsell collection, courtesy of Iron Island Museum.)

The *Empire State Express* sits in the shadows of Buffalo Central Terminal and enjoys the brief rest before it begins the daily routine of the 10-hour-and-55-minute trip from Cleveland to New York City, which will be 621 miles every day. Although all is quiet here for now, tomorrow will be December 7, 1941. (Mark Pempsell collection, courtesy of Iron Island Museum.)

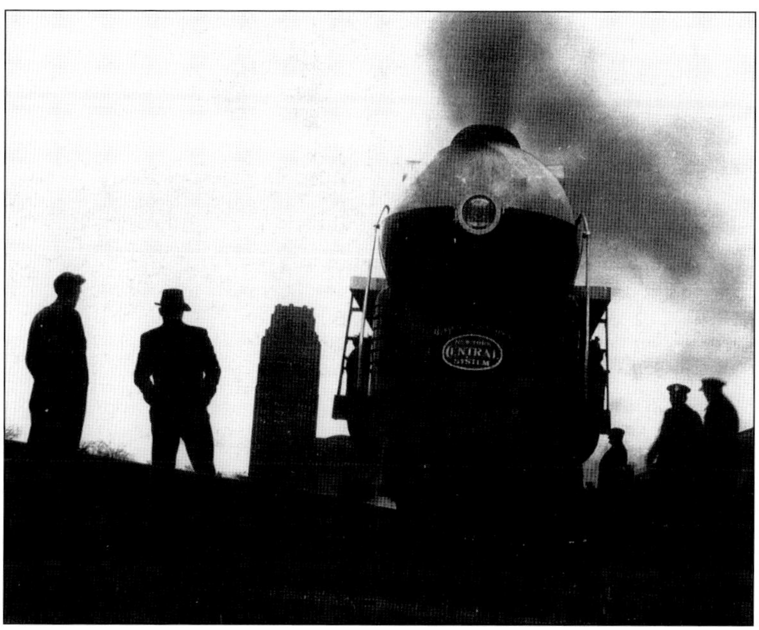

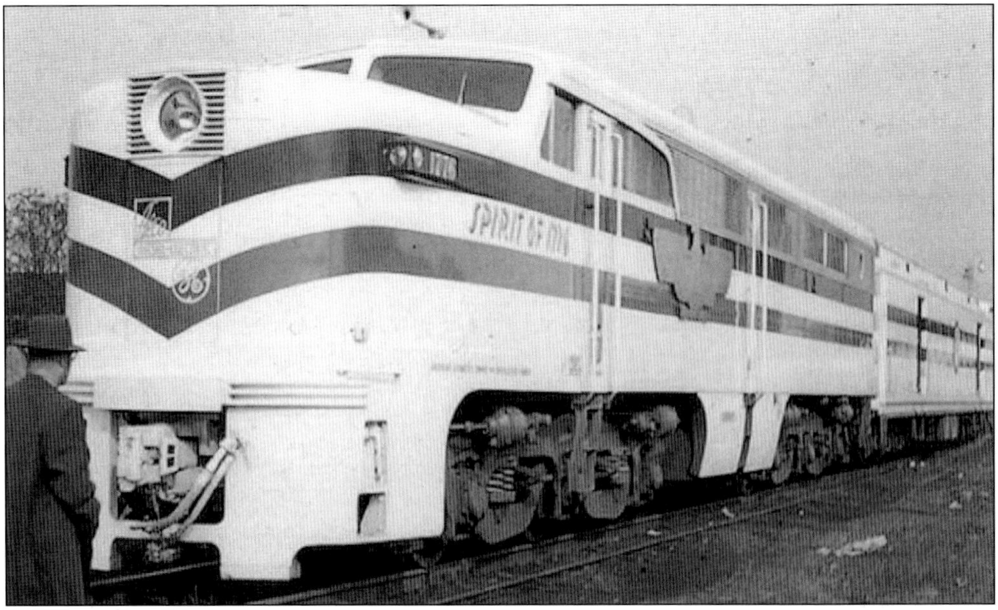

In a burst of post–World War II patriotic pride, President Truman and Attorney General Tom Clark promoted the idea of a train touring the nation carrying artifacts and documents precious to our history and freedom. The seven-car, privately financed *American Freedom Train* made a 37,160-mile tour across the country between September 11, 1947, and January 22, 1949. Here the train is on exhibit at Buffalo Central Terminal on November 7, 1947. (Nathan Vester Collection, Central Terminal Restoration Corporation.)

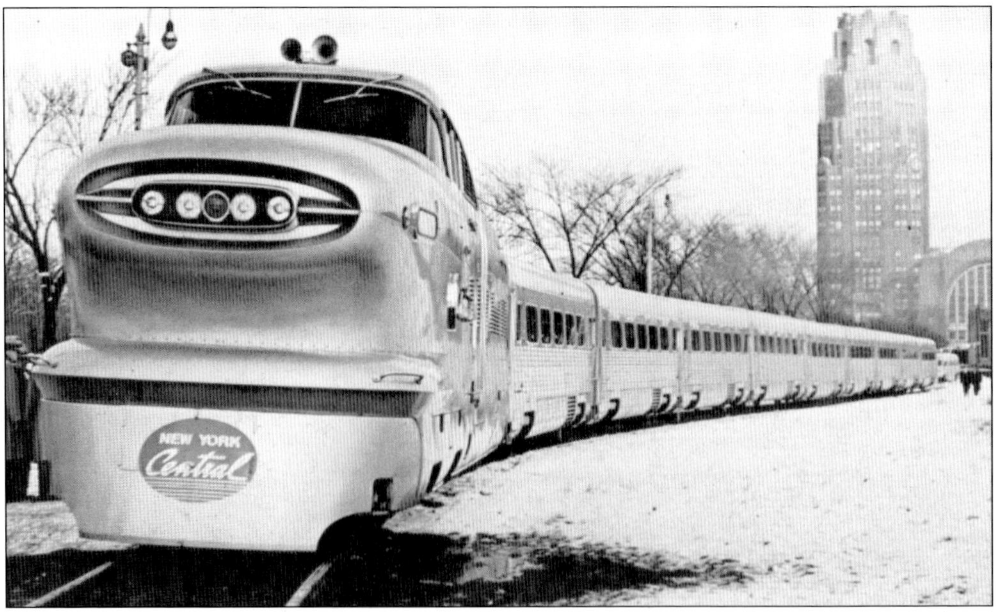


The *Empire State Express* and the *American Freedom Train* were not the only special trains displayed at Central Terminal. Here in winter 1956, New York Central's *Aerotrain*, built with automotive styling by General Motors, awaits public inspection. From here the train shortly entered service between Chicago and Detroit. The train's 10 coaches, made from widened GM bus bodies, made for rough riding, and the train was returned to GM in 1957. (John C. Dahl collection.)

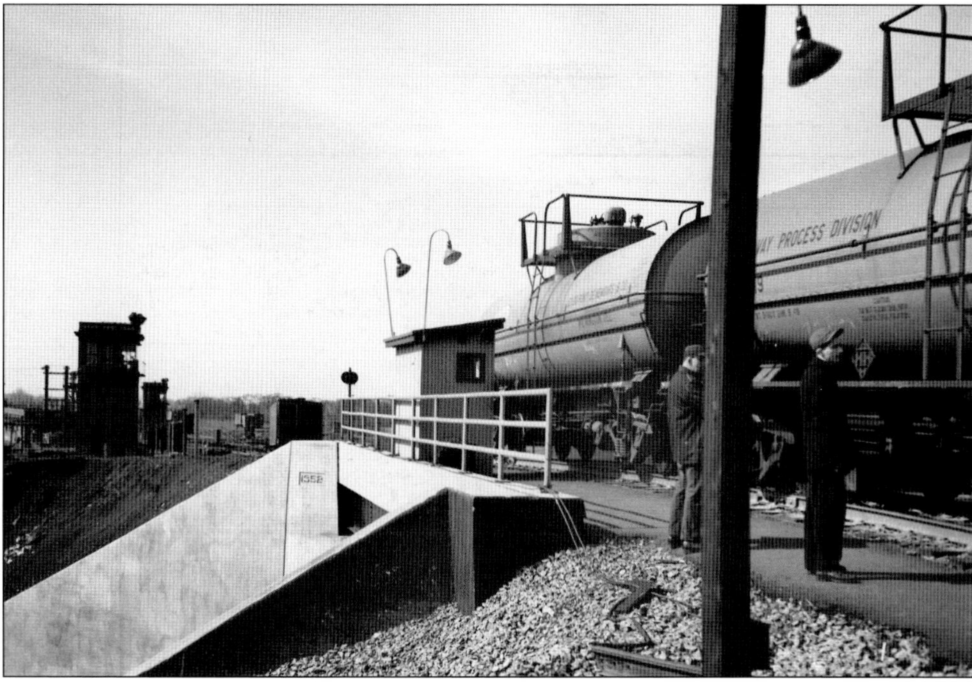


On June 12, 1895, New York Central Railroad interests incorporated the Terminal Railway of Buffalo, which built and opened an 11.02-mile line from Depew to Blasdell permitting many trains to bypass downtown Buffalo. The centerpiece of the project was a new yard in Gardenville. Here in 1953, cars were pushed over a hump and then permitted to drift to a classification track. (Jeremy Taylor photograph, courtesy New York Central System Historical Society.)

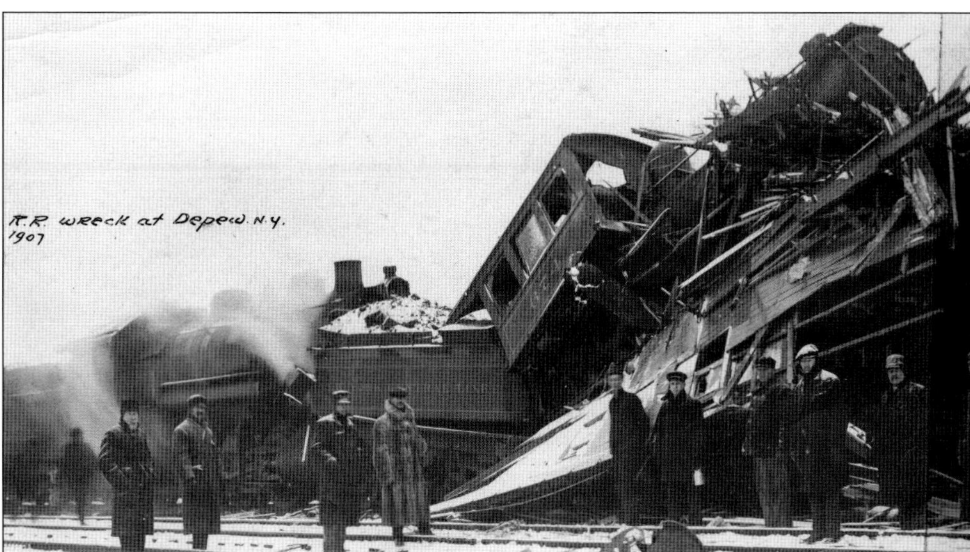


This scene from the cold winter of 1907 shows a train wreck on the NYC&HR in Depew, New York, just a few miles east of Buffalo. Several cold railroaders observe the damage of locomotive No. 674 as they anticipate how to clear the wreckage and restore service on the busy main line. (Village of Depew Historian collection.)

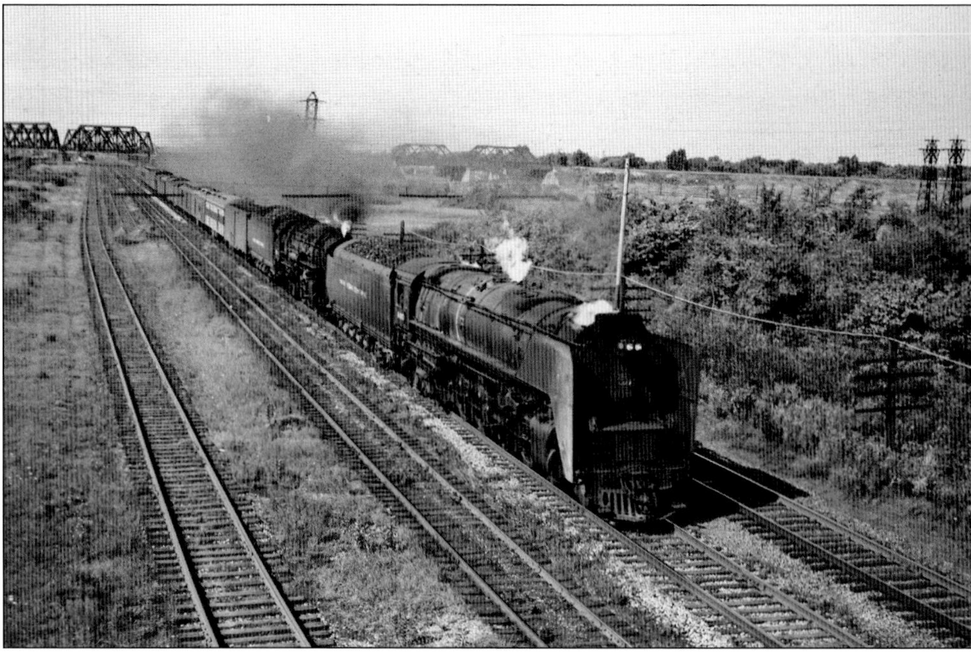

The Railway Express Agency was the UPS of its day. Nationwide, inexpensive, and fast, the express moved in trainload quantities, as demonstrated here. Niagara-type S-class No. 6017 leads train 137 with Hudson-type J-class No. 5263 and 19 cars of express west through Blasdell. The 185.16 miles from Buffalo to Cleveland, the first stop, will be covered in 3 hours and 30 minutes. (Jeremy Taylor photograph courtesy New York Central System Historical Society.)

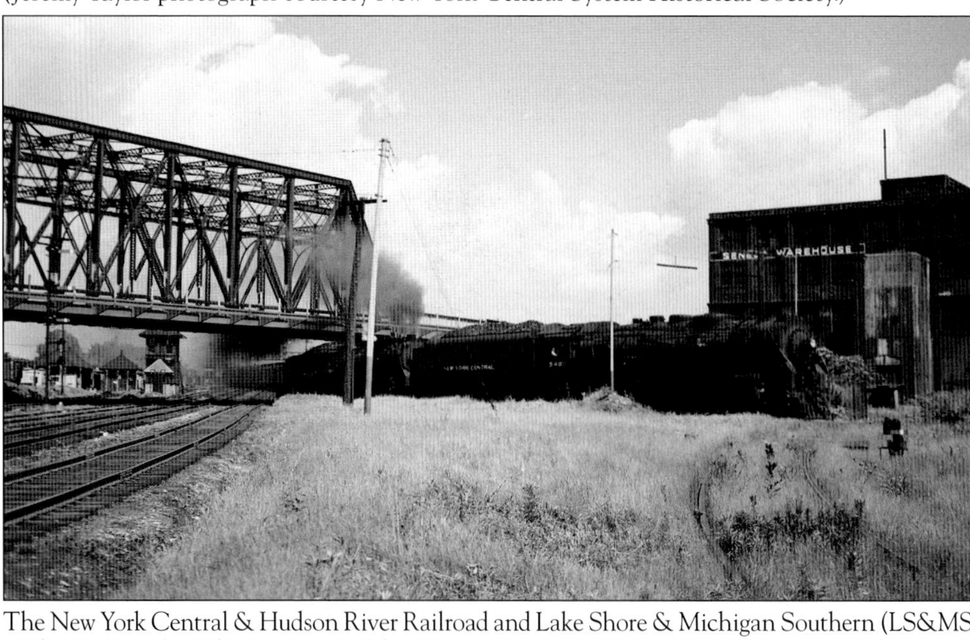

The New York Central & Hudson River Railroad and Lake Shore & Michigan Southern (LS&MS) Railway focused on downtown Buffalo. Creating a through route involved some tortuous track alignment. Here in 1953, Mail and Express train X-35 enters the aptly named "Compromise Track" connecting the original NYC&HR (to the left) with the LS&MS (out of sight to the right). (Jeremy Taylor photograph courtesy New York Central System Historical Society.)

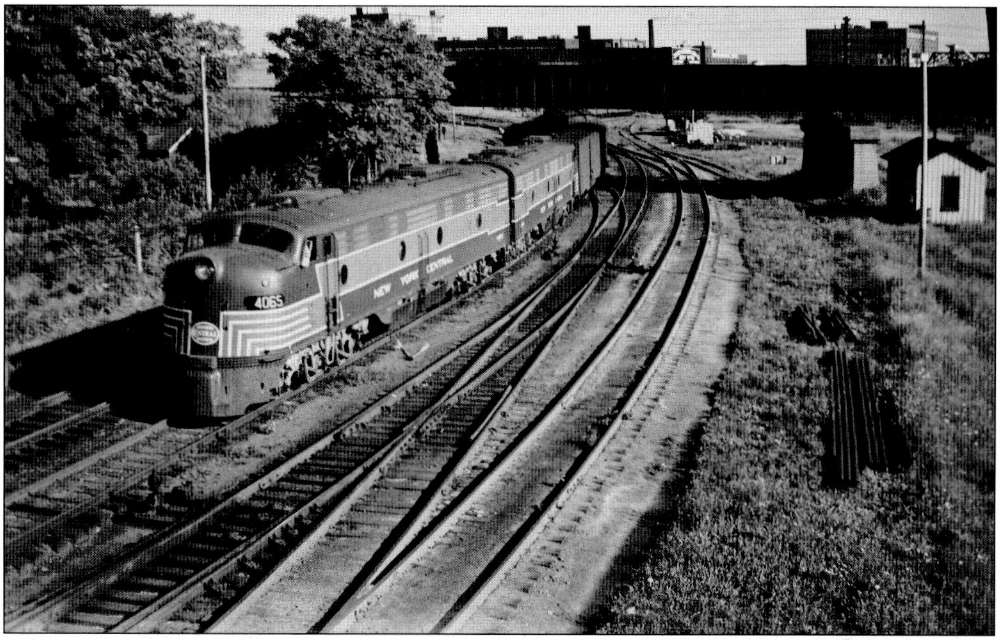

Later in 1953, and now powered by diesel-electric locomotives No. 4065 and No. 4064, train X-35 is leaving the Compromise Track. General Motors Electro-Motive Division built both locomotives with E-8 as their model. X-35 is passing under the Main Line of the Delaware, Lackawanna & Western Railroad in south Buffalo. (Jeremy Taylor photograph courtesy New York Central System Historical Society.)

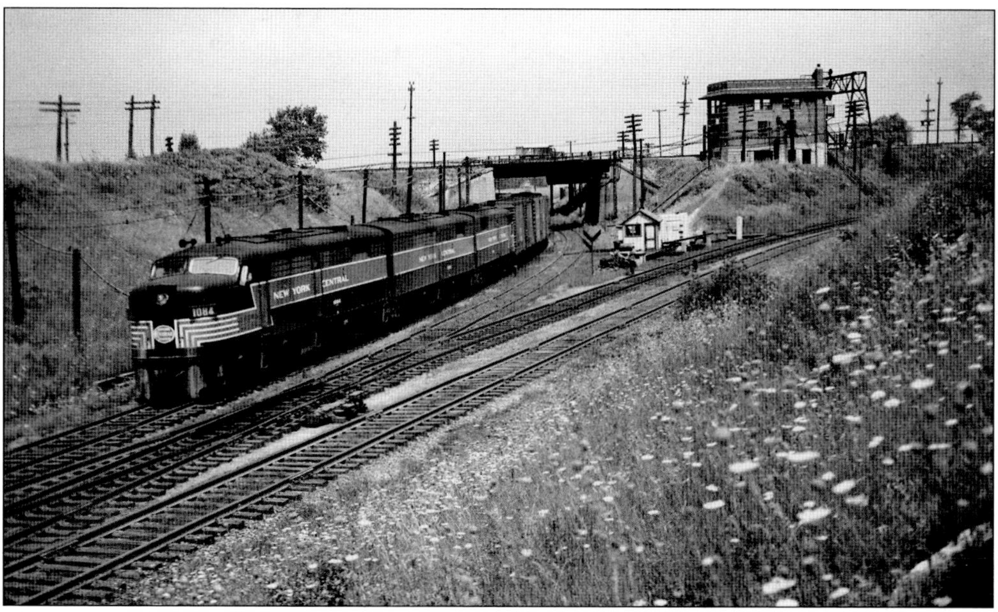

The New York Central's massive investment in the Gardenville Cut-off is on display in Depew in this 1953 view of First LS-1 westbound from the West Shore going under the NYC's New York City–Buffalo Main Line at Tower 46. LS-1 was a hot New York-to-Chicago through freight, as evidenced by its power: new Alco-built diesel-electric locomotives. (Jeremy Taylor courtesy New York Central System Historical Society.)

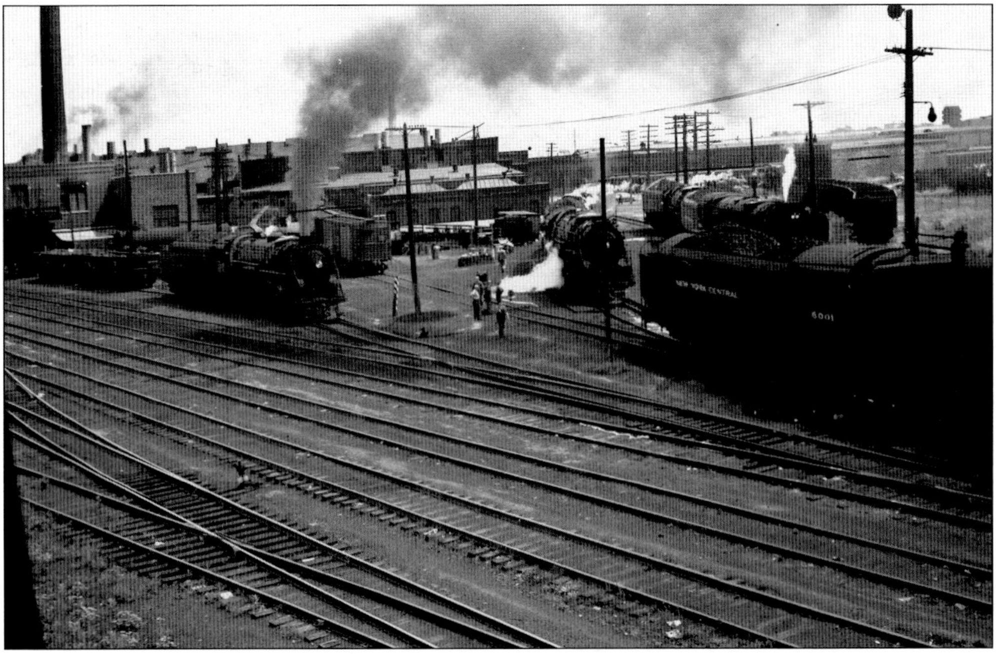

New York Central's 1953 operations in Buffalo were so intense that engine-serving facilities were needed at Gardenville, Central Terminal, Black Rock, and East Buffalo (shown here), commonly called the West Shore Roundhouse. The name reflected back to the 1883 opening of the New York, West Shore, and Buffalo Railway—the NYC's erstwhile competitor at almost all points between Albany and Buffalo. (Jeremy Taylor courtesy New York Central System Historical Society.)

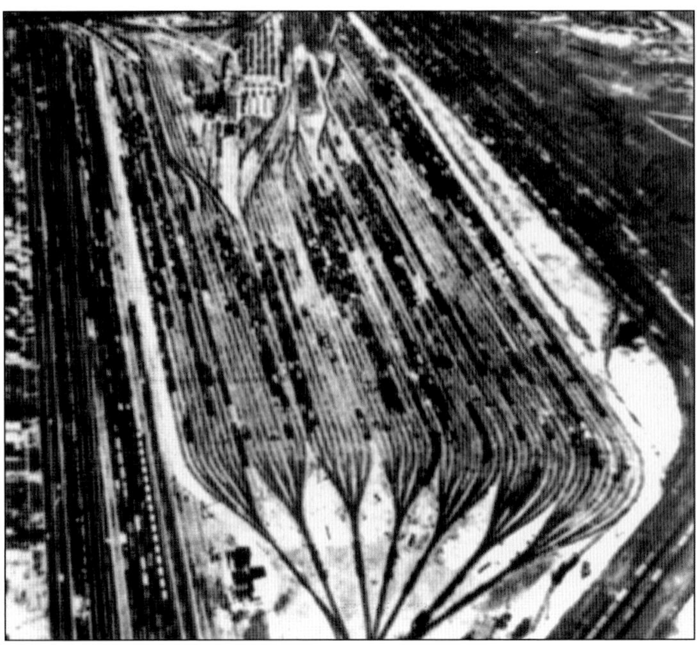

A major initiative of New York Central president Alfred E. Perlman's 1954–1968 administration was tackling inefficient and congested yards. Buffalo in the early 1950s was a textbook case of all that was wrong. Perlman and his team acted boldly to consolidate Buffalo operations by building the new and modern Frontier Yard, closing eight yards in Buffalo and sufficiently improving transit times. (Patrick Connors collection.)

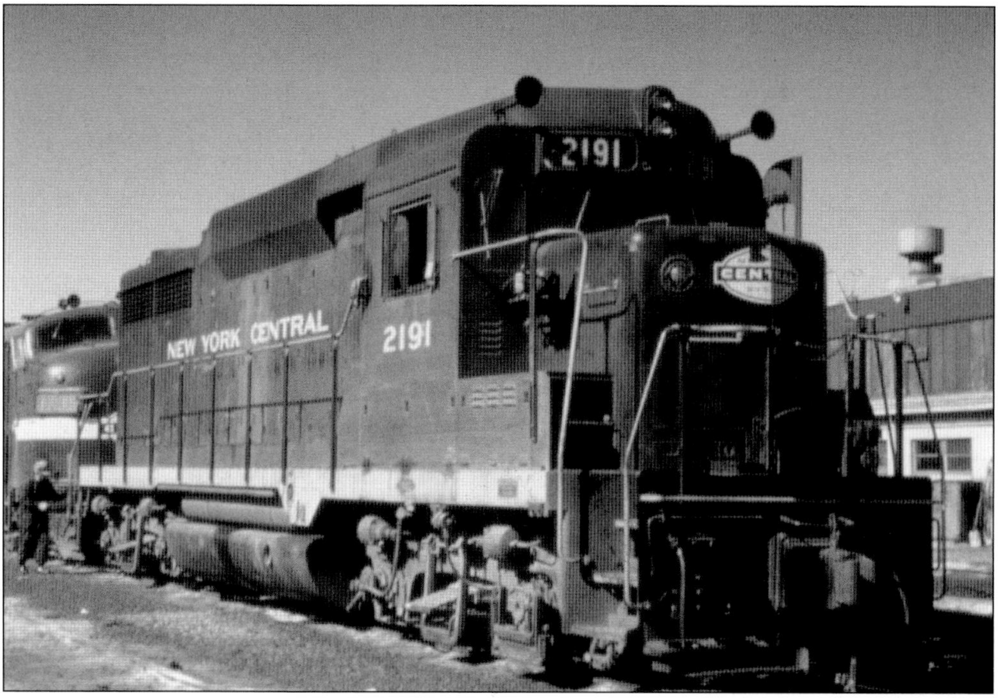


As the Penn Central merger approached, each railroad selectively renumbered locomotives to insure against duplicate numbers in the post-merger fleet. NYC 2191, here at the Buffalo engine terminal on October 22, 1969, has not been through the paint shop since the February 1, 1968, merger and still shows her NYC heritage. Built in August 1962 by EMD as NYC 6118, the 2,250-horsepower model GP-30 locomotive was renumbered in 1966. (Joseph Schveder collection.)

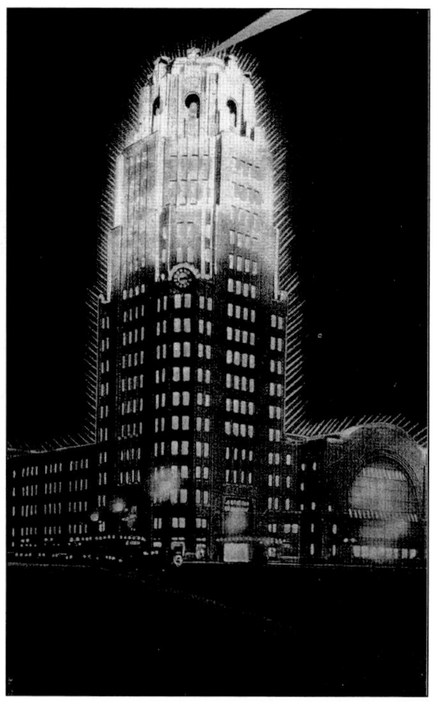

From its opening in 1929 through its closing in 1979, Buffalo Central Terminal has mirrored both railroad passenger traffic and the City of Buffalo. The postcard at right of the Terminal lighted as a beacon in the night skies reflects the optimism of the New York Central's managers that drove its location and construction. This image of Buffalo and the New York Central at their apex is what we remember. (Iron Island Museum collection.)

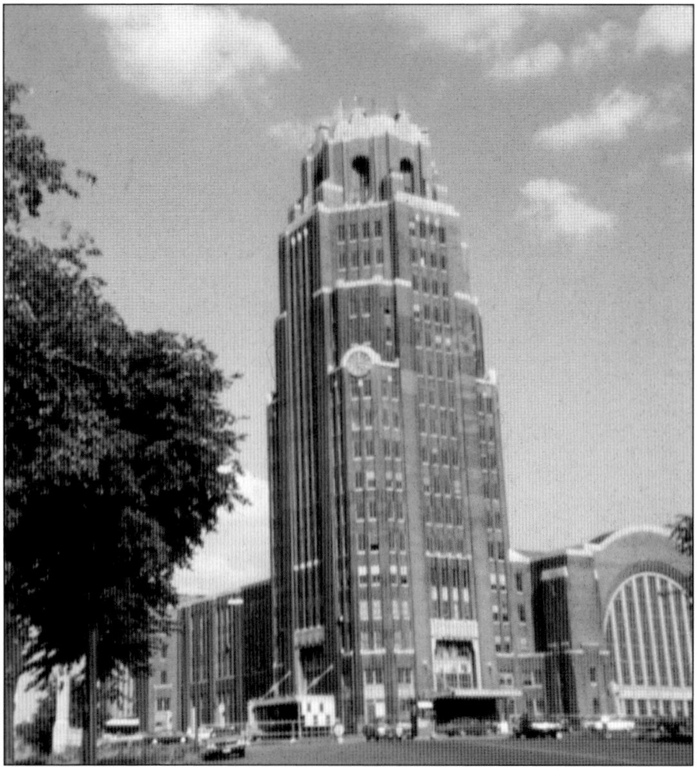

Buffalo Central Terminal's fall into virtual abandonment was a slow process. Besides its role as Buffalo's major passenger terminal, the building also housed the New York Central's System Car Accounting Department, the Buffalo Division Superintendent and Dispatchers, and many miscellaneous offices. This view of a still-active facility soon after the Penn Central merger emphasizes the Terminal Office Tower's 17 stories and 271-foot height. (Photograph by Roy O. Davis.)

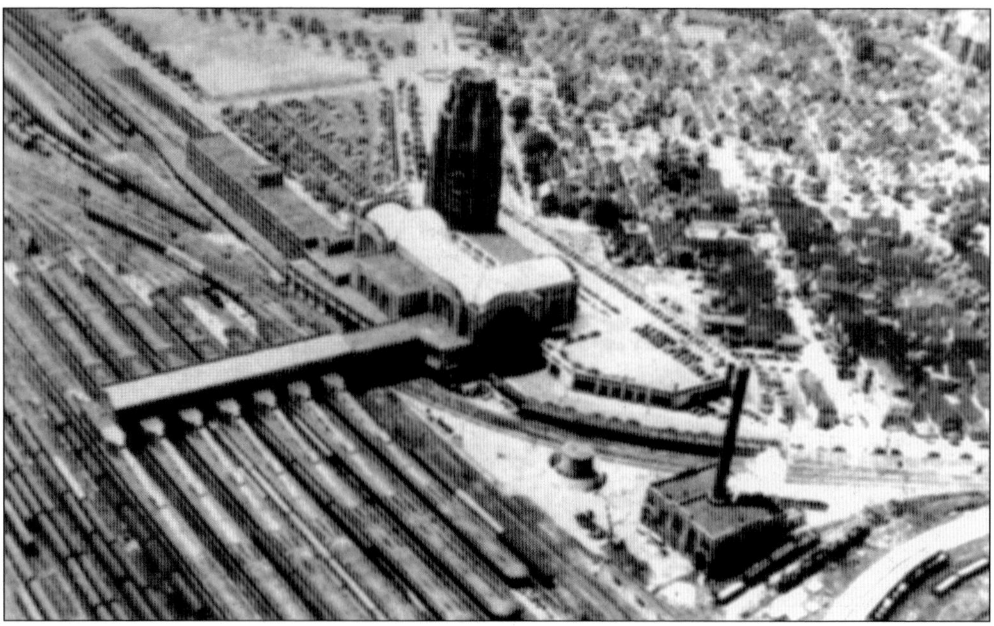

An aerial view of the Buffalo Central Terminal complex from the 1940s shows, moving up from lower right, the power house for steam and heat, the west leg of the NYC's Belt Branch, the concourse, the office tower, and the express building. To the lower left are the coach yards. Trains occupy several of the Terminal's 14 tracks. The non-commercial nature of the adjacent Buffalo neighborhood is painfully apparent. (Patrick Connors collection.)

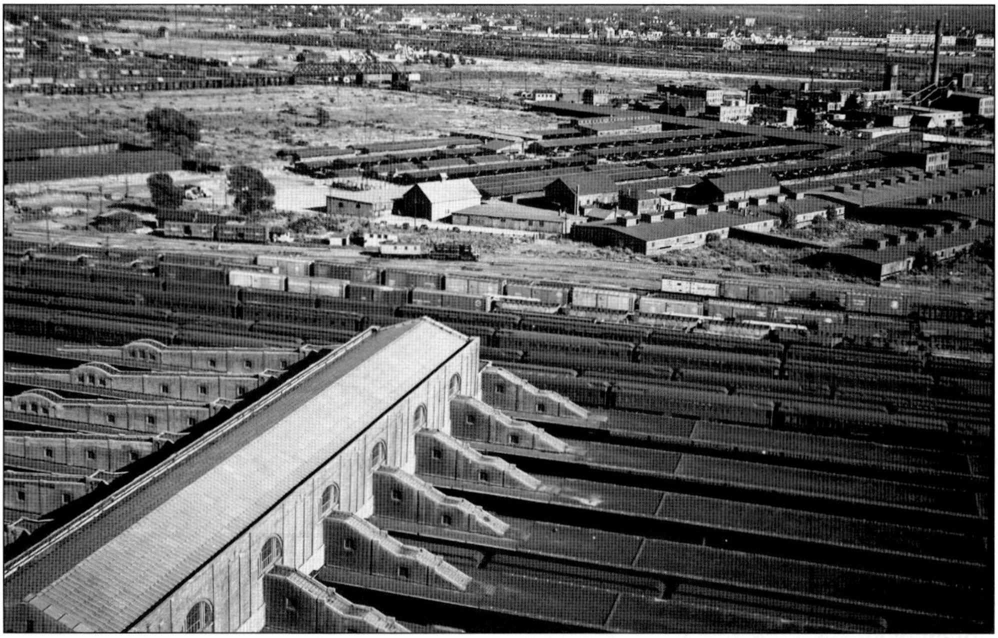

The New York Central (NYC) founded Buffalo Stockyards on December 25, 1863. Much of this 1953 scene looking southeast from the office tower of Buffalo Central Terminal is filled with a carload of hogs being unloaded. Under relentless government-supported trucking, the NYC closed the stockyards in June 1958. In the immediate foreground, passenger ramps and stairs to trackside platforms show part of NYC's 1927–1929 $14 million investment. (New York Central System Historical Society.)

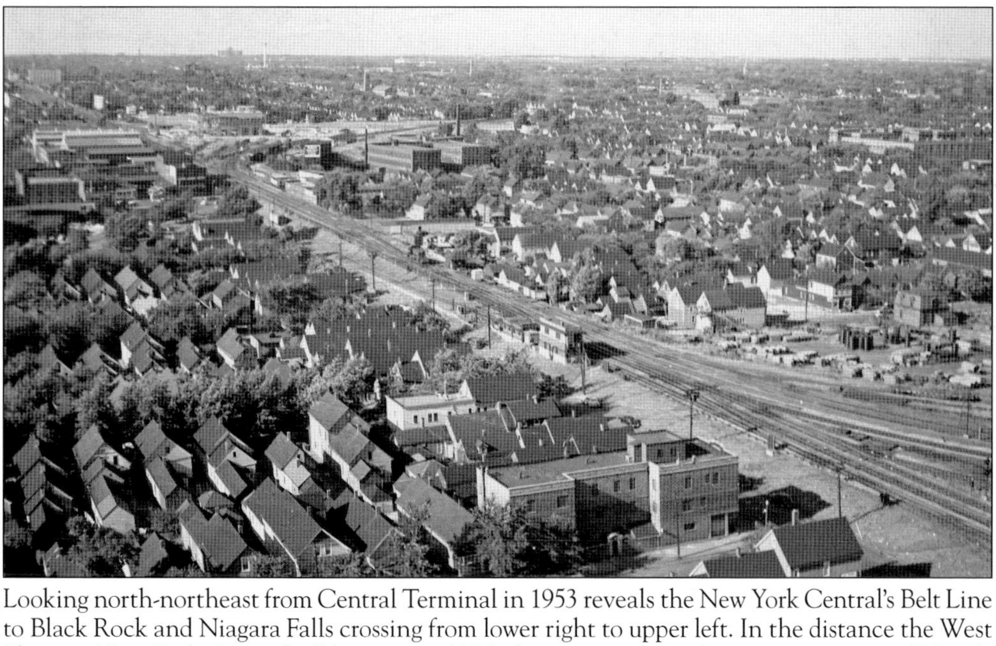

Looking north-northeast from Central Terminal in 1953 reveals the New York Central's Belt Line to Black Rock and Niagara Falls crossing from lower right to upper left. In the distance the West Shore, a New York Central affiliate since 1886, diverges to the right commencing its 426-mile route to New York Harbor at Weehawken, New Jersey. (Photograph by Jeremy Taylor, courtesy of the New York Central System Historical Society.)

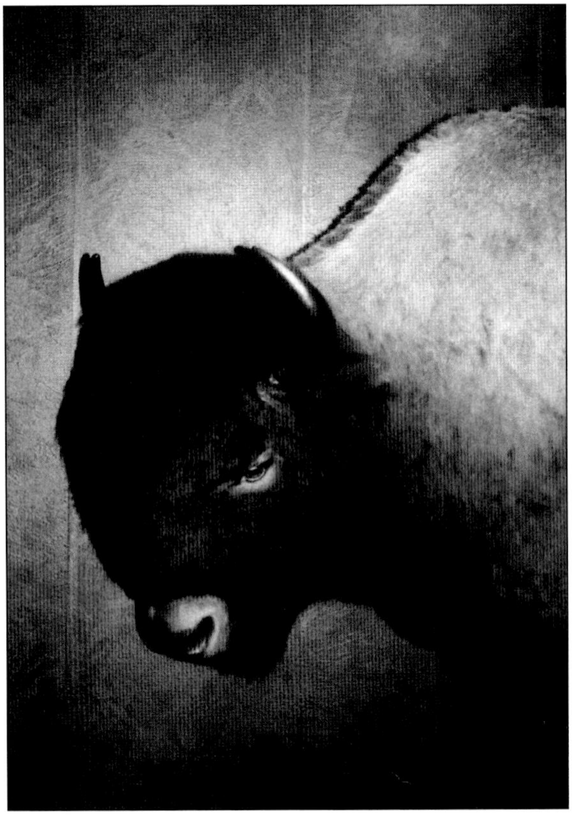

Stuffy the Buffalo was a stuffed bison that stood in the terminal concourse and welcomed weary travelers to his home city. As scores of young men boarded trains to depart for Europe and the Pacific, it was customary to pat Stuffy and grab a clump of hair off of him. Stuffy is currently on display at the Buffalo Museum of Science. (Iron Island Museum collection.)

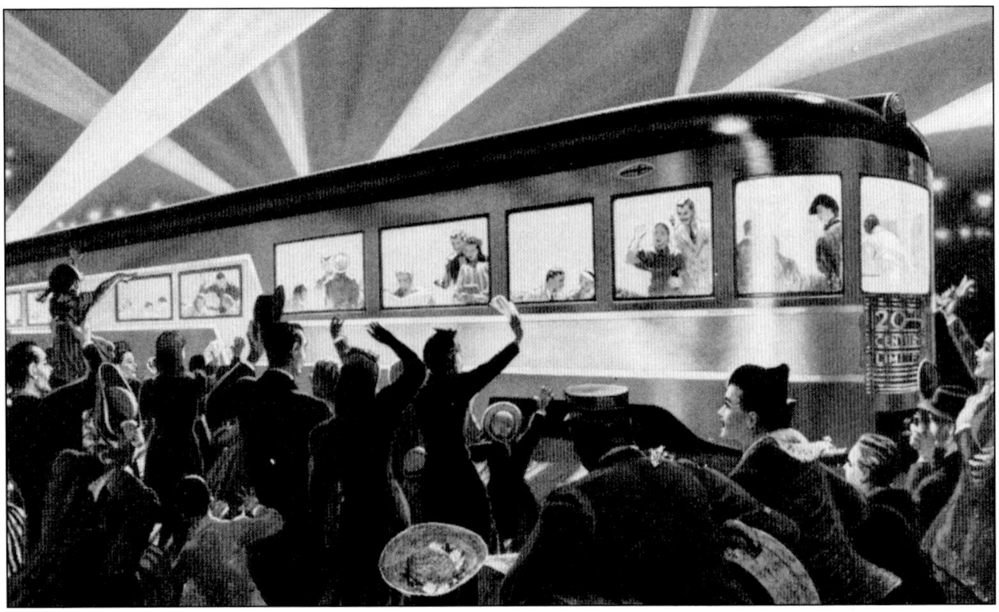

The New York Central 20th Century Limited was the true king of passenger rail travel in the world. This train sped between New York City to Chicago through Buffalo in a mere 16 hours or less and offered red carpet service. The Limited was the choice of travel for the rich and famous. It provided service from 1902 to 1967. ( Medina Railroad Museum. )

# Three

# Erie Lackawanna and Predecessors

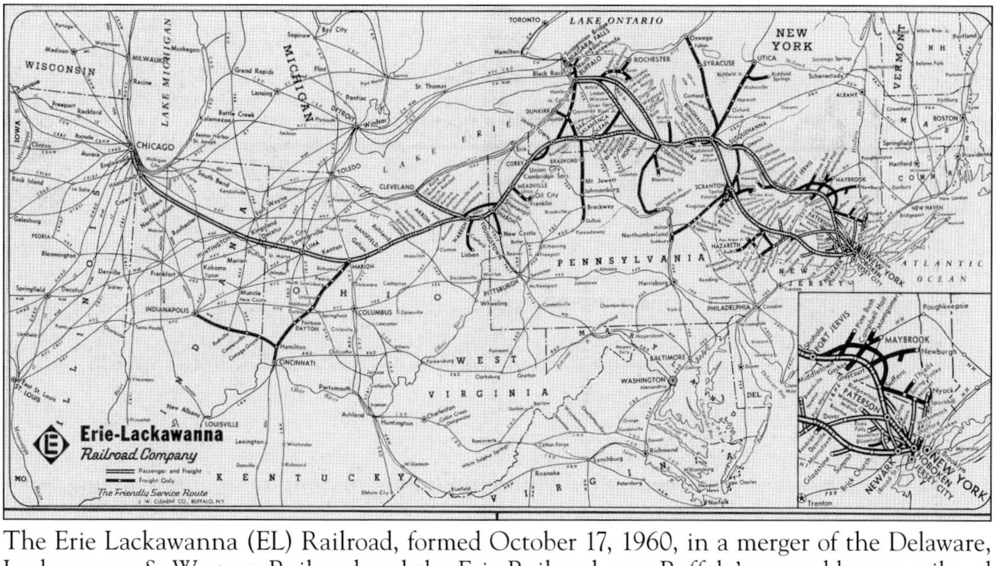


The Erie Lackawanna (EL) Railroad, formed October 17, 1960, in a merger of the Delaware, Lackawanna & Western Railroad and the Erie Railroad, was Buffalo's second-largest railroad during its brief life. Buffalo was important to the EL, and Bison Yard, an electronic hump yard in Sloan constructed in 1963, reflected that. Conrail absorbed the Erie Lackawanna's property in 1976, snuffing out this bright star of railroading. (Michael J. Connor collection.)

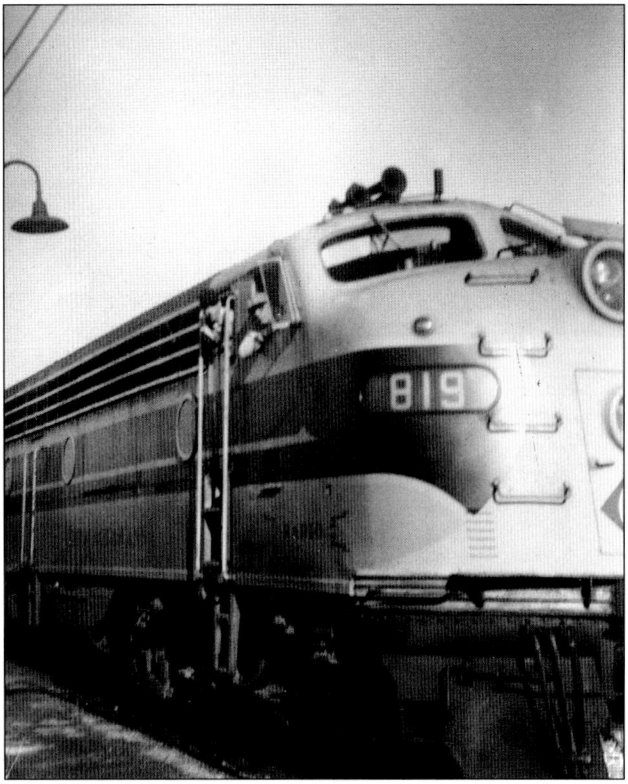


The early years of the Erie Lackawanna saw a continuation of the Delaware, Lackawanna & Western Railroad's Buffalo passenger service, albeit with some renumbering and renaming of the trains. On December 28, 1961, Fireman Joseph F. Seibert (left) and Engineer Frank W. Aberhone have train No. 32, the Buffalo section of the *Erie Lackawanna Limited*, formerly DL&W train No. 6, the *Phoebe Snow*, at Dansville, New York, 76.7 miles from Buffalo. (Photograph by Michael J. Connor.)

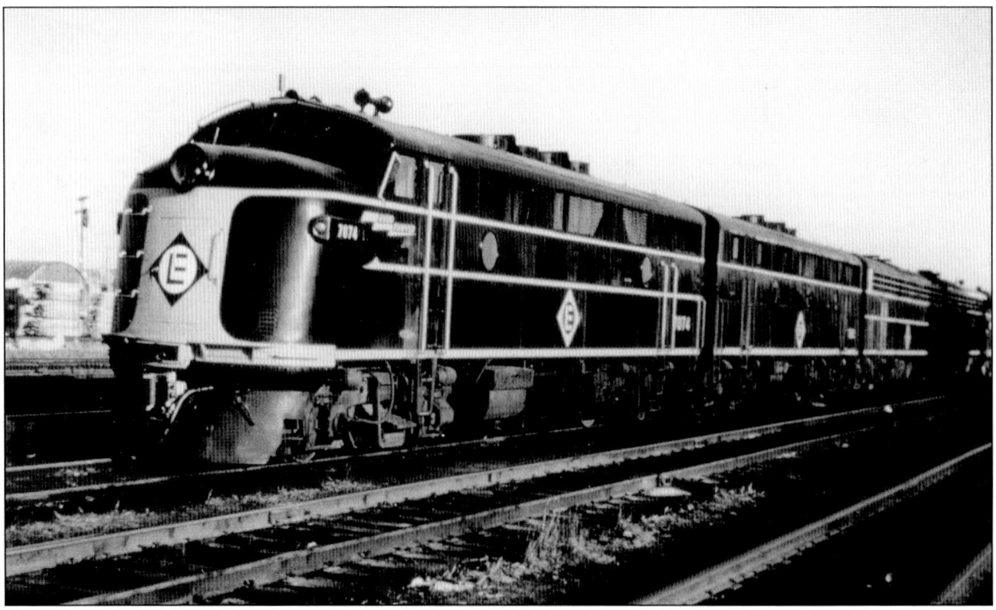

The Erie Lackawanna's October 17, 1960, merger melded the Delaware, Lackawanna & Western Railroad's 212 diesel-electric locomotives with the Erie's 484. Initially this required renumbering, mostly of former DL&W locomotives, and hurried painting and application of the EL diamond. No. 7074, a former Erie locomotive built by General Motors Electro-Motive Division in November 1947 and later retired in 1965, shows an initial merger livery. (Erie Lackawanna Historical Society.)

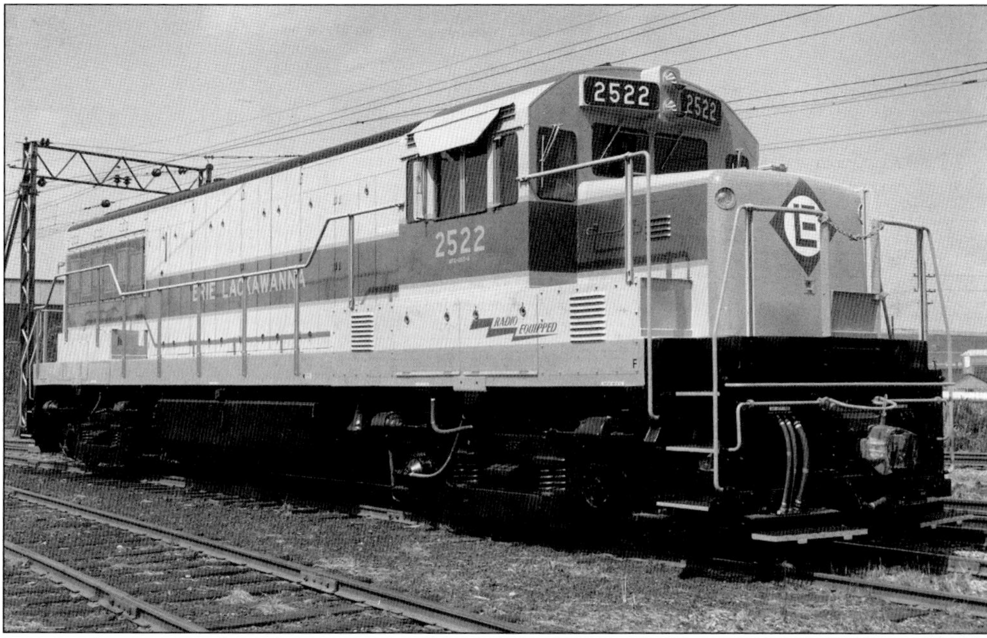


The initial years of the Erie Lackawanna's life resulted in massive deficits, but by 1964, the railroad began to turn around. One of the most visible and necessary examples of the turnaround was the purchase of new locomotives. No. 2522, a model U25B (nicknamed "U-Boats"), is pictured above in Erie, Pennsylvania, at its General Electric manufacturer, in September 1964. (Michael J. Connor collection.)

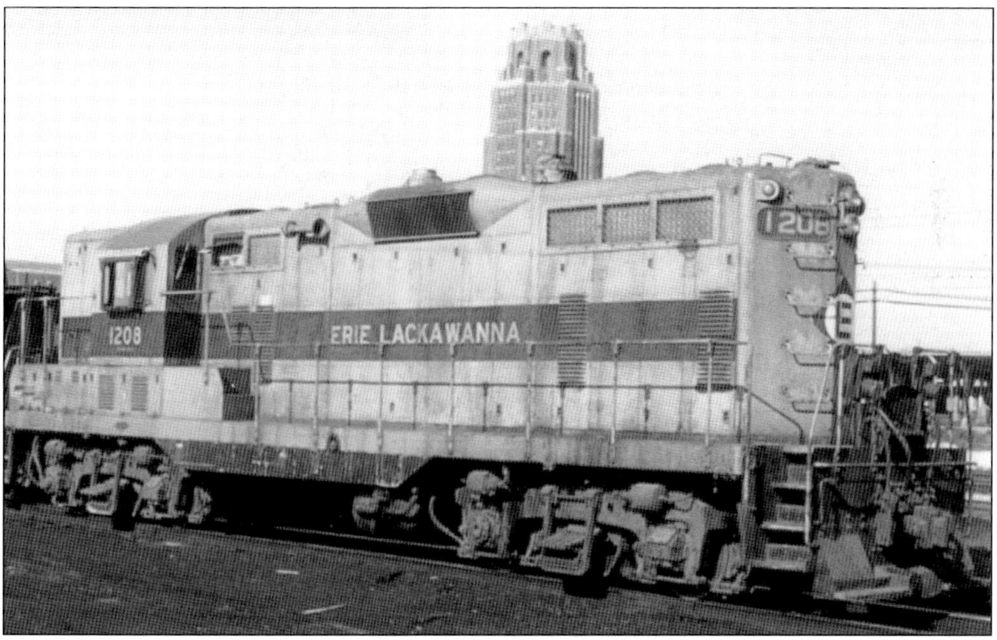


The Erie Lackawanna's October 17, 1960, merger was strongly opposed by some railroads and the EL's unions. The resulting court cases delayed full implementation of the merger until at least December 1961. An Erie Lackawanna EMD GP-7 built in October 1950 sits near Central Terminal. (Nathan Vester collection; Central Terminal Restoration Corporation.)

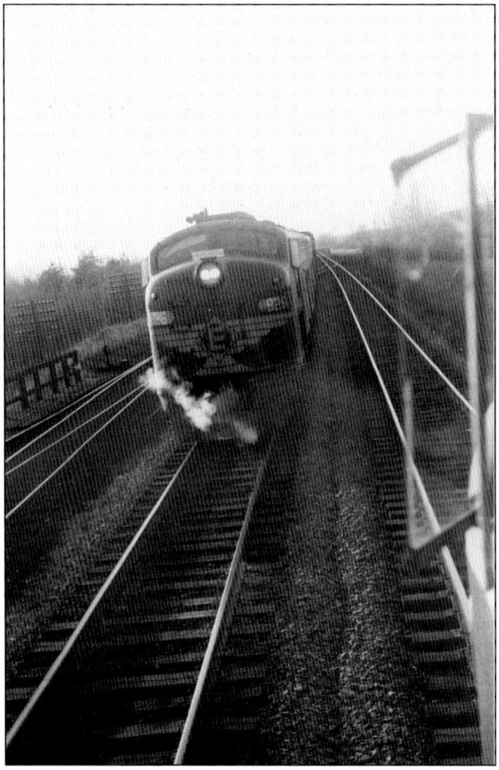

Despite its name, Erie Lackawanna train No. 10, the *New York Mail*, offered excellent passenger amenities and a convenient schedule from Buffalo to communities in New York's Southern Tier. Here on a snowless December 28, 1961, train No. 10, led by former Erie model E-8 diesel-electric locomotive No. 826, arrives in Dansville as train No. 31 departs. The trains are 76.7 miles from Buffalo. (Photograph by Michael J. Connor.)

While the Delaware, Lackawanna & Western Railroad (DL&W) was smaller than its Erie Railroad merger partner, it stood behind no Buffalo railroad in its superior track, streamlined trains, and reliable service. The DL&W's 395.2-mile route was the shortest of any railroad to New York Harbor and its signature passenger train, *The Phoebe Snow*, was a Buffalo travel institution. (Michael J. Connor collection.)

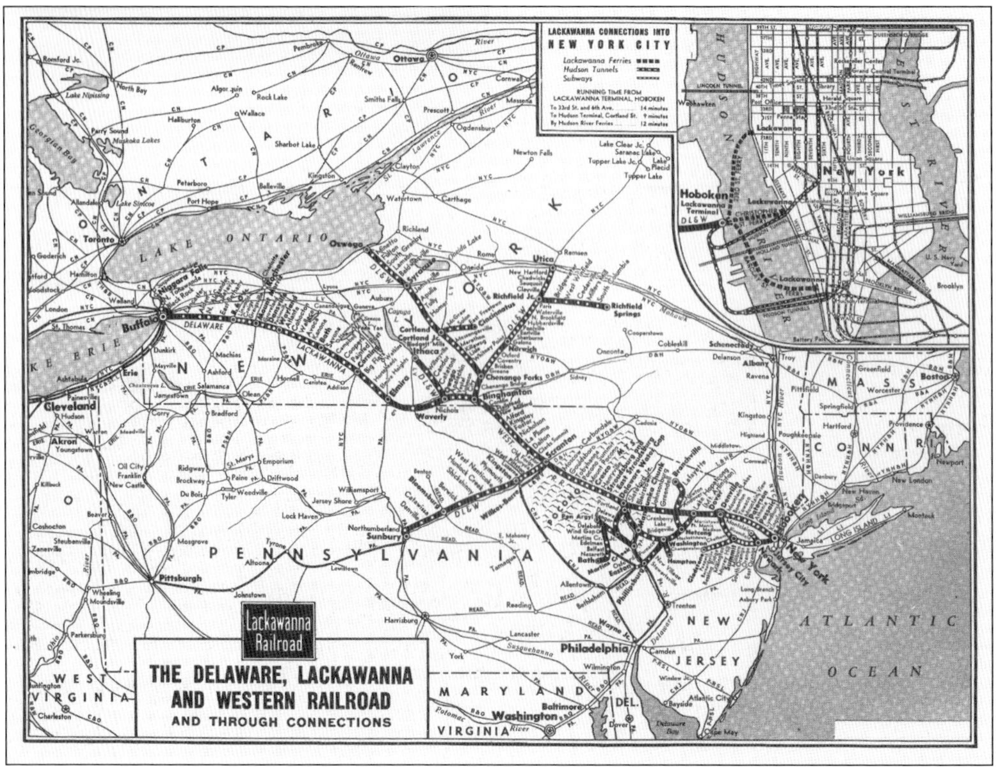

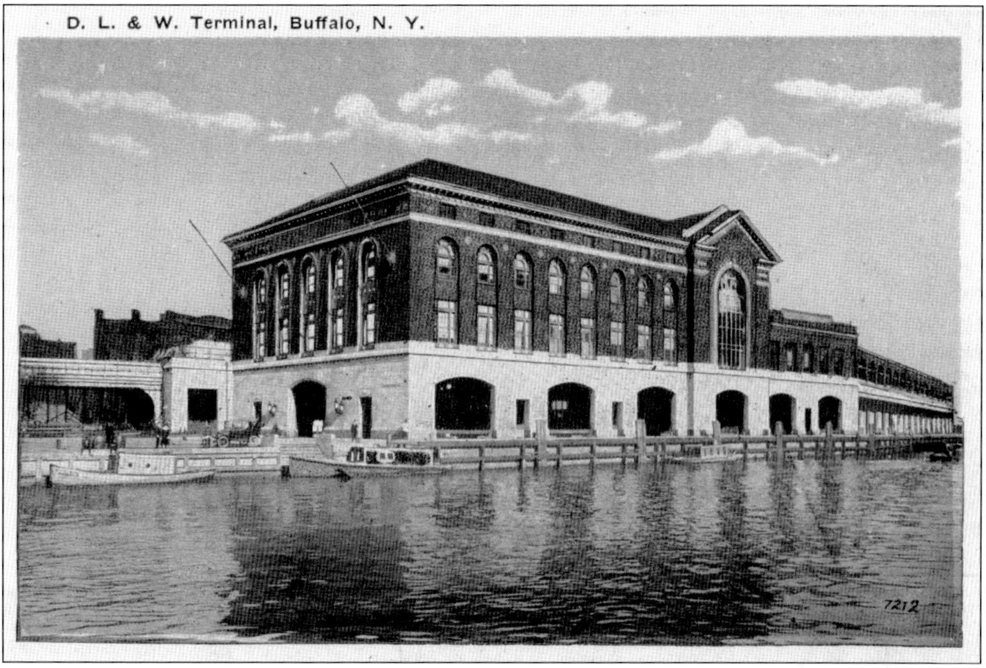


The Delaware, Lackawanna & Western Railroad was a relatively well-off railroad. Reflecting the DL&W's creative use of investment capital was its monumental Buffalo passenger terminal at the foot of Main Street, convenient to downtown Buffalo, used by passenger trains of the DL&W, the Wabash, Nickel Plate, Baltimore & Ohio, and South Buffalo railroads, and featuring frontage on the Buffalo River with direct rail-boat connections. (Stephen G. Myers collection.)

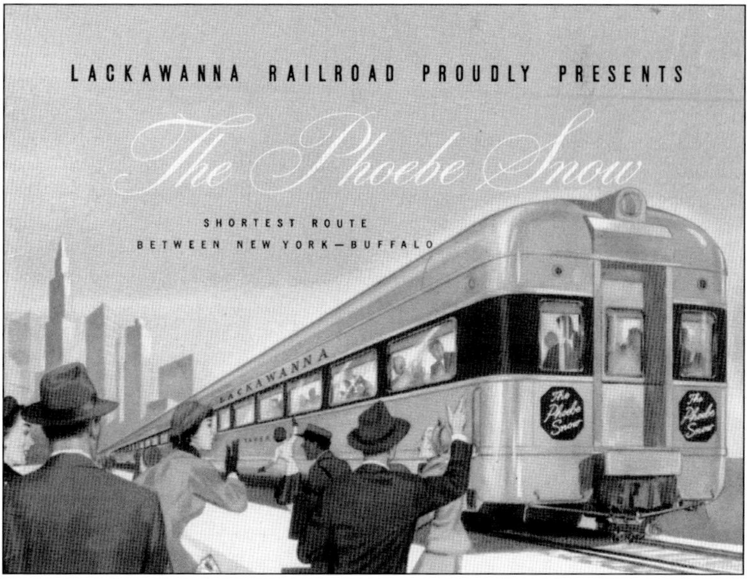


*The Phoebe Snow* was the premier passenger train offered on the Delaware, Lackawanna & Western and showcased the shortest route between New York and Buffalo. She provided a double track steel boulevard 396 miles in length between the two cities as she passed through three states and six major rivers. (Medina Railroad Museum.)

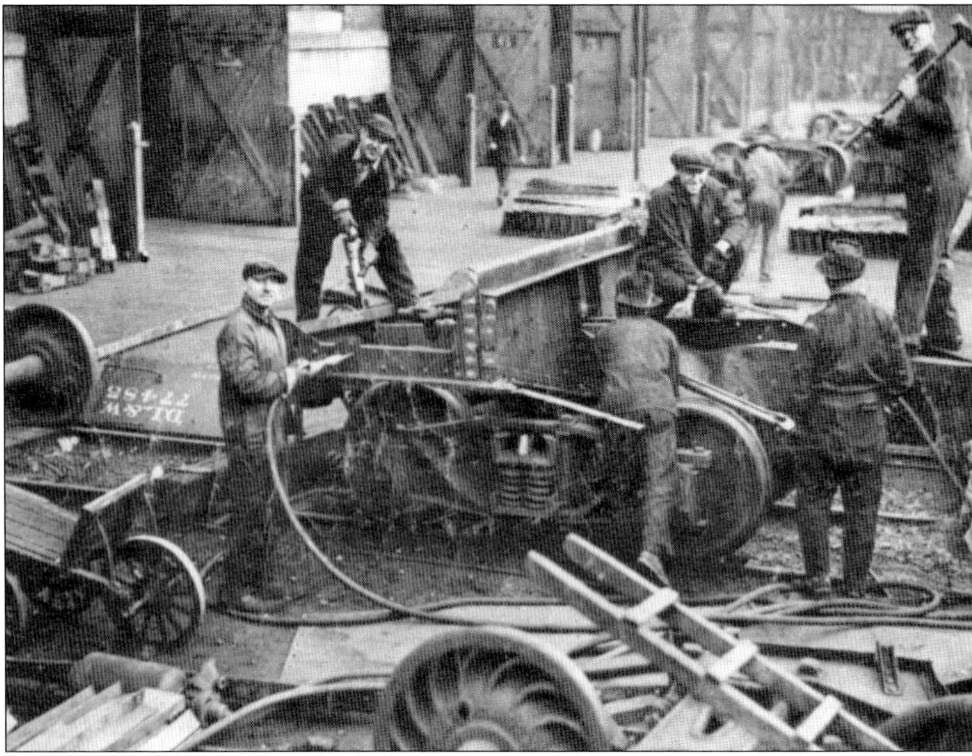

A group of Delaware, Lackawanna & Western car men work in the shop at Buffalo to build and repair train cars. A railway car man was and still is responsible for the inspection and repairs of railway cars. Despite their hard labor, this team looks happy to smile for the camera in this 1907 photograph. (Western New York Heritage Press, Inc. Used by Permission.)

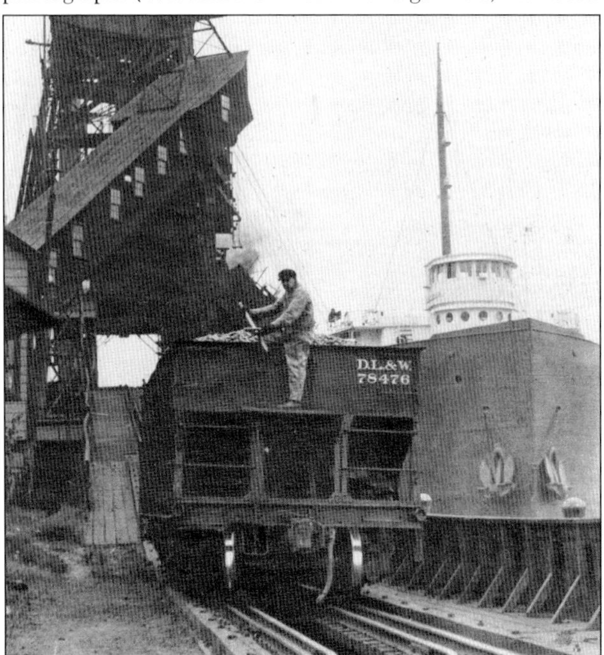

The Delaware, Lackawanna & Western Railroad was the only railroad to provide a rail-to-water coal transfer facility in Buffalo. The DL&W's dumper was just west of its Buffalo passenger terminal on the Buffalo River. Here *c.* 1925, a brakeman rides a 50-ton capacity hopper car to the rotary dumper. Besides trainloads of DL&W originated anthracite coal, the facility also handled bituminous coal delivered by the Buffalo, Rochester, and Pittsburgh Railway. (Western New York Heritage Press, Inc. Used by Permission.)

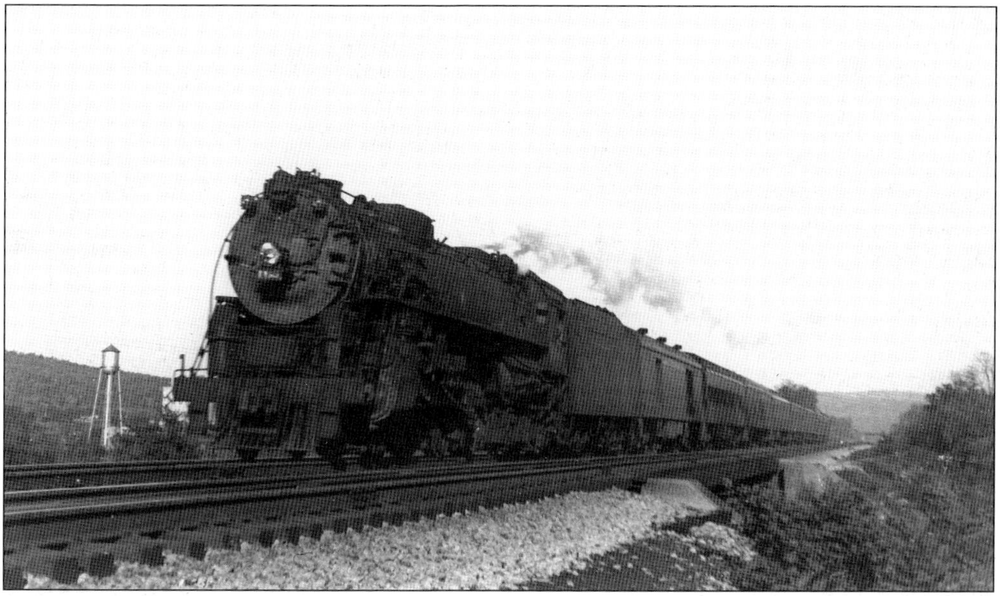

Delaware, Lackawanna & Western Train No. 3, known in this 1949 view as *The Lackawanna Limited*, races through Big Flats, New York, with Buffalo 135 miles and 2.5 hours away. Within months this train would be totally re-equipped with new General Motors model E8A diesel-electric locomotives and sleek Budd-built cars. In new attire, No. 3 (and eastbound counterpart No. 6) would be christened *The Phoebe Snow*. (Photograph by Jeremy Taylor.)

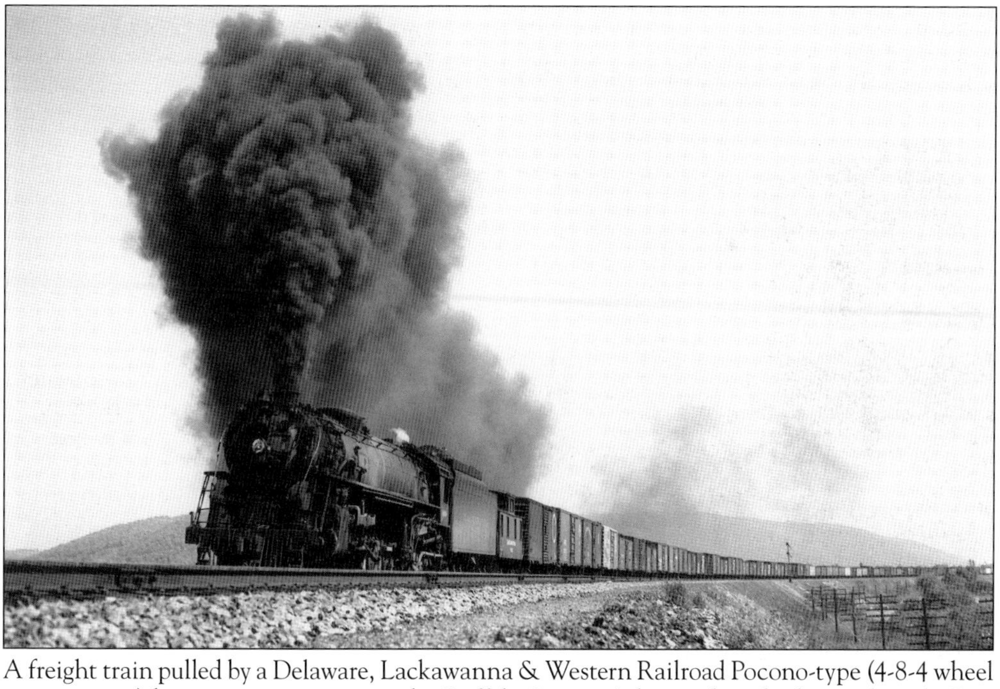

A freight train pulled by a Delaware, Lackawanna & Western Railroad Pocono-type (4-8-4 wheel arrangement) locomotive moves over the Buffalo Division's heavy-duty, high-speed track. East Buffalo yard is 135 miles west of this location near Horseheads, New York. With a fresh Elmira-based crew, the DL&W dispatchers and train crews will bring this train in on time. (Photograph by Jeremy Taylor.)

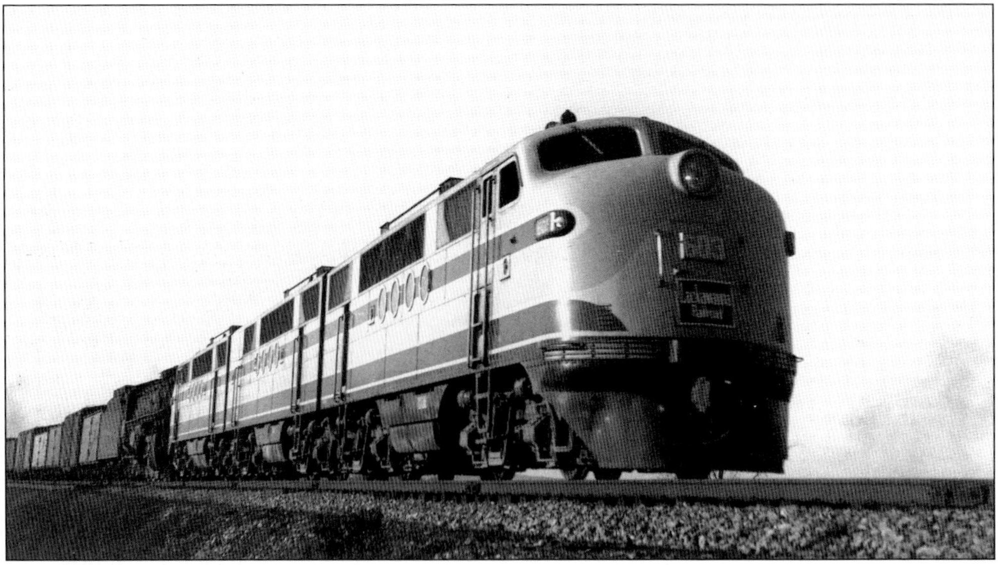

The DL&W was effectively dieselized by 1951. In the years immediately prior, it was common to see diesel-electric locomotives double-headed with steam locomotives. Here No. 603, a three-unit 4,500-horsepower locomotive, is assisting a Pocono-type (4-8-4 wheel arrangement) steam locomotive with an eastbound freight train near Corning, New York, with cars of perishable traffic (meat, fruit, and vegetables), received from connecting railroads at Buffalo. (Photograph by Jeremy Taylor.)

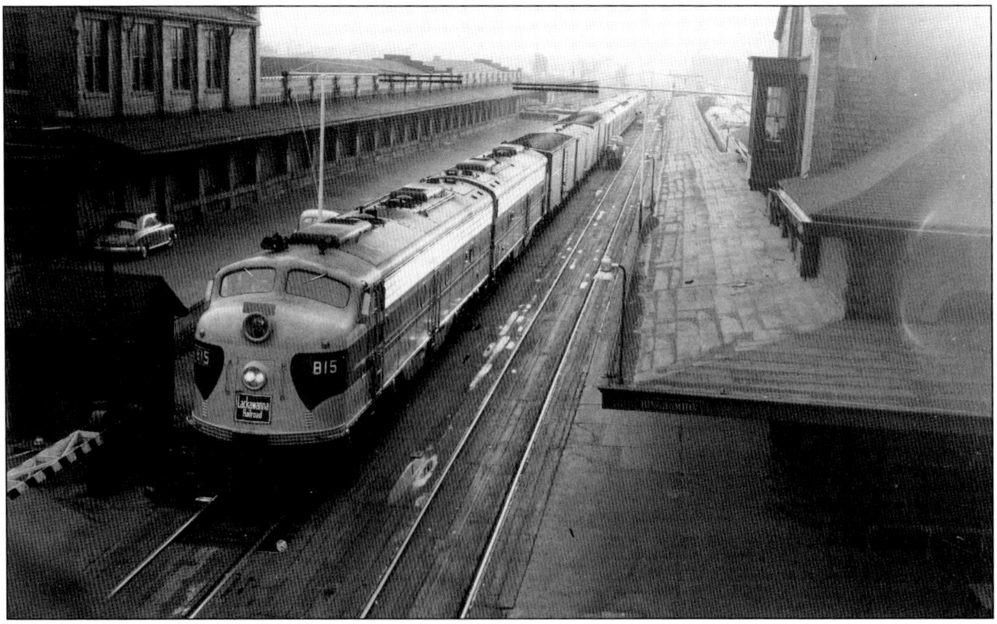



Buffalo's influence on the Delaware, Lackawanna & Western Railroad was system-wide. In this 1952 scene from the Chenango Street bridge in Binghamton, Train No. 3, the *Phoebe Snow*, is serviced while changing crews and receiving passengers, mail, baggage, and express. Immediately behind the locomotives are express boxcars equipped for passenger train service—at Buffalo they as well as a coach and sleeping car will be passed on to connecting railroads. (Photograph by Jeremy Taylor.)

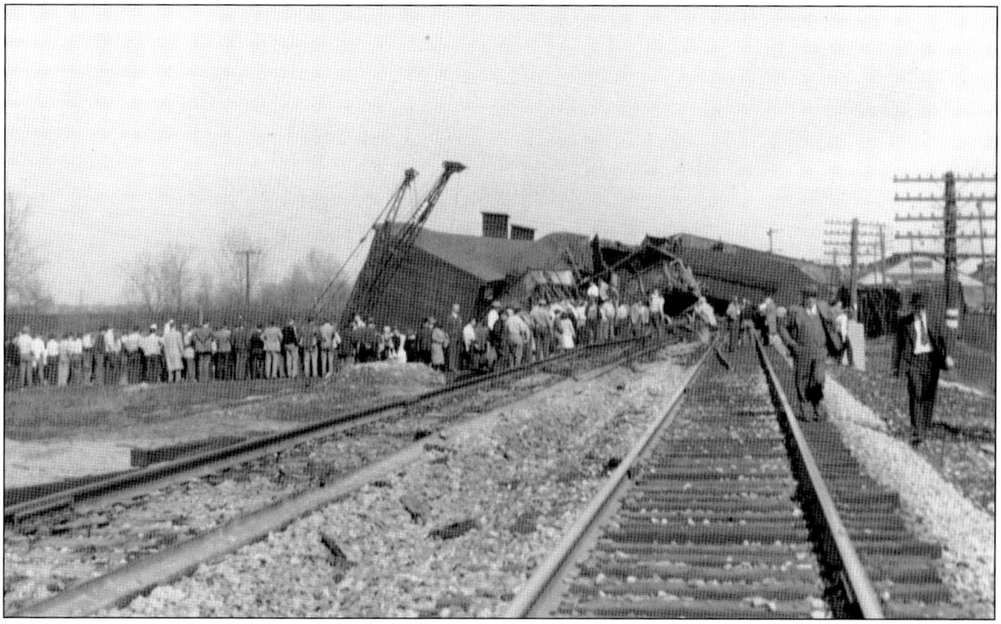

This large derailment garnered much attention on April 12, 1949, when a DL&W train wreck fell into the William F. Dougherty Coal Company in Depew, New York, causing much damage to the coal sheds and blocking the main line of the railroad. Village residents watch as the railcars are cleared. (Village Of Depew Historian collection.)

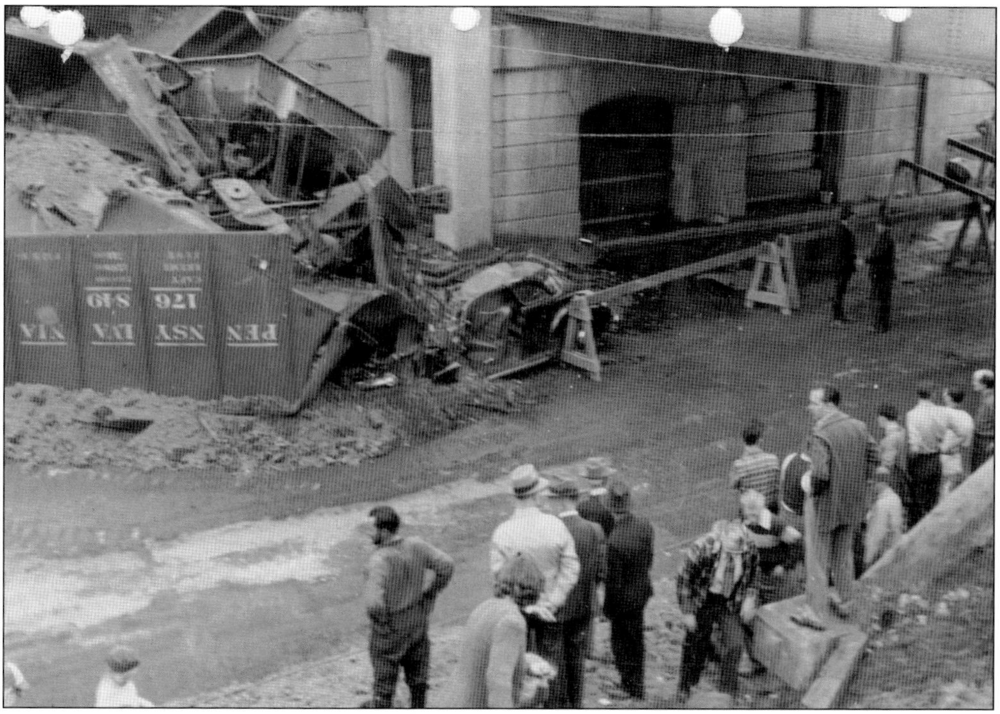

Not only did the derailment cause cars to plow into the coal sheds, but this event turned into tragedy when several cars fell from the Transit Road bridge and onto an automobile. Heavy equipment and cranes were rushed to the sight to remove the debris. (Village Of Depew Historian collection.)

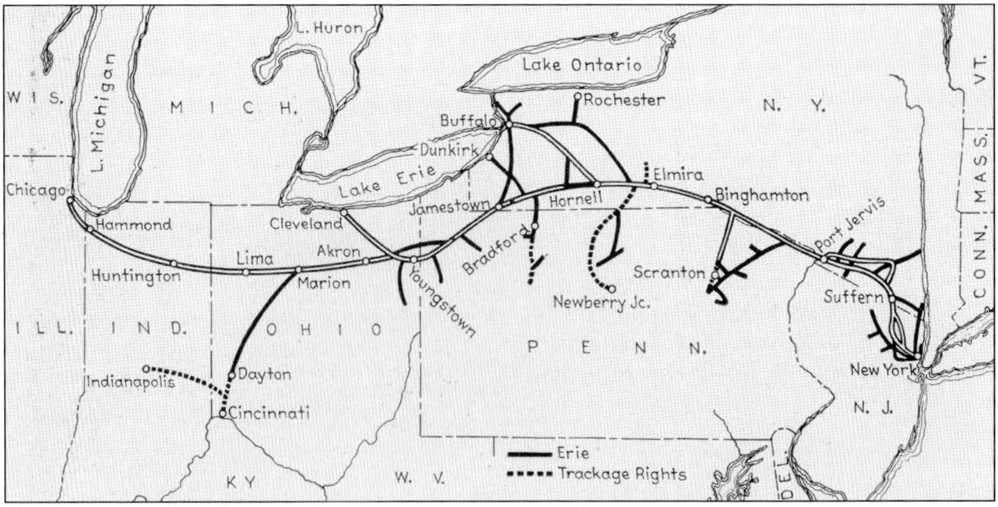


The 2,352-mile Erie Railroad was the second railroad to reach Buffalo. At its peak, the Erie employed 2,500 people in the area and handled over 200,000 carloads to, from, and through Buffalo annually. From Buffalo the Erie operated a main line to Jersey City, New Jersey, and secondary main lines to Jamestown, Black Rock, Suspension Bridge, and Lockport. Its 425-mile line was the second-shortest route to New York Harbor. (Michael J. Connor collection.)

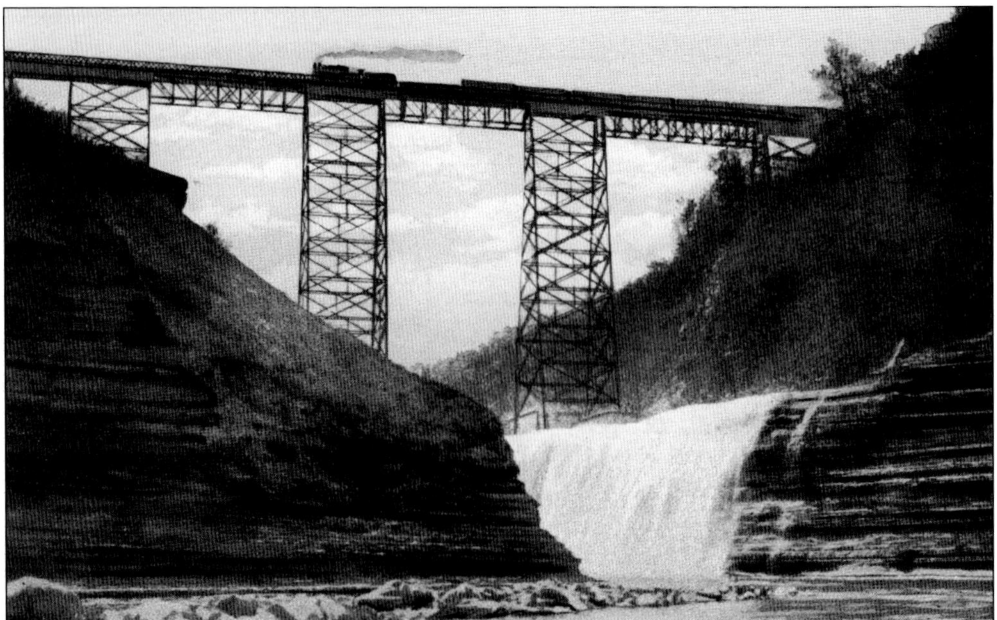

The 1876 iron and steel Portage Viaduct, pictured *c.* 1915, over the Genesee River in today's Letchworth State Park, carries today's much heavier locomotives and cars and its replacement is imminent. Originally carrying the Erie's unique 6-foot gauge tracks, it has been standard gauge since the early 1880s. It is the last remaining of a number of long and high railroad trestles in Western New York. (Stephen G. Myers collection.)

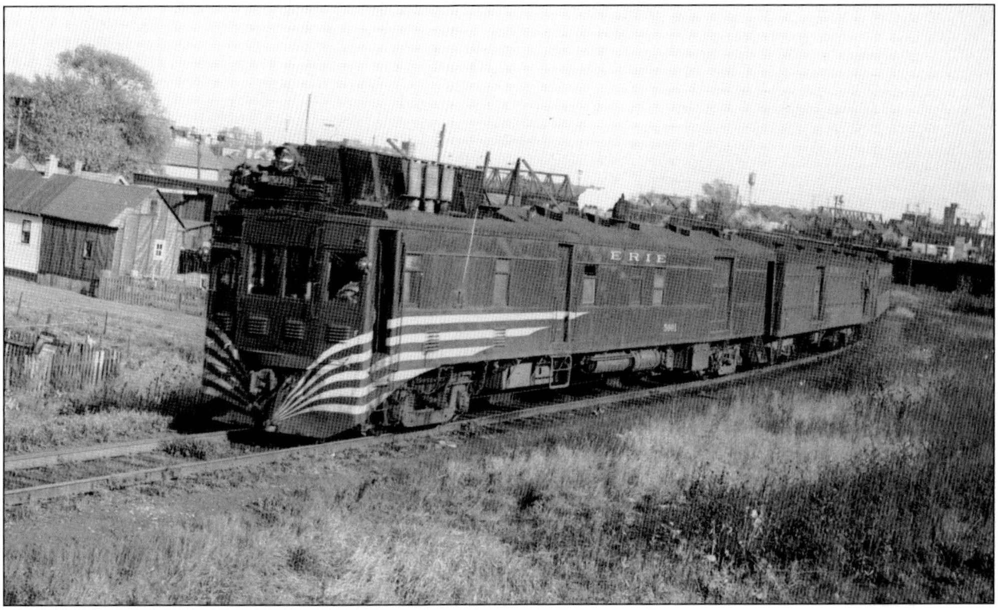


The Erie Railroad, like all railroads, was constantly seeking to reduce costs, especially with the decline in passenger ridership. The gas electric car 5001 was one of those innovations. Rather than the expense and labor to operate a steam locomotive, the 5001 was a self-propelled car that also had a baggage area. In her life, the baggage area was used as a railway post office. (Phil Soyring collection.)

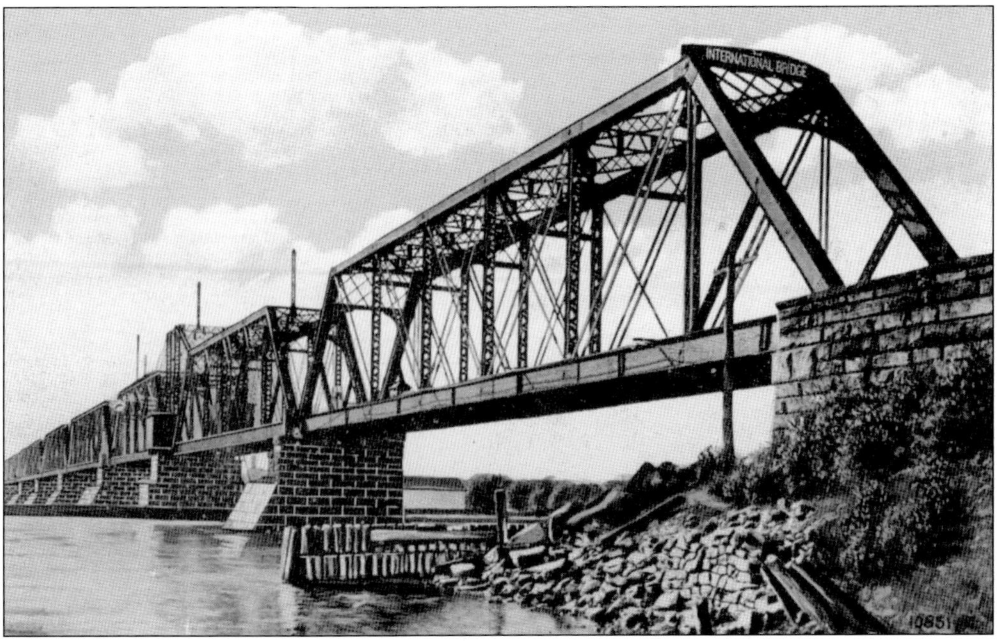


The International Railroad Bridge linking Fort Erie, Canada, with Buffalo's Black Rock District was the goal of several railroads. Erie rails reached the bridge in 1874, eight years before the Delaware, Lackawanna & Western Railroad. The Erie's International Bridge branch diverged from its Buffalo-to-Niagara Falls Main Line south of Kenmore Avenue. Conrail abandoned the grade-separated and almost curveless line in the 1980s. (Stephen G. Myers collection.)

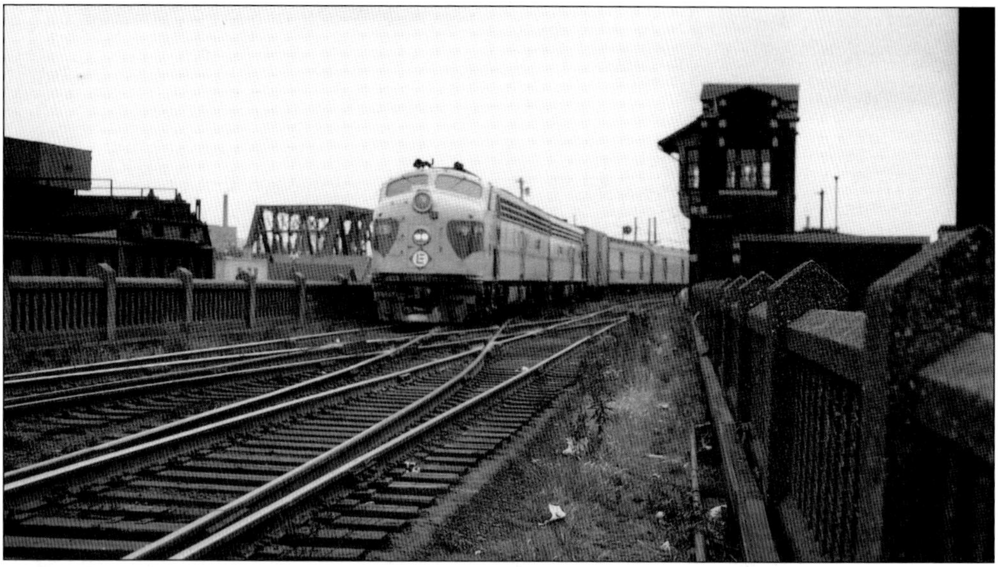

Just after the Erie and DL&W merger, locomotive No. 812, an EMD E-8A locomotive, is approaching the Delaware, Lackawanna & Western's Buffalo terminal with her train. The terminal was located on the shore of the Buffalo River. Most of the terminal was demolished in 1979. (Phil Soyring collection.)

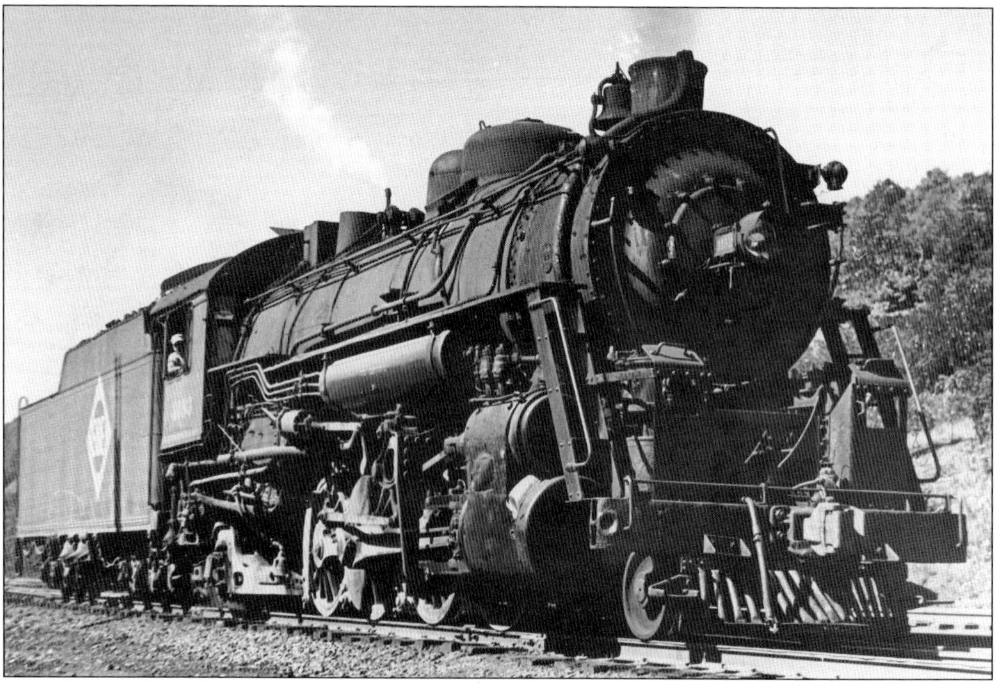

Steam locomotive No. 3193, pictured in 1949 at Clarion Junction, Pennsylvania, was a regular visitor to Buffalo before 1944. The Portage Viaduct over the Genesee River in Letchworth State Park was unable to handle any engines heavier than these Mikado-type (2-8-2 wheel arrangement) and then only when not double-headed. Emergency wartime improvements opened the bridge to the Erie's biggest locomotives. (George W. Thornton photograph, courtesy Erie Lackawanna Historical Society.)

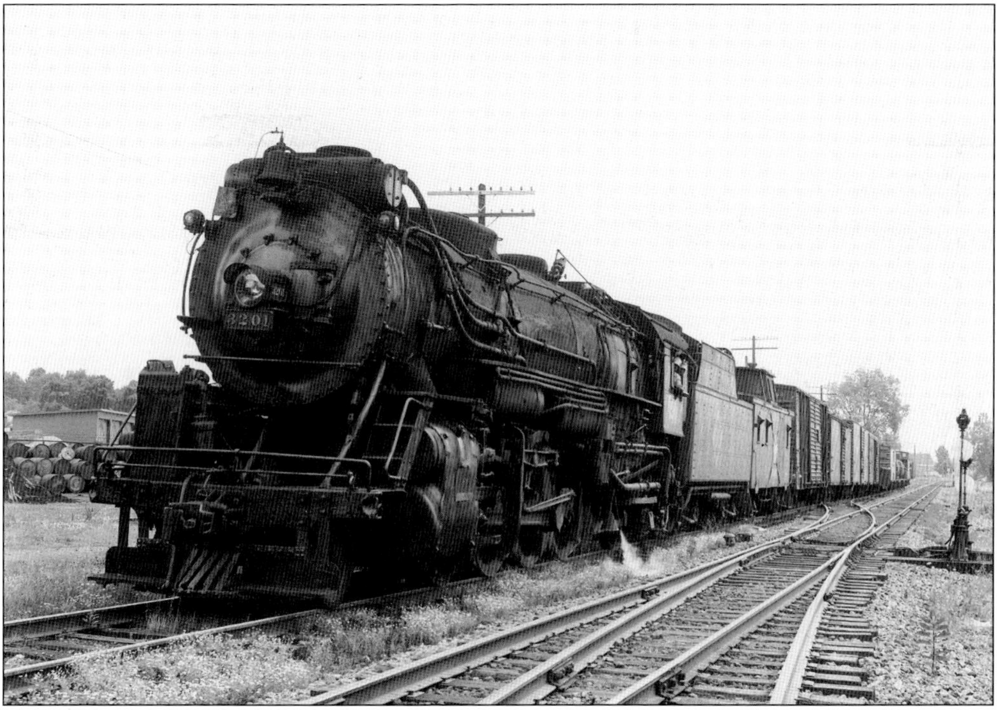

The Erie was a player for Buffalo-to-Chicago freight via its Buffalo and Southwestern line, which linked its main line at Jamestown with Buffalo via Hamburg. Here in 1949, No. 3201, a Mikado-type (2-8-2 wheel arrangement) locomotive, is in Hamburg in charge of the way freight, the Erie's name for the trains that served all customers between major cities. (Photograph by James Van Brocklin.)

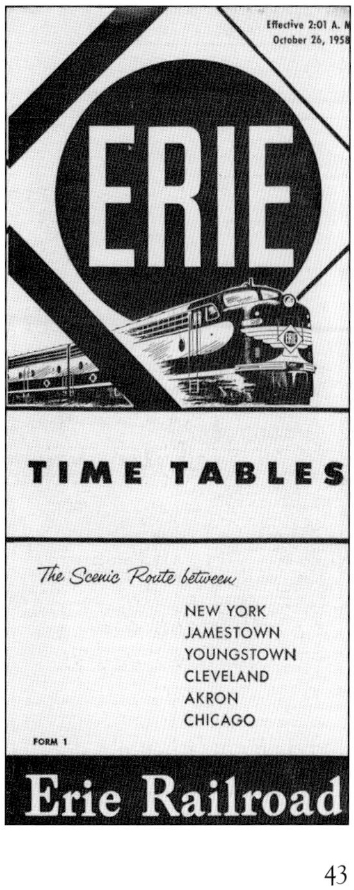


The Erie Railroad was a New York to Chicago route and had much competition from other rail lines like the New York Central Railroad and Pennsylvania Railroad. As a national highway system and airlines began to develop, the Erie found herself in an even fiercer situation. A 1958 timetable still proudly hails her passenger trains as *The Scenic Route*. (Joshua T. Myers collection.)

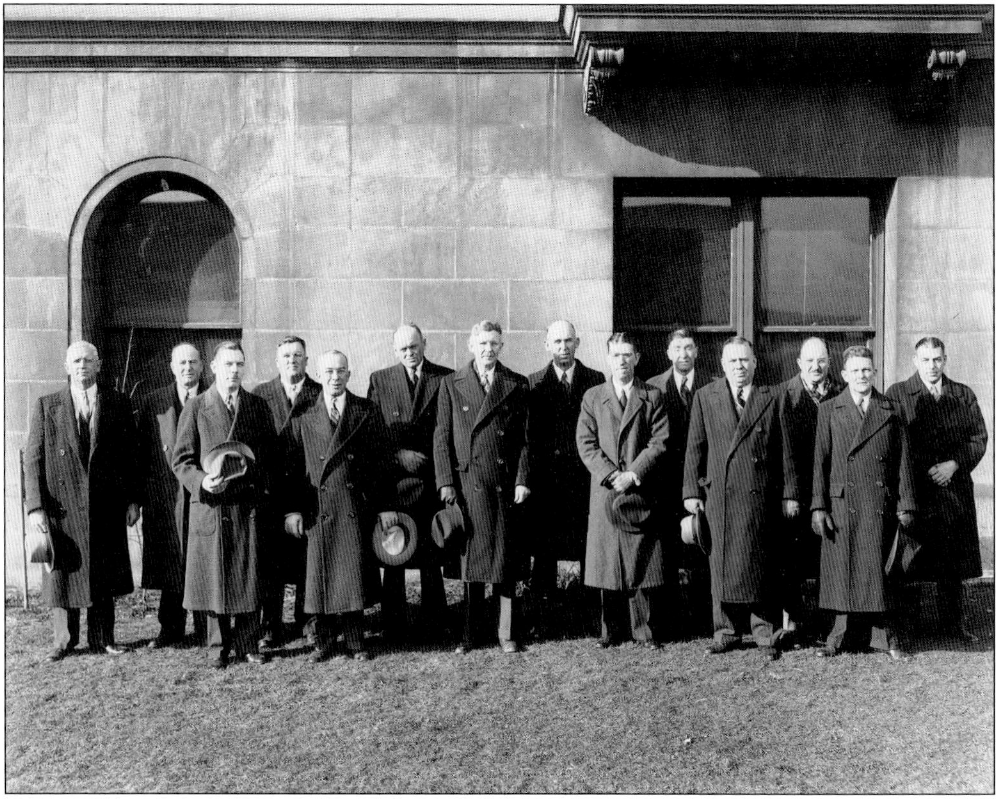

Buffalo and Rochester Division Engineer George E. Righter (seventh from left) and staff, here in January 1939, were responsible for the Division's track, bridges, signals, and buildings, on 268 miles of railroad line containing over 500 miles of track. Coauthor Connor's grandfather, Charles L. Connor Sr. (sixth from left) was responsible for the 147.3 miles from Attica and Rochester to Painted Post, New York. (Michael J. Connor collection.)

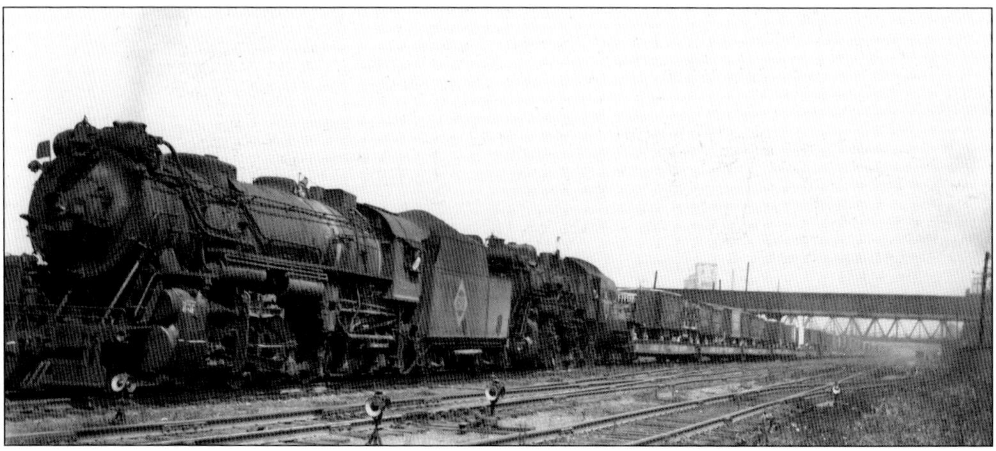

Besides reliable freight and passenger transportation, the railroads brought the circus to town. Here in 1949 double-headed Erie steam locomotives are westbound with the Strates Brothers Circus for a performance at the Erie County Fair in Hamburg. The train is running on Buffalo Creek rails and has just gone under the DL&W. Further in the distance is the South Park Avenue bridge. (Richard H. Ganger photograph, courtesy William C. Kessel.)

## *Four*

# PENNSYLVANIA, PENN CENTRAL, AND CONRAIL

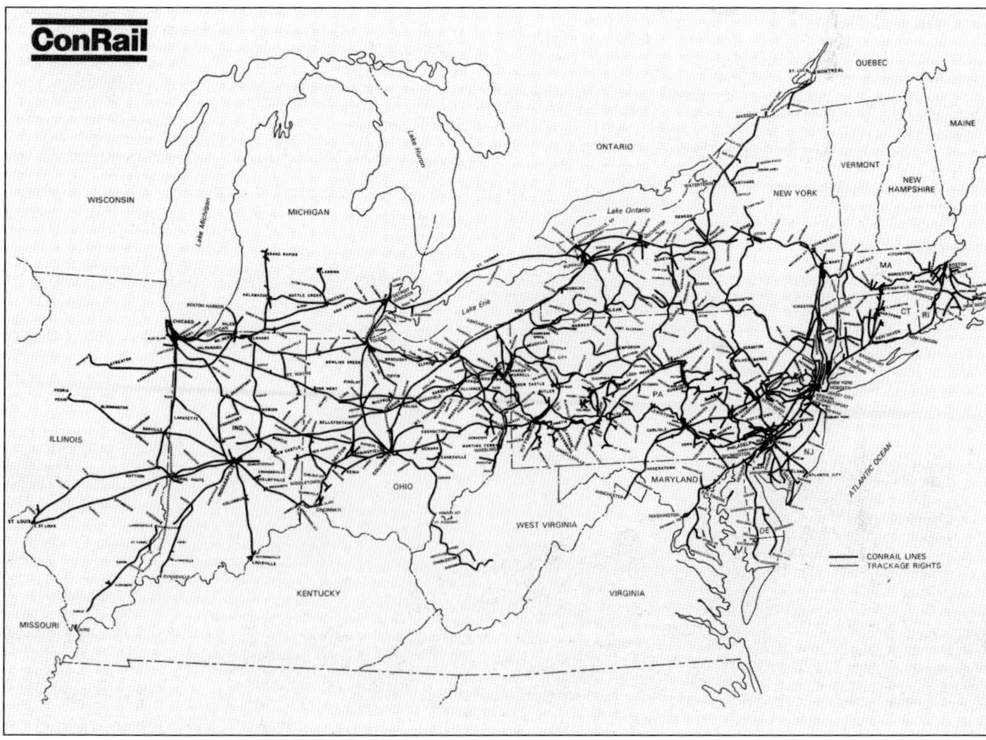


Decades of restrictive economic regulation, excessive taxation, and intensive government promotion of competing transportation modes brought bankruptcy to Buffalo's Penn Central, Lehigh Valley, and Erie Lackawanna railroads between 1970 and 1973. Conrail was federally chartered on April 1, 1976, to acquire assets of the bankrupt railroads and meld a profitable system from them. Conrail's ultimate financial success was partially at the price of greatly diminished railroad service in Buffalo. (Michael J. Connor collection.)

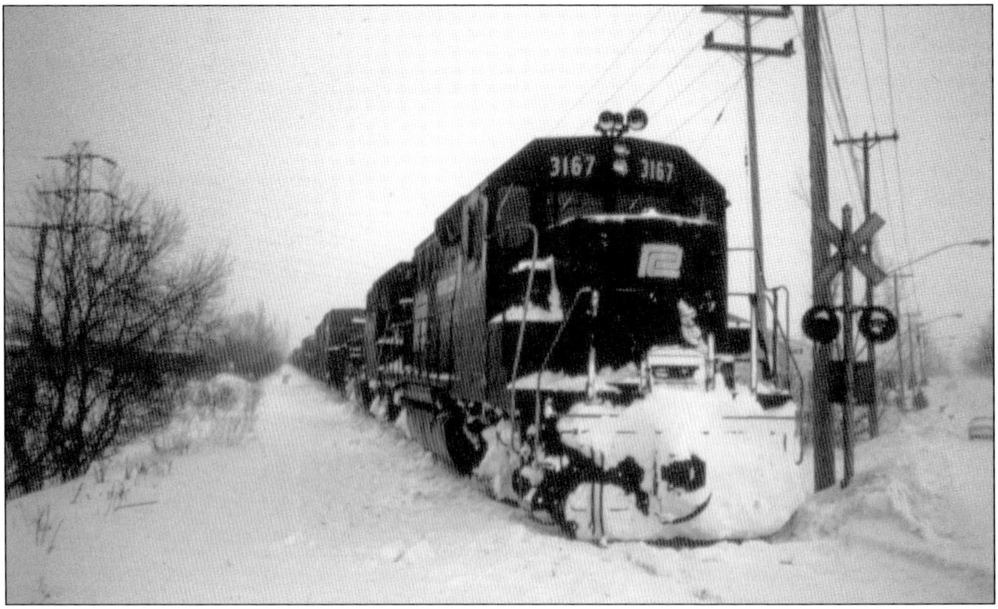


The first winter under Conrail leadership turned into an operational nightmare with the Blizzard of 1976–1977. The storm's blockage of terminals caused even trains on clear track to outlaw. In February 1977, a train on the former Erie Lackawanna, a route only lightly affected by the storm, stands with no crew near Lancaster awaiting a relief crew and a clear arrival track. (Photograph by Michael J. Connor.)

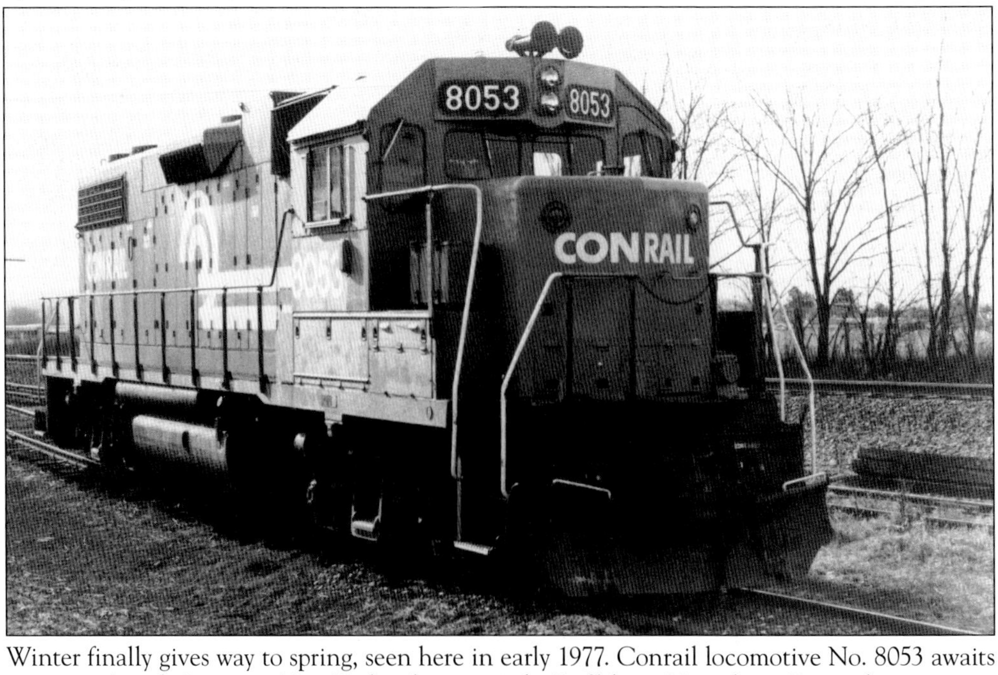


Winter finally gives way to spring, seen here in early 1977. Conrail locomotive No. 8053 awaits a crew at Arcade Junction, New York, adjacent to the Buffalo-to-Harrisburg, Pennsylvania, main line. Here one-year-old Conrail connected with the 60-year-old Arcade & Attica Railroad. No. 8053, a 2,000-horsepower locomotive, was one of 223 GP 38-2s built for Penn Central and acquired by Conrail. (Photograph by Patrick Connors.)

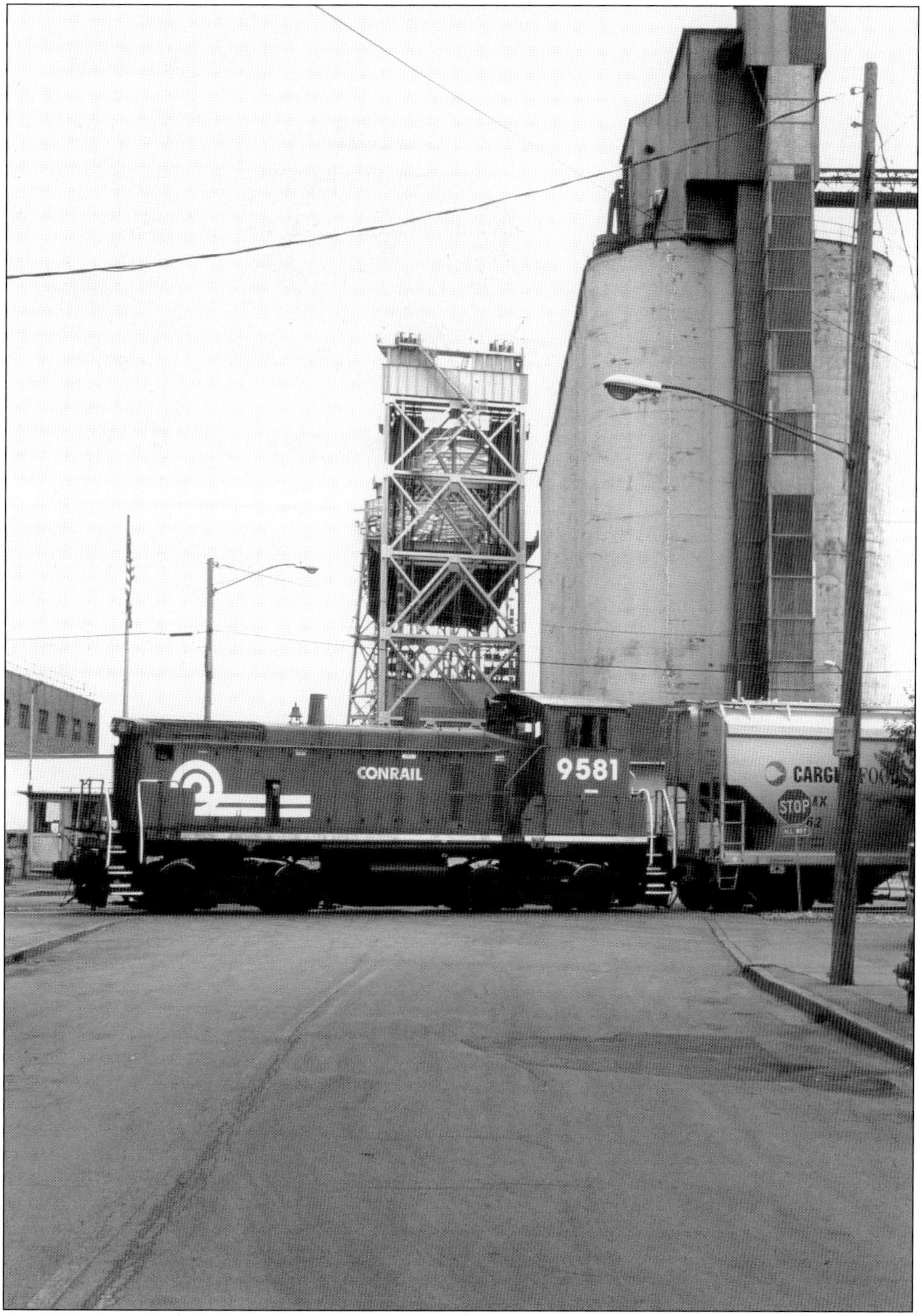


A Conrail EMD SW1500 locomotive at Michigan Street has train OS 11 switching local industries on September 9, 1997. This former Penn Central locomotive was built by General Motors and has 1,500 horsepower. Conrail kept a fleet of switcher locomotives in the Buffalo area due to the vast number of railroad-served industries. (Photograph by Stephan M. Koenig.)

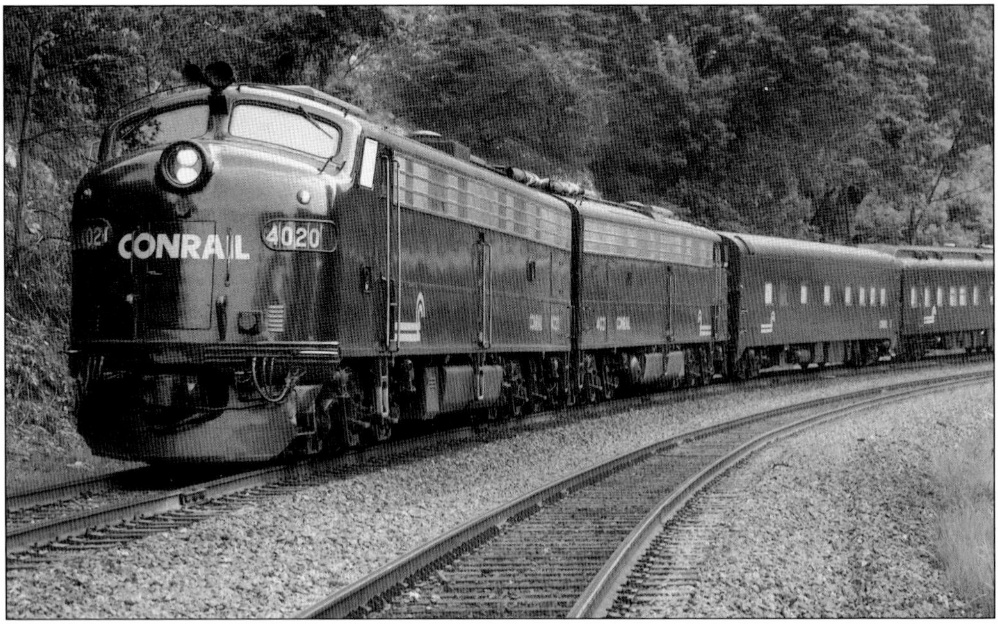


Conrail did not operate passenger service but was a host railroad for several Amtrak routes, including service through Buffalo. For formal inspections of the railroad Conrail operated this inspection train, which featured E8A locomotives including locomotives inherited from the former Erie Lackawanna and Pennsylvania railroads. It was an elegant way to meet the utilitarian task of long-distance railroad inspection. (Michael J. Connor collection.)

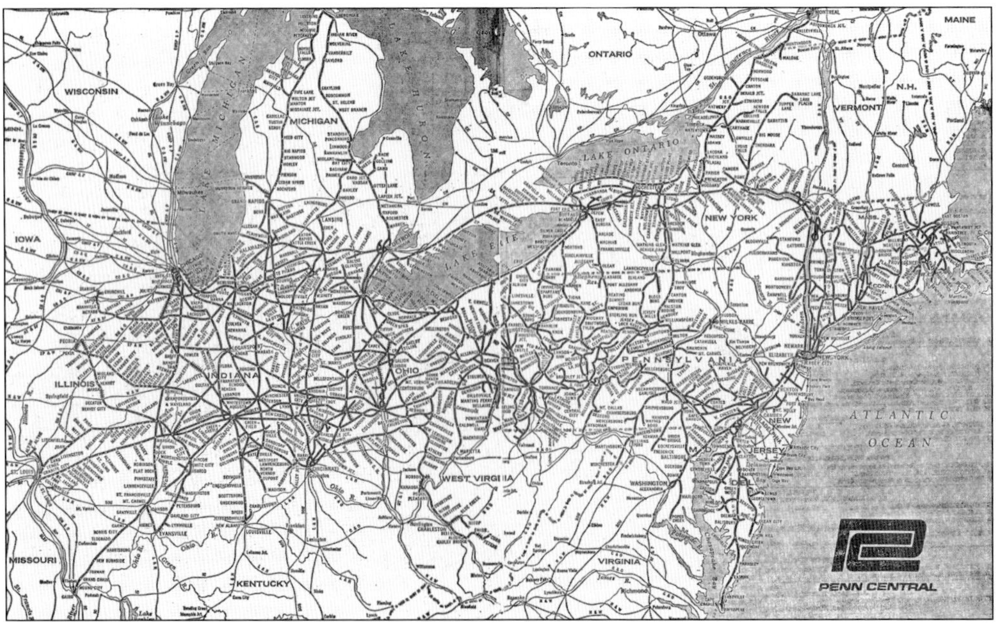


The February 1, 1968, merger of the New York Central and Pennsylvania railroads to form the 19,177-mile Pennsylvania New York Central Transportation Company was quickly renamed Penn Central. Initially it was viewed as a new era in railroading but the nation's largest railroad was doomed by a number of serious issues and entered bankruptcy 871 days later on June 21, 1970. (Michael J. Connor collection.)

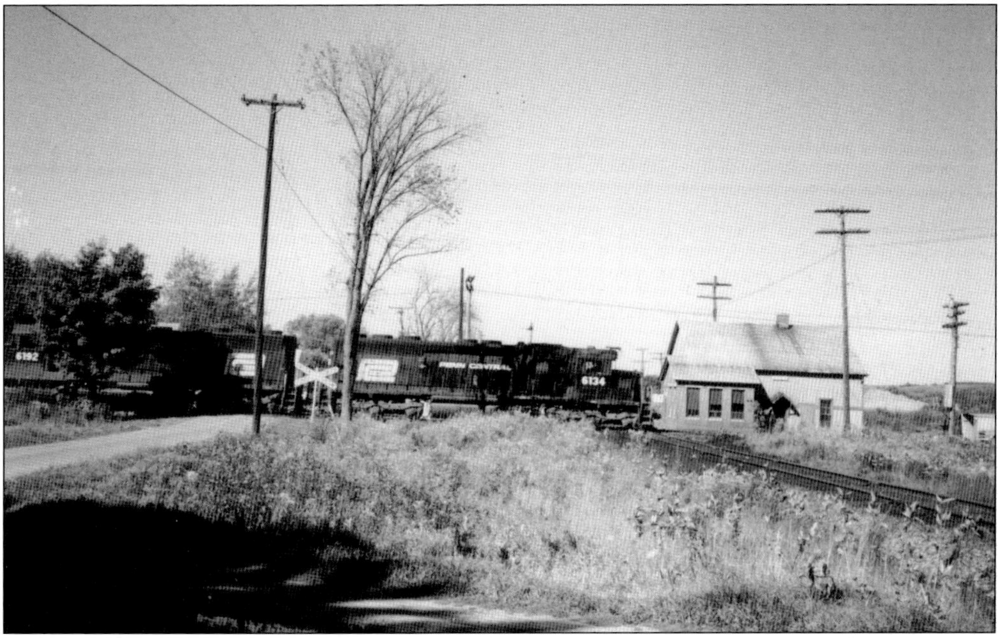

Despite bankruptcy, the Penn Central had a big job to do and traffic actually grew during its years in bankruptcy. In 1974, SD-45 model locomotives 6134 and 6182, originally built by General Motors Electro-Motive Division for the Pennsylvania Railroad, lead a Buffalo-bound freight over the B&O crossing diamonds at Machias Junction, New York. PC's Frontier Yard is 48 miles ahead. (P. Templeton photograph, courtesy Patrick Connors.)

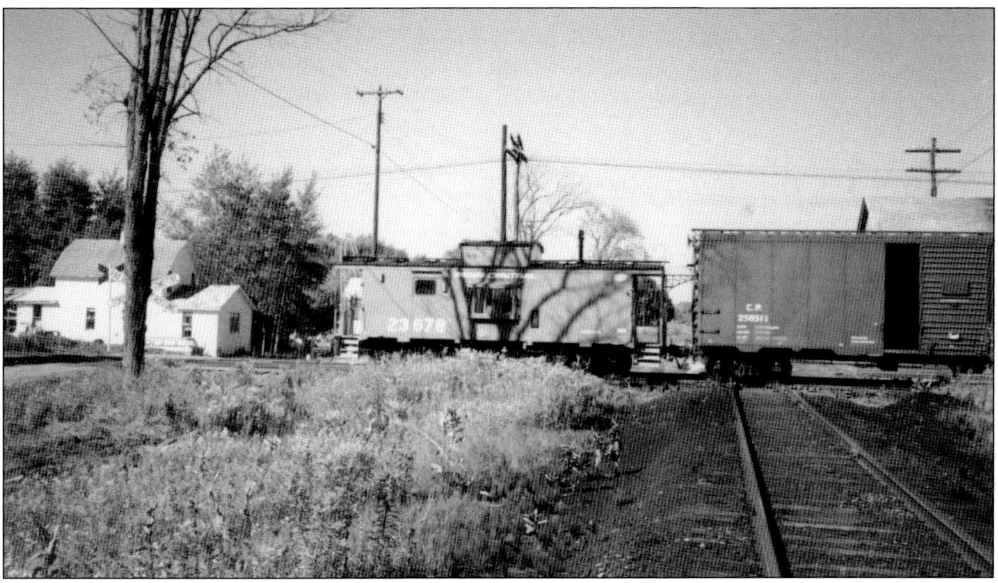

In 1974, still at Machias Junction, New York, the cabin car, as the caboose was known on the former Pennsylvania Railroad, illustrates the Penn Central's (PC) frugality. Forced to absorb the bankrupt New Haven Railroad on January 1, 1969, the PC rebuilt a number of former New Haven cabooses, blanking out the cupola and installing bay windows and new running gear. Caboose 23678 painted in PC emerald green illustrates the result. (P. Templeton photograph, courtesy Patrick Connors.)

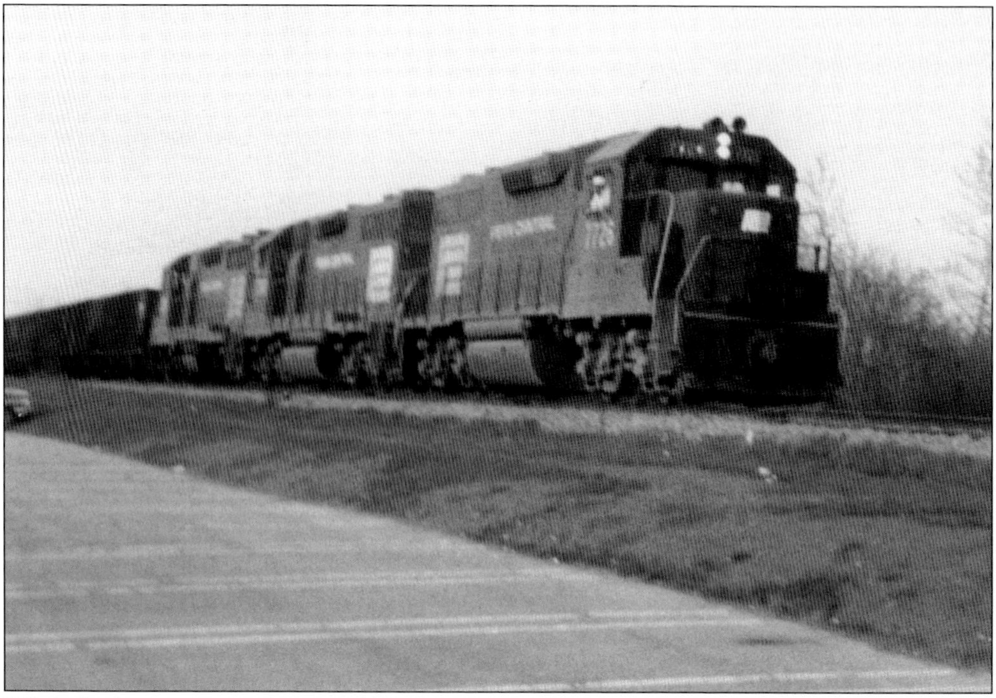

While the former New York Central lines serving Buffalo were primarily multiple-track, the former Pennsylvania's Buffalo-Harrisburg, Pennsylvania, line had long stretches of single-track. Here in 1974, No. 7726, a GP-38 model locomotive built by General Motors Electro-Motive Division in 1969 for Penn Central and two of its model SD-38 sisters, moves a coal train north of Arcade towards the Bethlehem Steel plant in Lackawanna. (P. Templeton photograph, courtesy Patrick Connors.)

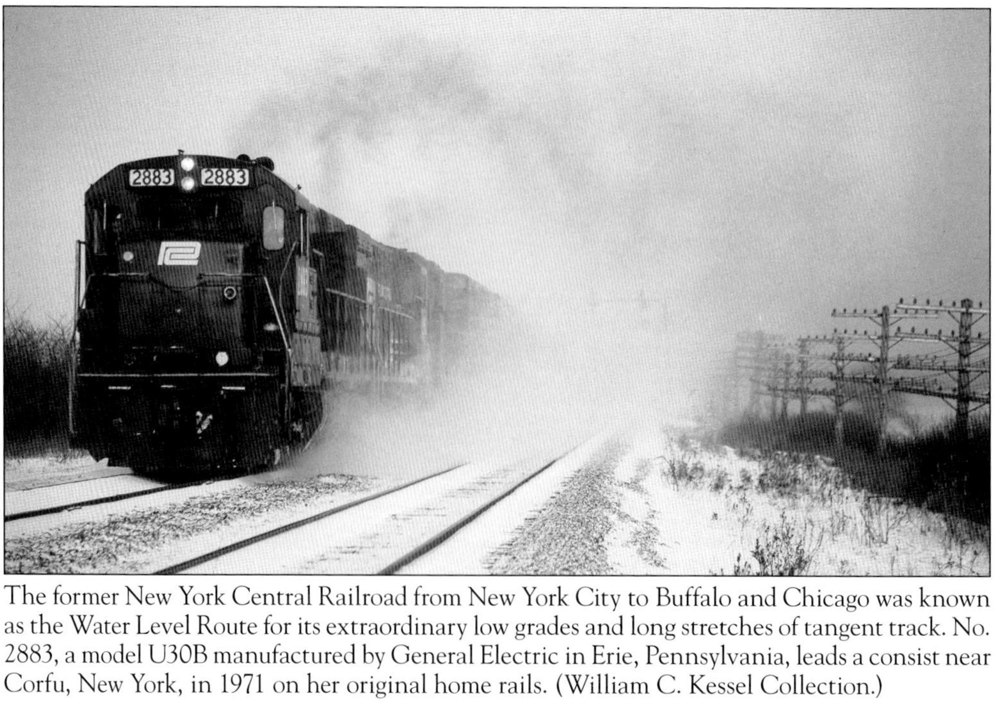


The former New York Central Railroad from New York City to Buffalo and Chicago was known as the Water Level Route for its extraordinary low grades and long stretches of tangent track. No. 2883, a model U30B manufactured by General Electric in Erie, Pennsylvania, leads a consist near Corfu, New York, in 1971 on her original home rails. (William C. Kessel Collection.)

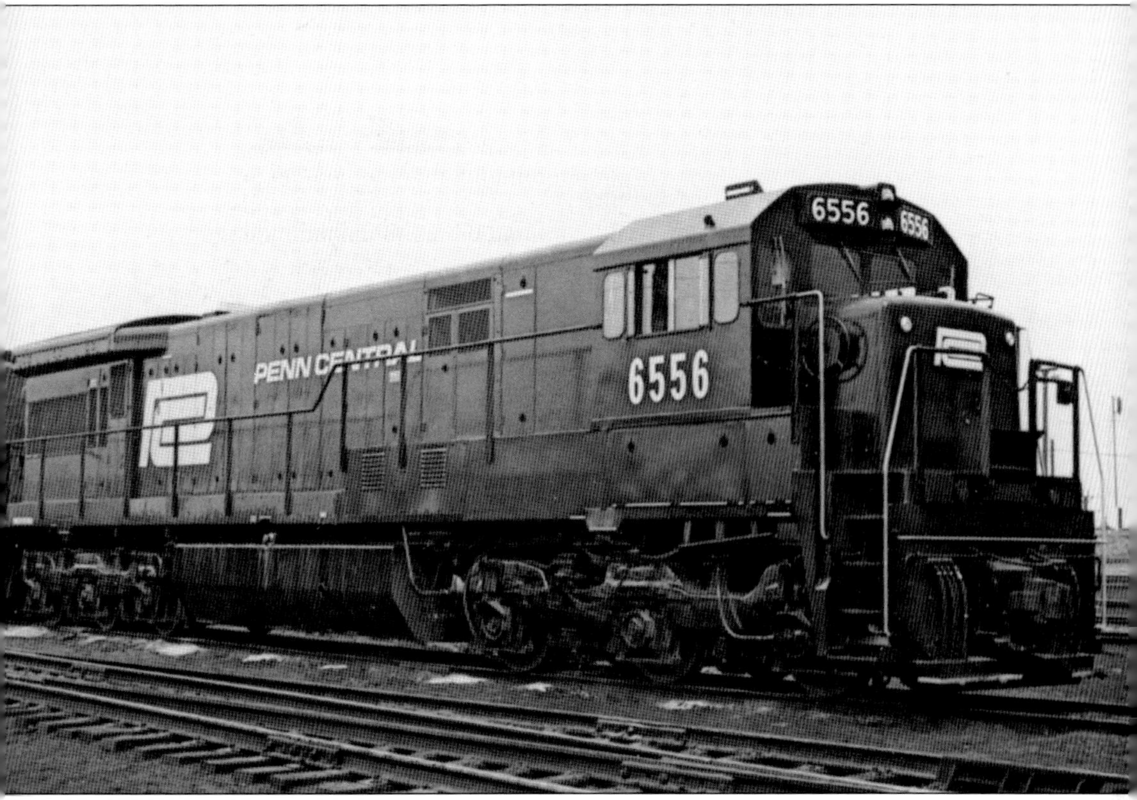


More powerful locomotives were acquired by railroads to reduce costs, like this General Electric U33C built in Erie, Pennsylvania, which could produce 3,300 horsepower. The Penn Central had a strong presence in Buffalo, with both Pennsylvania and New York Central properties, but due to poor management, strangling labor contracts, and government policies that favored other modes of transportation, the Penn Central was destined to fail. (Michael J. Connor collection.)

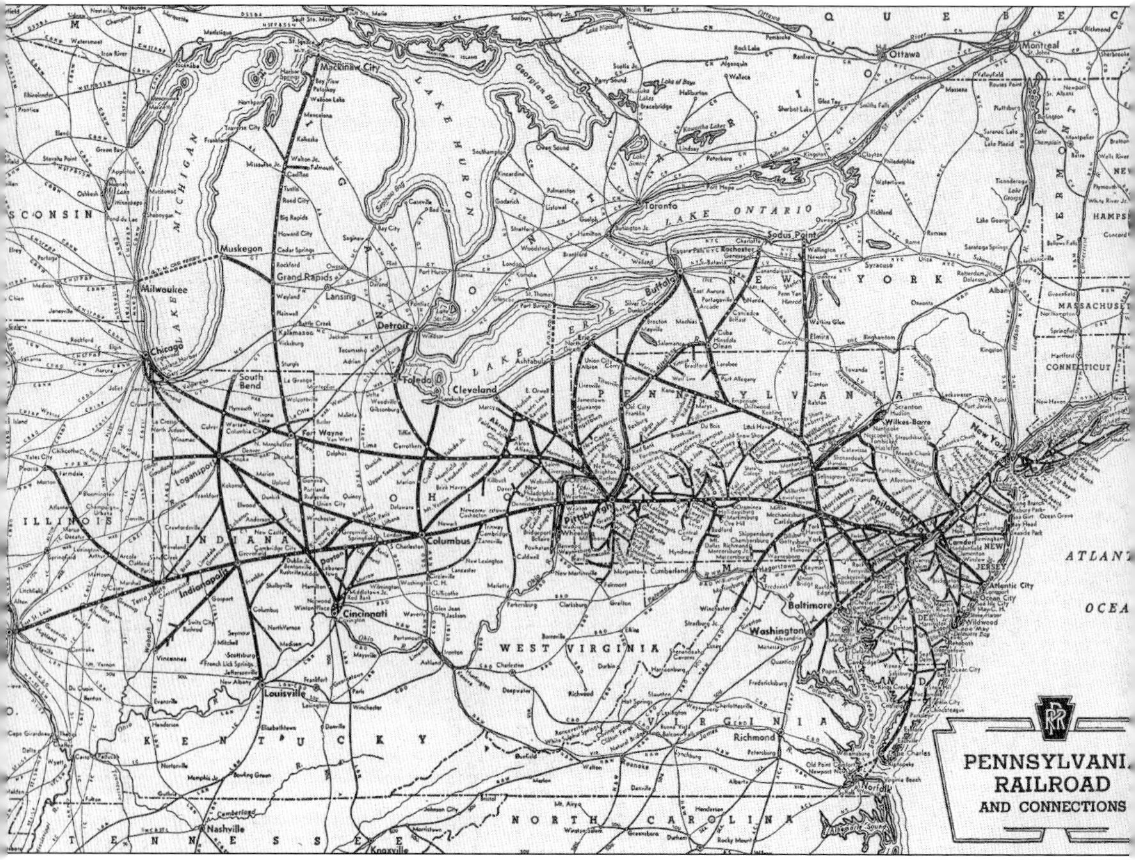


The Pennsylvania Railroad was a 9,538-mile railroad at the time of its 1968 merger with the New York Central Railroad to form Penn Central. The PRR reached Buffalo over its Buffalo-Harrisburg, Pennsylvania, main line through East Aurora and its Buffalo-Pittsburgh Chautauqua Branch through Angola. Its principal yard was in Ebenezer, supported by four others. Passenger service was focused on Buffalo Central Terminal-Harrisburg-Baltimore-Washington trains. (Michael J. Connor collection.)

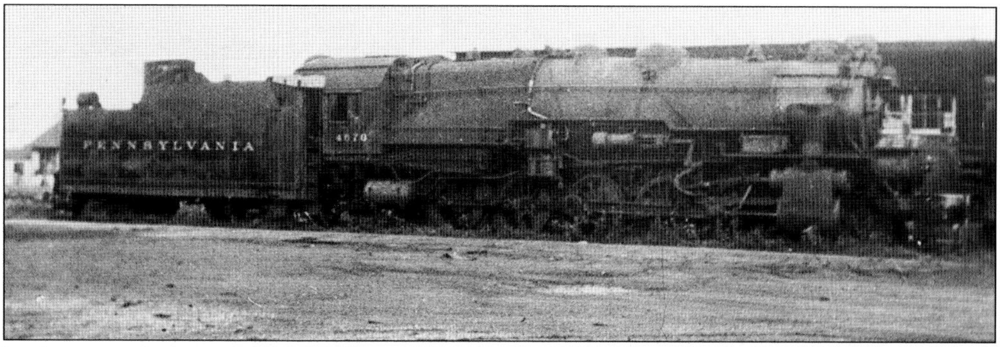


Lacking an elegant appearance but exuding brute force, the Decapod-type 2-10-0 locomotive No. 4670 rests in Ebenezer Yard in 1951. The Pennsylvania Railroad owned the largest fleet of steam locomotives in North America. 4670 and her 597 Class I1s sisters each weighed 193 tons and significantly reduced double-heading on heavy coal and ore trains. (Photograph courtesy Western New York Railway Historical Society)

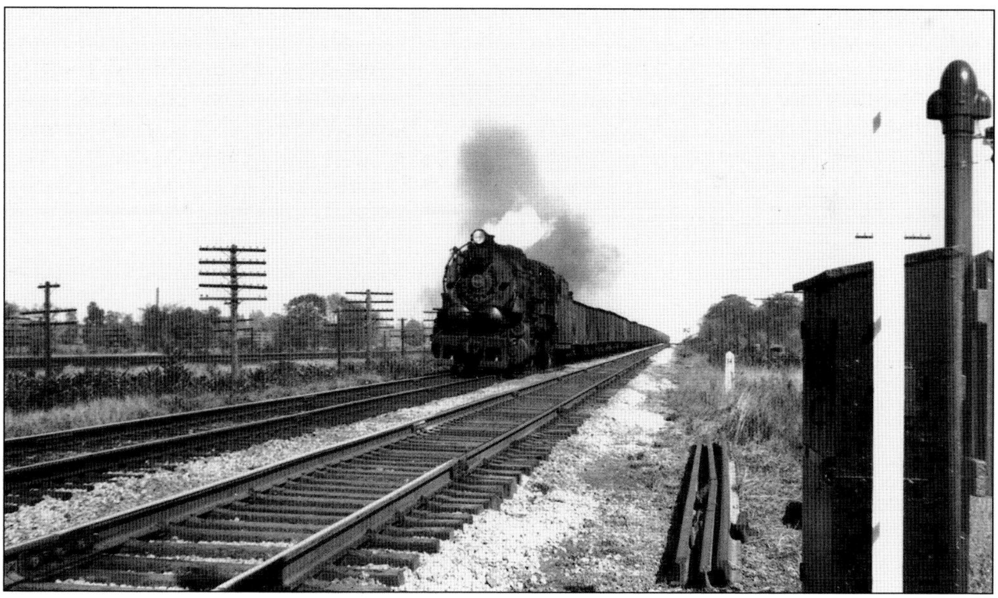

A Pennsylvania Railroad Decapod-type (2-10-0 wheel arrangement) locomotive is about to cross Pleasant Avenue/Heltz Road in Wanakah on October 14, 1951. The train of mostly empty coal hoppers en route to Pittsburgh via Corry, Pennsylvania, is on the jointly operated Nickel Plate Road (NKP)-PRR double-track between Buffalo and Brocton, New York. The NKP owned the westbound track while the PRR owned the eastbound track. (Photograph by James A. Van Brocklin.)

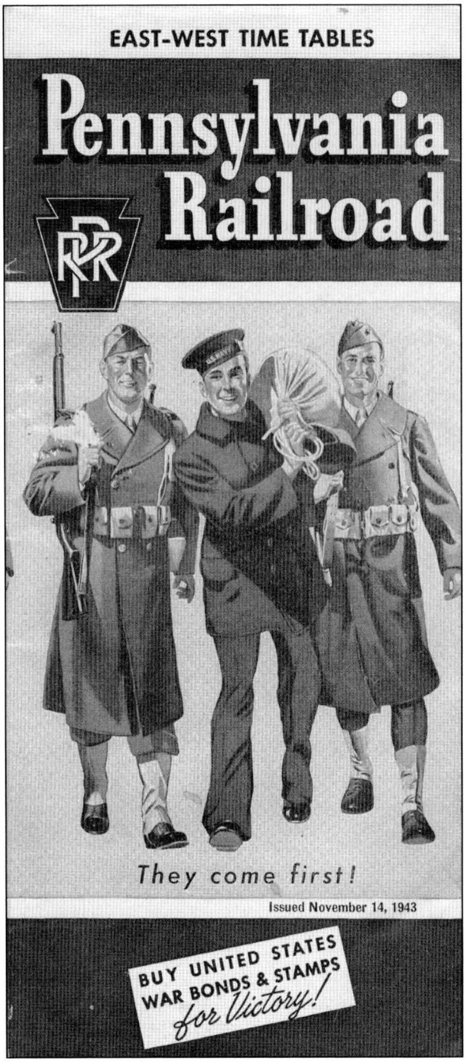


This 1943 Pennsylvania timetable reminds passengers that any train delays could be the cause of moving troop trains or military equipment ahead of their passenger train. The war effort was the priority and Buffalo was in the forefront of war production with its large industrial base. (Medina Railroad Museum.)

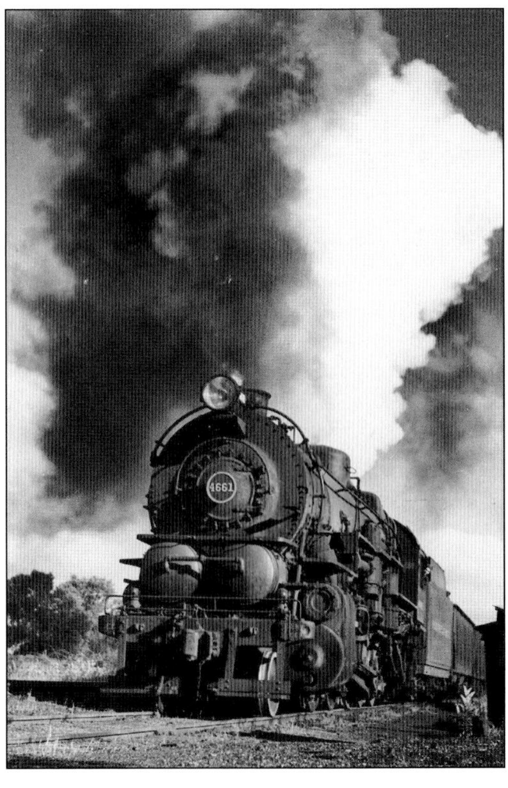


Class I1s steam locomotives were ubiquitous on the PRR Northern Region centering in Buffalo. Here No. 4661 gathers up cars for movement. The PRR did not reach Buffalo until 1900 when it leased the much smaller Western New York and Pennsylvania Railway. The PRR's arrival paralleled the growth and development of the steel industry in Lackawanna. (Photograph by George W. Thornton; courtesy Erie Lackawanna Historical Society.)

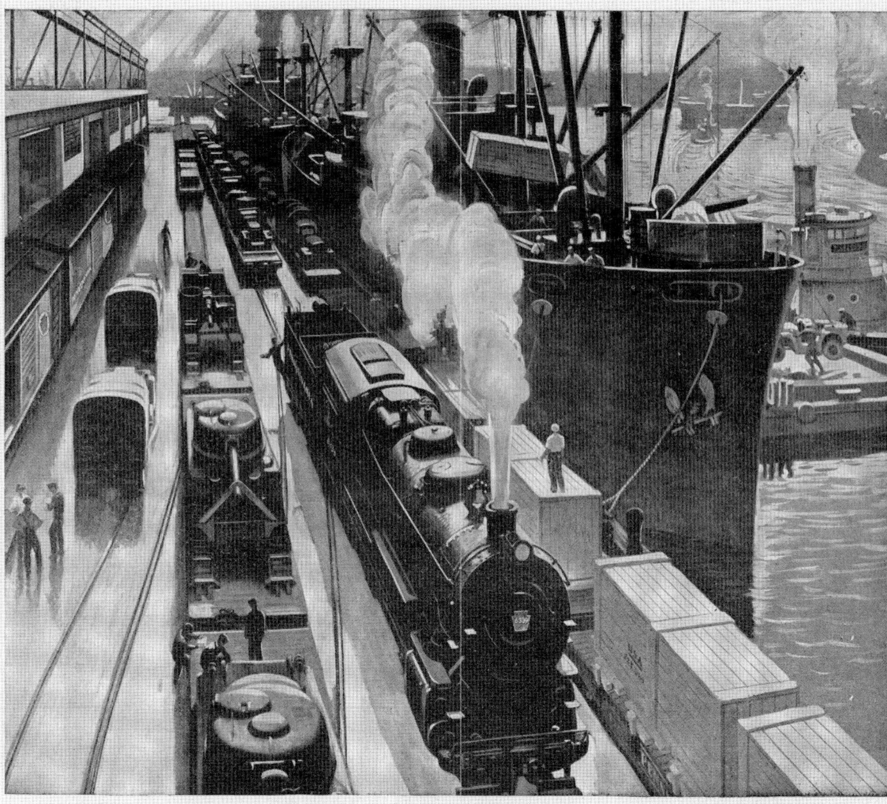

## KEEPING APPOINTMENTS WITH CONVOYS

In a day's combat, an infantry division fires about 300 tons of ammunition . . . 100 37 mm. anti-aircraft guns, 127½ tons . . . and the thousands of army vehicles "passing the ammunition" and other supplies each burn up an average of 10 gallons of gasoline . . .

All of these materials — the guns, the "gas", the ammunition, the vehicles — *plus 700,000 other different military items* — must come by sea.

A gigantic supply task without parallel in the history of the nation, this job calls for the finest coordination of American railroads with ships.

The railroads must bring everything to ship sidings exactly as needed — and when needed. Any slip, any delay, may hold up a convoy sailing.

So keeping appointments with convoys is one of the most important jobs railroads have these days.

If pushing a "convoy train" through ahead of your passenger train caused you to be a little late for an early-morning business appointment, the Pennsylvania Railroad feels sure you will gladly overlook it. The demands of war must have not only railroad equipment — but the right-of-way!

**BUY UNITED STATES WAR BONDS AND STAMPS**

In a Pennsylvania magazine advertisement, the railroad shows its importance and support of the war effort. Moving freight from Lake Erie and the many heavy industries of Buffalo that had switched production to war related materials depended on railroads to keep the nation moving. (Medina Railroad Museum.)

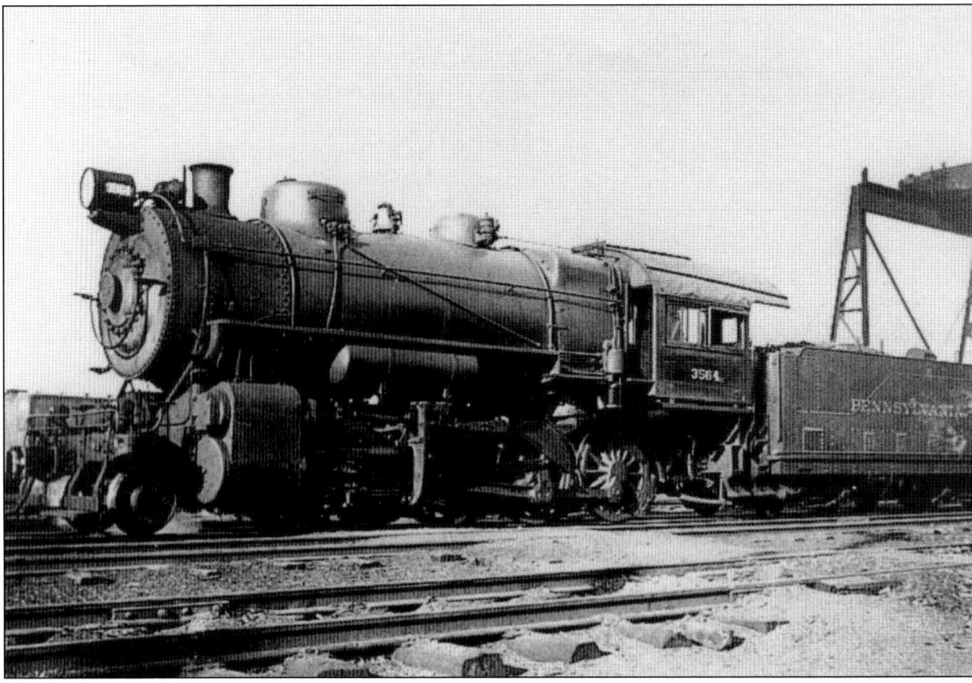

For an industrial city like Buffalo there was a great need for coal and coke to power the factories and heat the homes. The Pennsylvania Railroad, like her competitors, was ready to move the materials in and take the finished products from Buffalo to the world. No. 3564 is a Pennsy H8-b steam locomotive and awaits her next assignment at Northumberland, Pennsylvania. (Stephen G. Myers collection.)

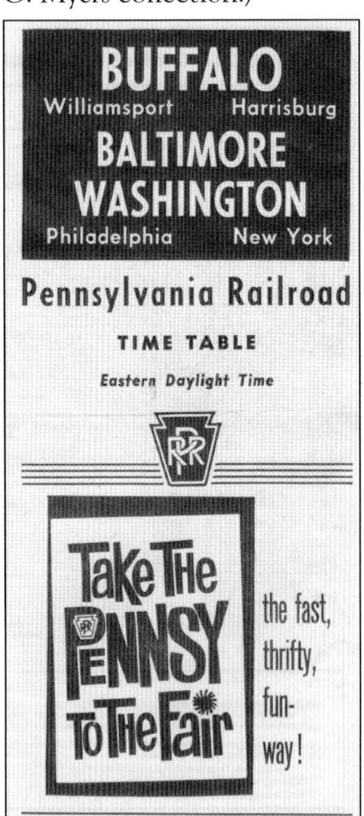


The Pennsylvania Railroad was known as The Standard Railroad Of The World. The Pennsy offered passenger trains from Buffalo Central Terminal to Washington, D.C. via Harrisburg and Baltimore. In an era before our highway systems and modern airports, the railroad was the preferred mode of travel. (Medina Railroad Museum.)

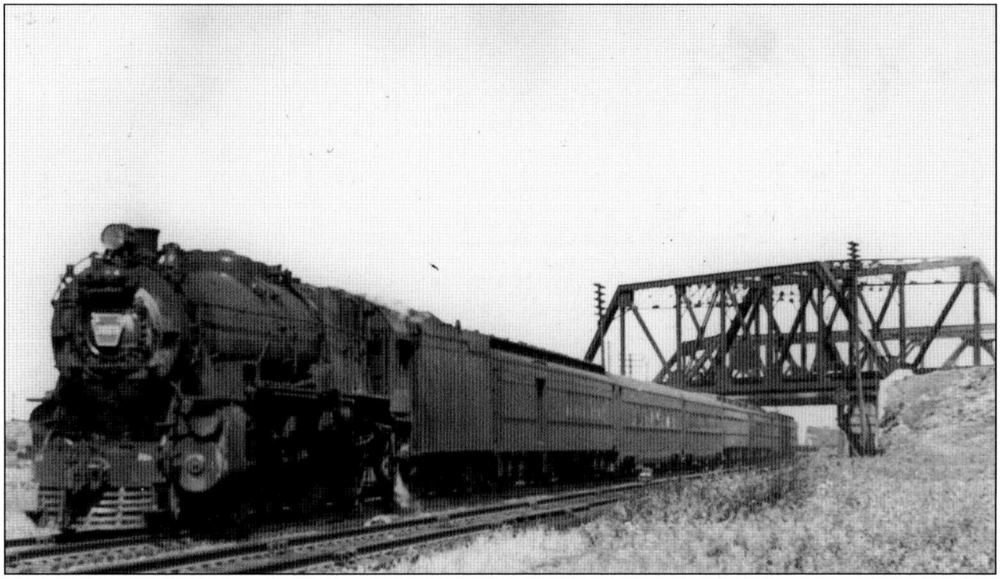

The beautiful Pennsylvania Railroad K4 Pacific No. 3676 leads this passenger train past DM tower. The Pennsy built these K4s at its shops in Altoona, Pennsylvania. Even though the 3676 was built in 1918, she is still up to the task in this summer of 1942. (R. Ganger photograph, Michael J. Connor collection.)

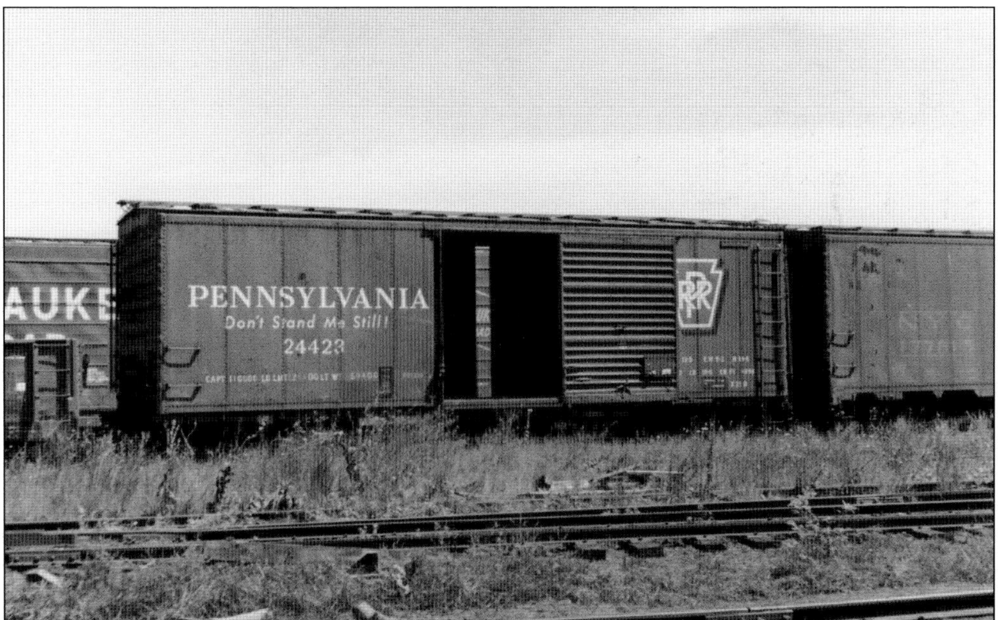


With the well known PRR keystone logo and a slogan of "Don't Stand Me Still" on her side, a typical 50-foot boxcar sits in the yard at Buffalo. The Pennsylvania was ready with a fleet of rolling stock to provide for the needs of local shippers; anything from grain to furniture could end up in a boxcar. (Ronald R. Dukarm collection.)

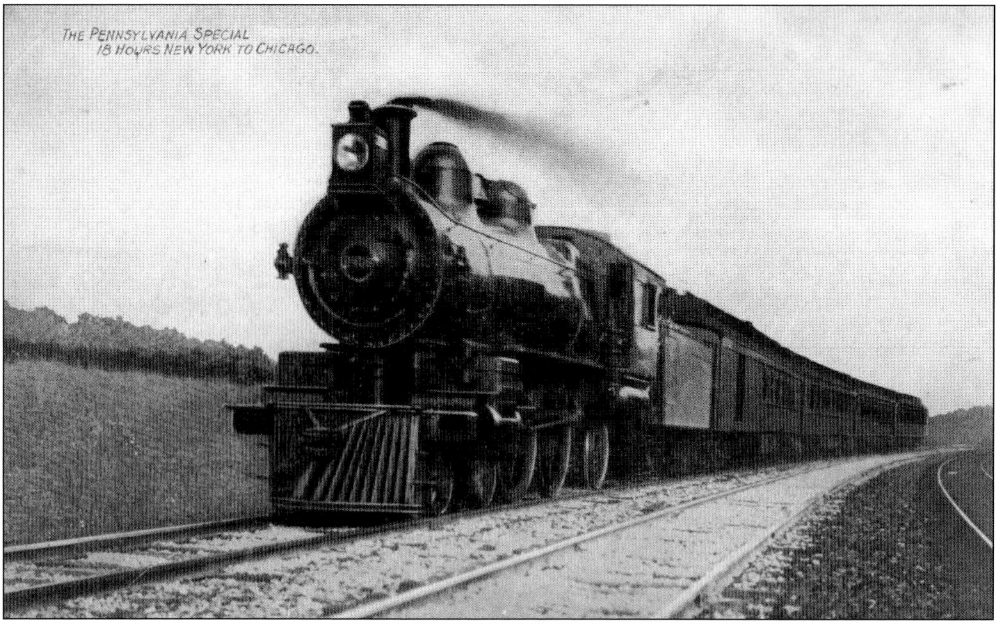


The *Pennsylvania Special* carrying four cars flies through the countryside while relaxed passengers await their final destination. With room to stretch, walk, or enjoy a meal in the dining car, there is no better way to travel. For 175 years, people have travelled on trains at Buffalo. (Stephen G. Myers collection.)

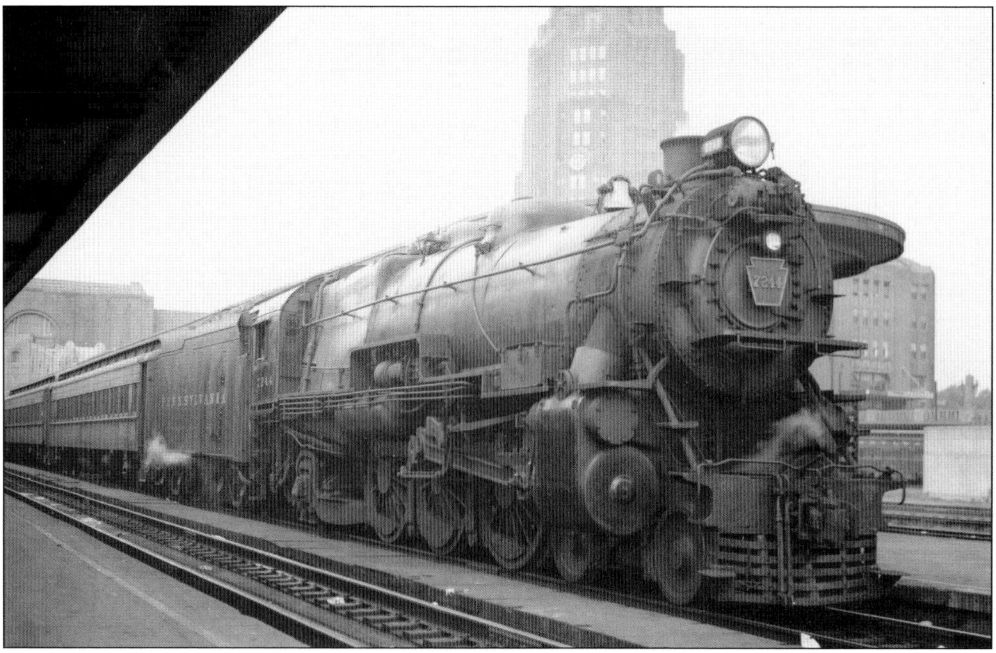

A Pennsylvania passenger train pulled by locomotive No. 7244 K4 Pacific is awaiting her departure from the Buffalo Central Terminal platform. Buffalo's beloved train station is seen in the background in better days. The building still stands and hopes remain that the Central Terminal Restoration Corporation will one day find a buyer to utilize the facility. (Nathan Vester Collection, Central Terminal Restoration Corporation.)

# *Five*

# THE LEHIGH VALLEY AND BUFFALO & SUSQUEHANNA

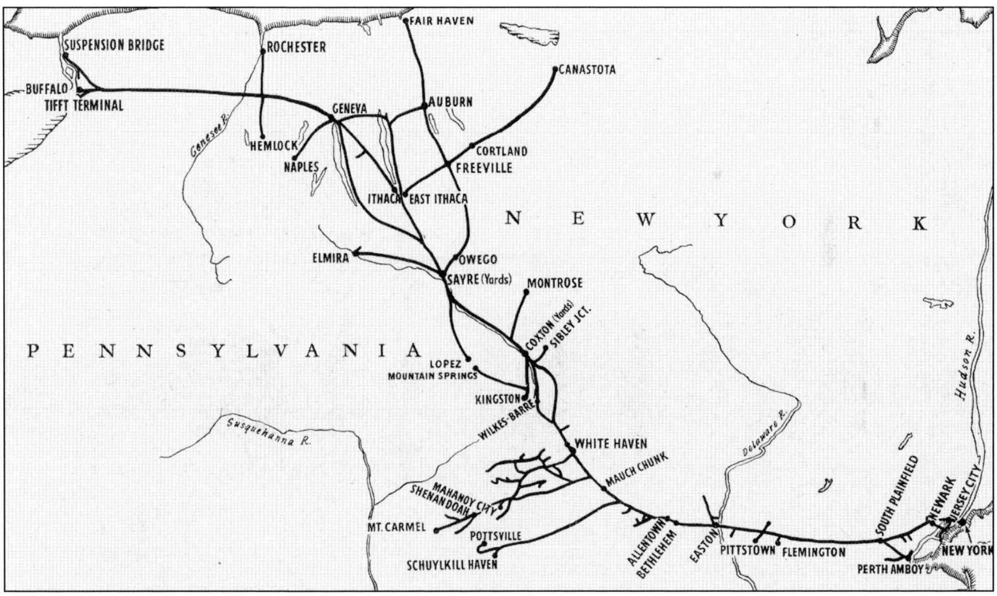


The Lehigh Valley Railroad was chartered September 20, 1847, in Pennsylvania as the Delaware, Lehigh, Schuylkill and Susquehanna Railroad Company, which changed its name on January 7, 1853 to the Lehigh Valley Railroad Company. The LV reached Buffalo in September 1892, establishing its passenger terminal on Scott Street in downtown Buffalo, freight yards at Tifft Farm in south Buffalo, and a Buffalo bypass route to Suspension Bridge via Williamsville. (Michael J. Connor collection.)

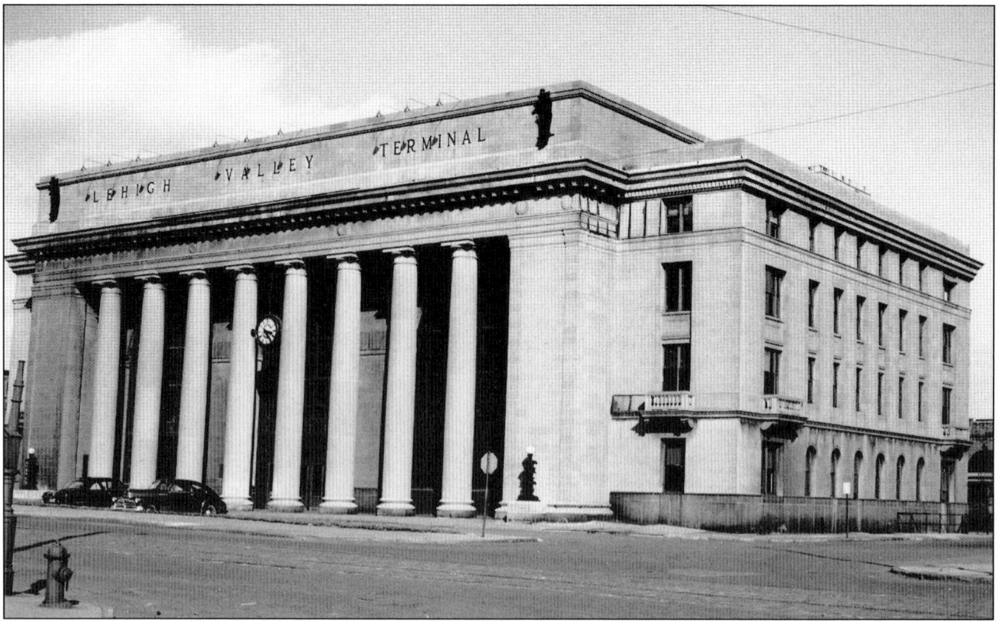


In 1912, after the failure of a movement for a Buffalo Union Station, the Lehigh Valley decided to build a new terminal. Opened August 29, 1916, it was unique in that the main station, above, was separated from the train shed by Scott Street, which the ever-recalcitrant City of Buffalo refused to vacate. Passengers passed under Scott Street in a pedestrian tunnel. The magnificent terminal was closed August 11, 1955. (Phil Soyring collection.)

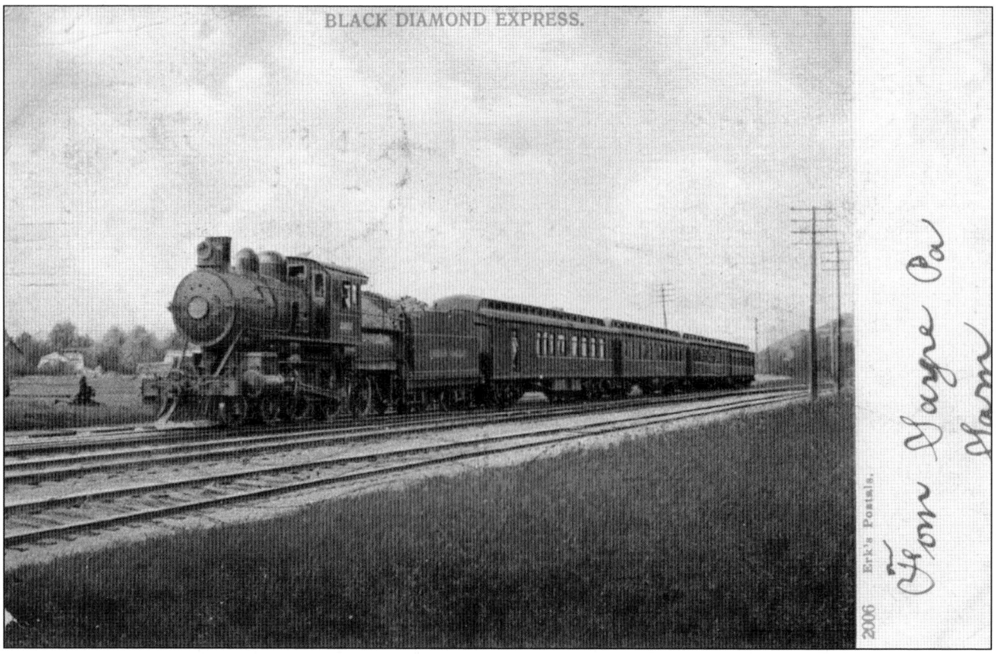


The Lehigh Valley was the last major railroad to reach Buffalo and needed a premier passenger train to compete against the other large roads. The result was the *Black Diamond Express*, which began on Monday, May 18, 1896; she traveled Lehigh rails between New York and Buffalo for 63 years. (Stephen G. Myers collection.)

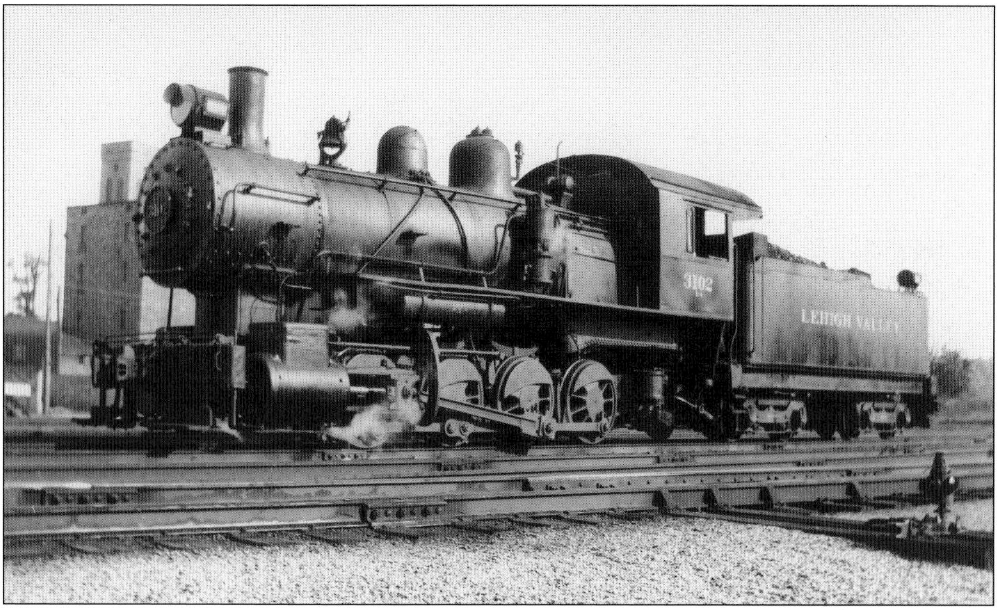



Switching passenger and freight cars is the seemingly eternal job of switch engines. The Lehigh Valley (LV) rostered over 1,500 locomotives in its 130-year life. No. 3102 awaits her next move in the mid-1930s; she was an LV Class L 0-8-0 wheel arrangement locomotive. She was built in February 1912 by the LV's own forces in Sayre, Pennsylvania, but was scrapped in February 1938. (Phil Soyring collection.)

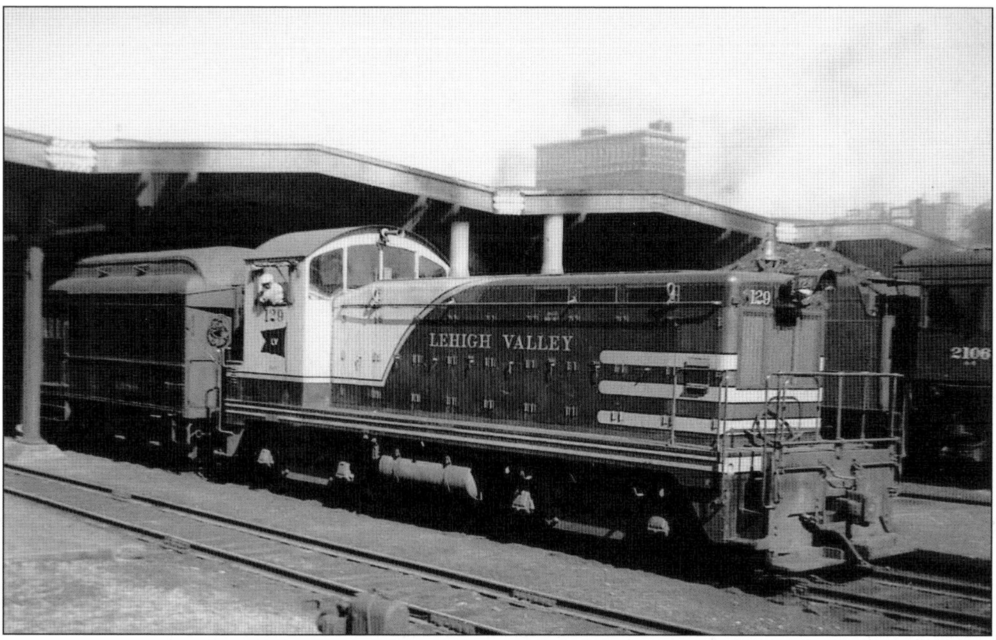



The Lehigh Valley began its dieselization program in earnest in 1937 with switch engines. No. 129, a 900-horsepower locomotive manufactured by General Motors Electro-Motive Division in August 1938, earned its living in 1945 switching the 10-track Buffalo passenger terminal. The locomotive would be retired in November 1953. Class K-5 Pacific (4-6-2 wheel arrangement) 2106 stands by fully coaled for the next train out. (Phil Soyring collection.)

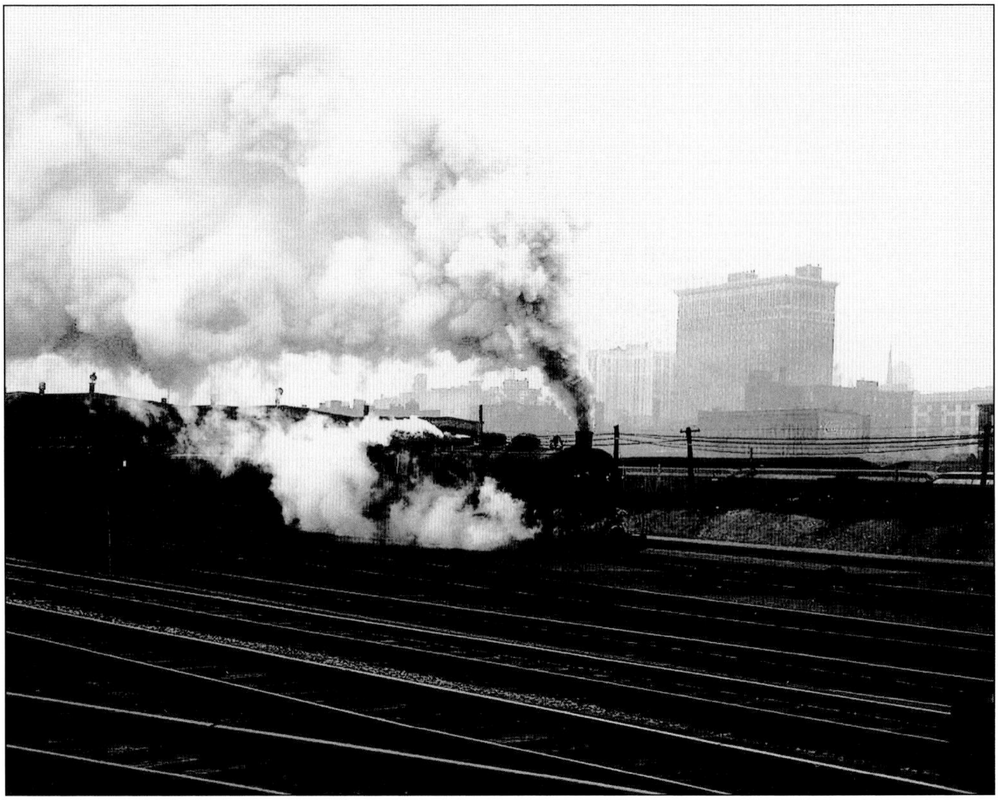

Overseen by the Main Seneca Building, a 17-story skyscraper erected in 1927, the Buffalo section of Erie Railroad Train 2, the *Erie Limited*, departs in this 1946 view. The Erie closed its Buffalo passenger terminal fronting on Michigan Avenue in 1935 and moved its eight daily trains to Lehigh Valley Terminal, where they stayed until the Erie exited the Buffalo passenger train market in 1951. (Phil Soyring collection.)

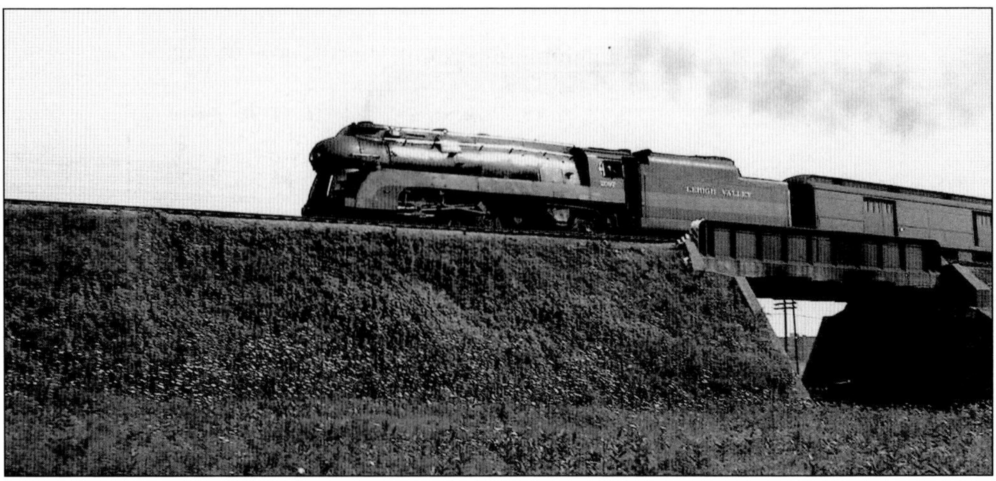


Working in 1939–1940 with noted industrial stylist Otto Kuhler, the Lehigh Valley streamlined several of its passenger trains, most notably the *Black Diamond*, the LV's premier train between Buffalo and New York City. No. 2097, an LV Class K-6B Pacific built in February 1924, streamlined in 1940, and retired in 1951, leads the *Black Diamond* out of Buffalo in 1946. (Phil Soyring collection.)

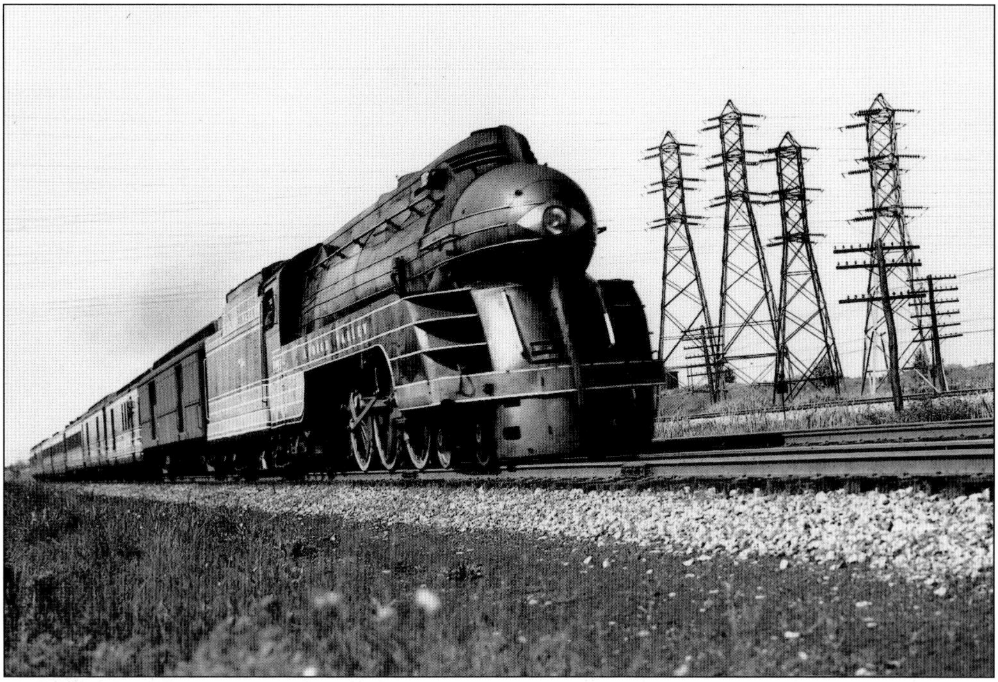

No. 2097, a Lehigh Valley Class K-6B Pacific 4-6-2 wheel arrangement built in February 1924, streamlined in 1939, and retired in January 1951, leads train No. 10, the *Black Diamond*, east of Depew in 1945. Train No. 10 is moving at the authorized 70 miles per hour to Batavia. 2097 was the first streamlined locomotive in her class. (Phil Soyring collection.)

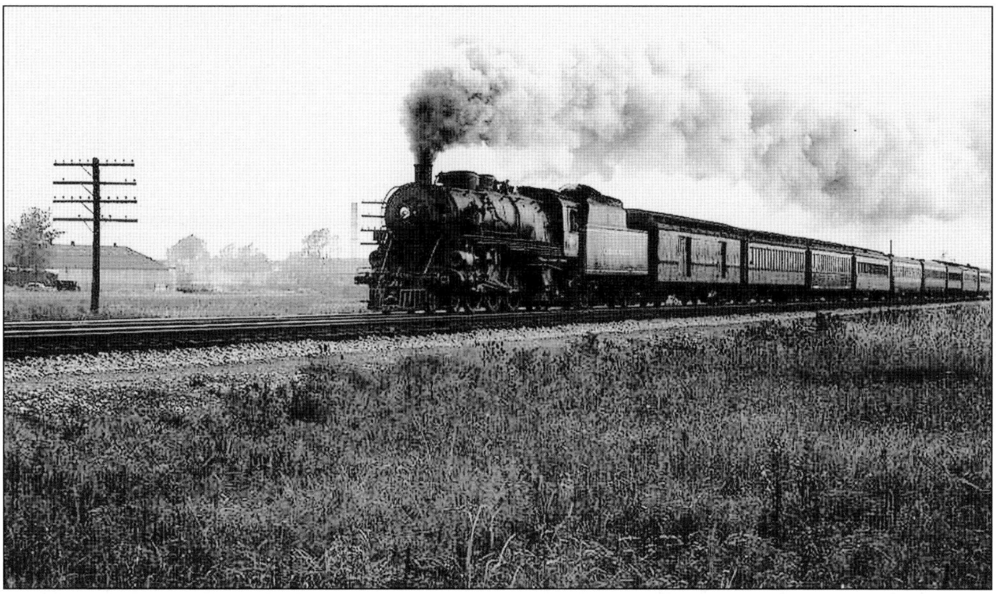

With four passenger trains daily in each direction, the Lehigh Valley's five streamlined Pacific-type steam locomotives could not cover all assignments. Even the most famous train, the *Black Diamond*, was occasionally pulled by a non-streamlined locomotive. Here an LV's K-class Pacific leads the *Diamond* east near Lancaster, New York. The train's nine cars will require a helper on some of the challenging grades in Pennsylvania. (Phil Soyring collection.)

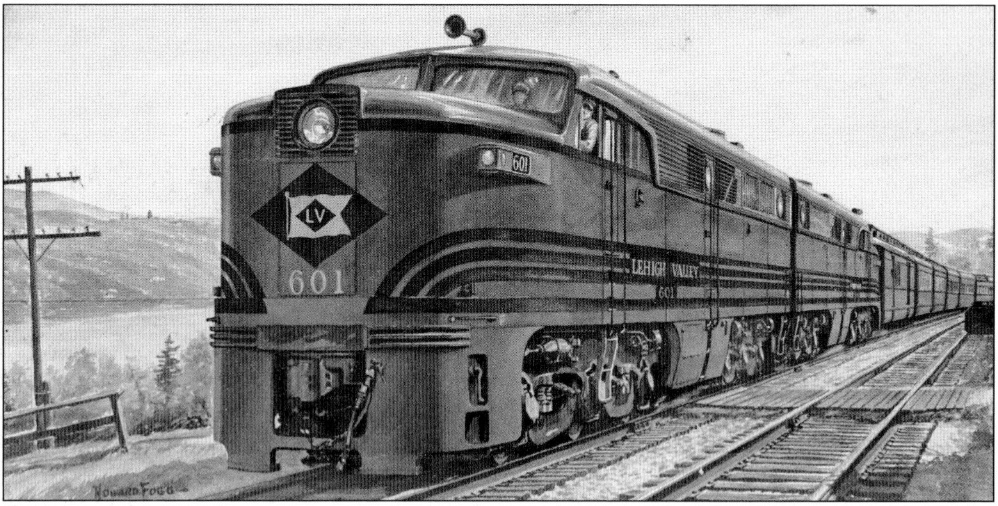

The Lehigh Valley's passenger service was dieselized almost overnight with the purchase of 14 Alco model PA-1 2,000-horsepower diesel-electric locomotives. Their arrival in March 1948 ultimately consigned the well-worn K-class Pacifics to scrapping. The LV ordered the new diesels painted a striking Cornell red livery with black accent striping. (Medina Railroad Museum.)

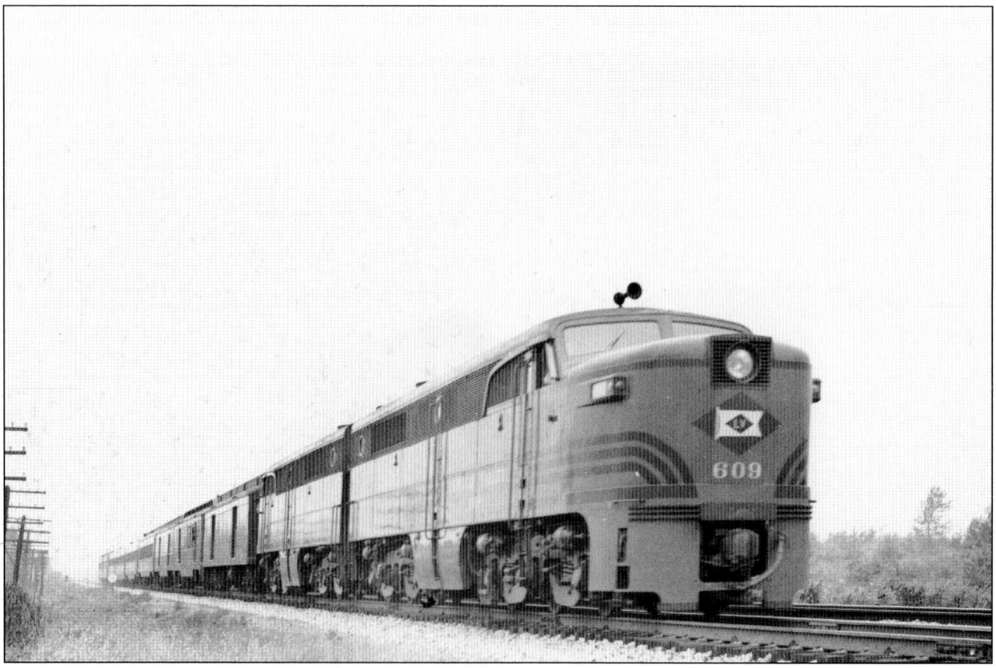

Lehigh Valley No. 609 and an unknown mate, both Alco PA-1 type diesel-electric locomotives, move train No. 10, the *Black Diamond*, east of Depew in 1949. Unlike the Lackawanna and the New York Central railroads, the LV's post-war modernization program got little further than dieselization as a look at the trailing cars shows. This ultimately helped to bring the early (1961) end of LV passenger service. (Phil Soyring collection.)

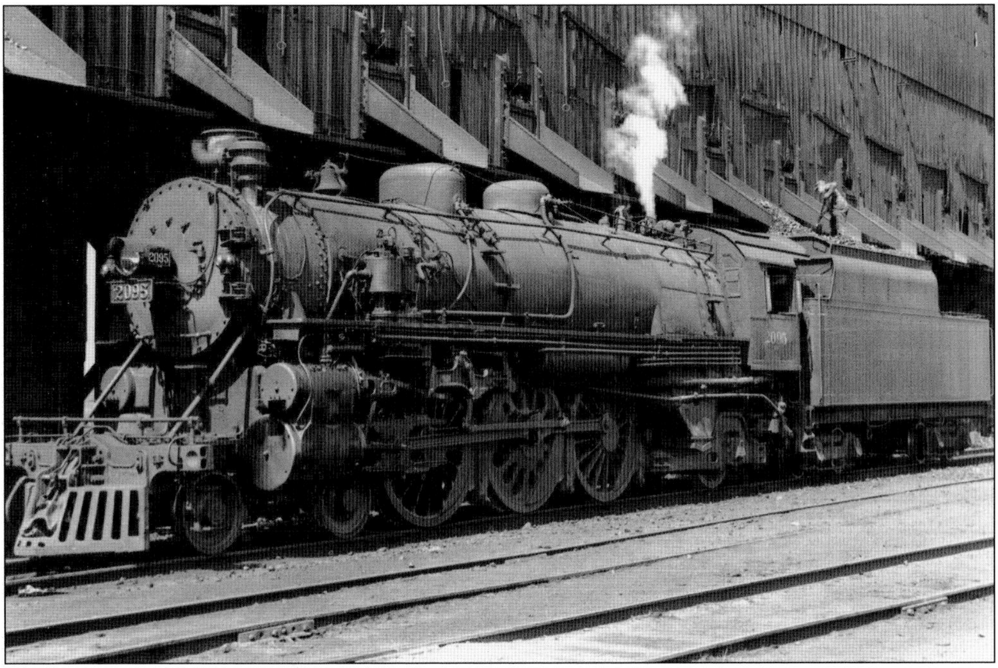

Here is Lehigh Valley K-6B No. 2095, built by American Locomotive Company in 1924. She is taking on coal at the massive coal chutes in Cheektowaga, New York, on April 20, 1940. The 2095 lasted until February 1952, when she succumbed to the scrapper's torch. (Phil Soyring collection.)

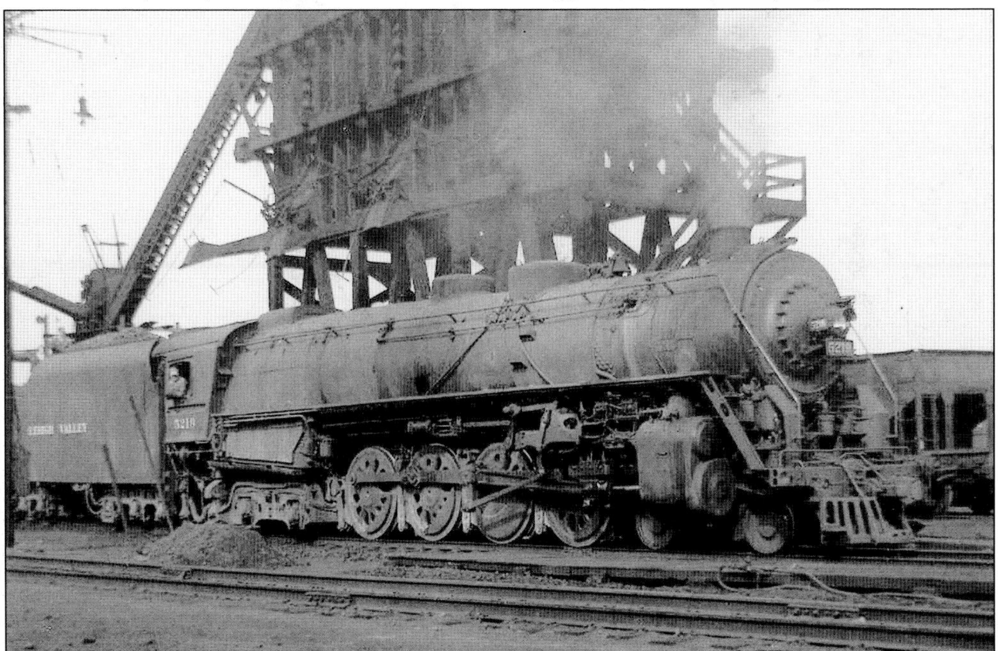

The Lehigh Valley was primarily a freight railroad—that meant that No. 5218, a Class T-2B Wyoming-type locomotive, would soon be leaving the coal dock to lead another freight train. No. 5218 was one of 10 Wyomings built in October 1943 to handle the LV's burgeoning war traffic. Diesels and the post-war traffic declines sent her to scrap in March 1952. (Phil Soyring collection.)

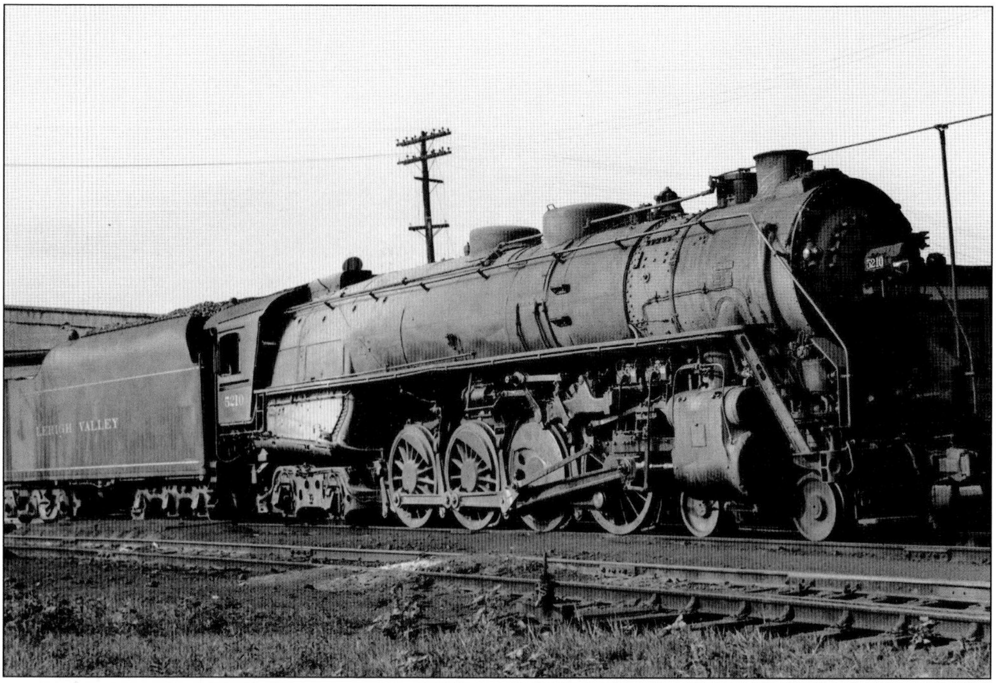


Lehigh Valley No. 5210 was a Wyoming-type 4-8-4 wheel arrangement locomotive. Engines of similar wheel arrangement were known by at least a dozen other names. On the Lackawanna, they were Poconos; on the New York Central, they were Niagaras; on most other railroads, 4-8-4s were known as Northerns. In an era when locomotives seldom left home rails, this created much pride among railroad employees. (Phil Soyring collection.)

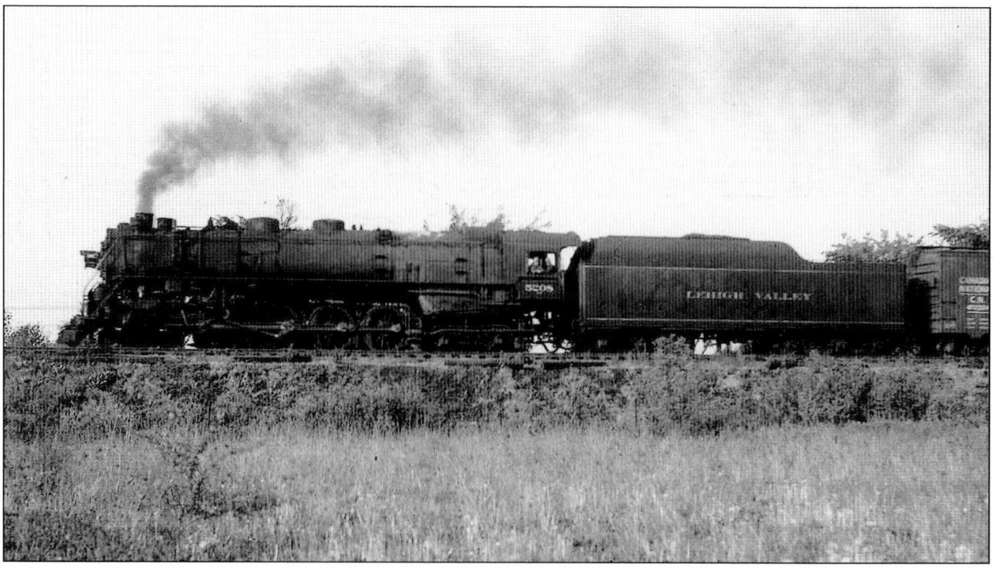


Lehigh Valley Class T-2 Wyoming-type No. 5208 was built in May 1932. She is headed westbound near Wende with a freight train for Suspension Bridge, the LV's vital Canadian National Railway connection. The LV's Niagara Falls Branch diverged from the main line immediately west of Depew, reaching Niagara Falls via Williamsville, North Tonawanda, and the New York Central Railroad. (Phil Soyring collection.)

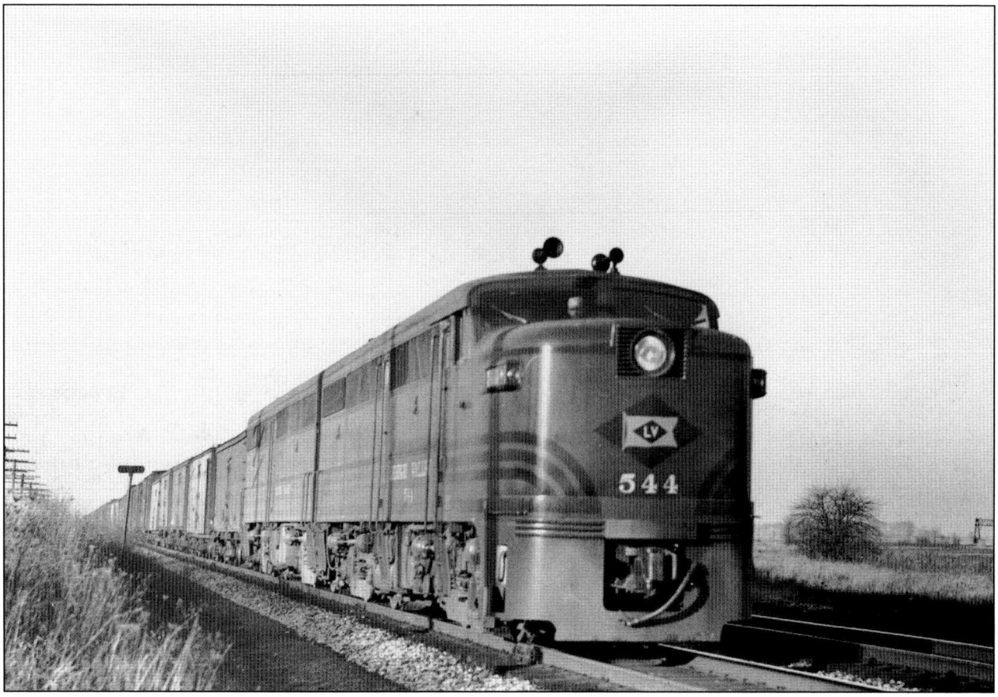


Dieselization of the Lehigh Valley's road freight service dates to 1948 with the arrival of No. 544, an Alco model FA-1 1,500-horsepower locomotive, and 19 of her sisters. By 1951, the last LV steam locomotive banked its fires for good. No. 544 leads symbol freight BM-2 (Buffalo-Manchester) east through Wende in 1949. (Phil Soyring collection.)

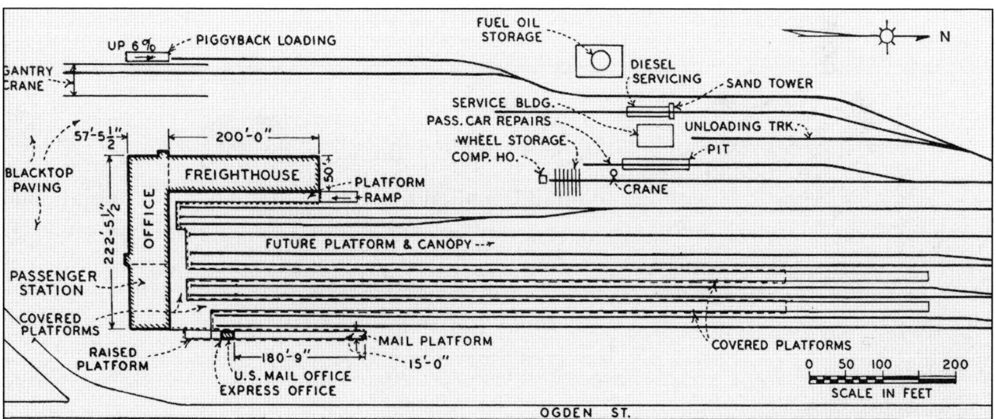


The New York State Thruway purchased the Lehigh Valley's Buffalo Terminal and 4.25 miles of main line for $6.9 million in 1954. Failing to negotiate access to the Delaware, Lackawanna & Western or New York Central passenger terminals, the LV built this new facility at Dingens and South Ogden Streets in east Buffalo. The new terminal opened August 11, 1955. (Michael J. Connor collection.)

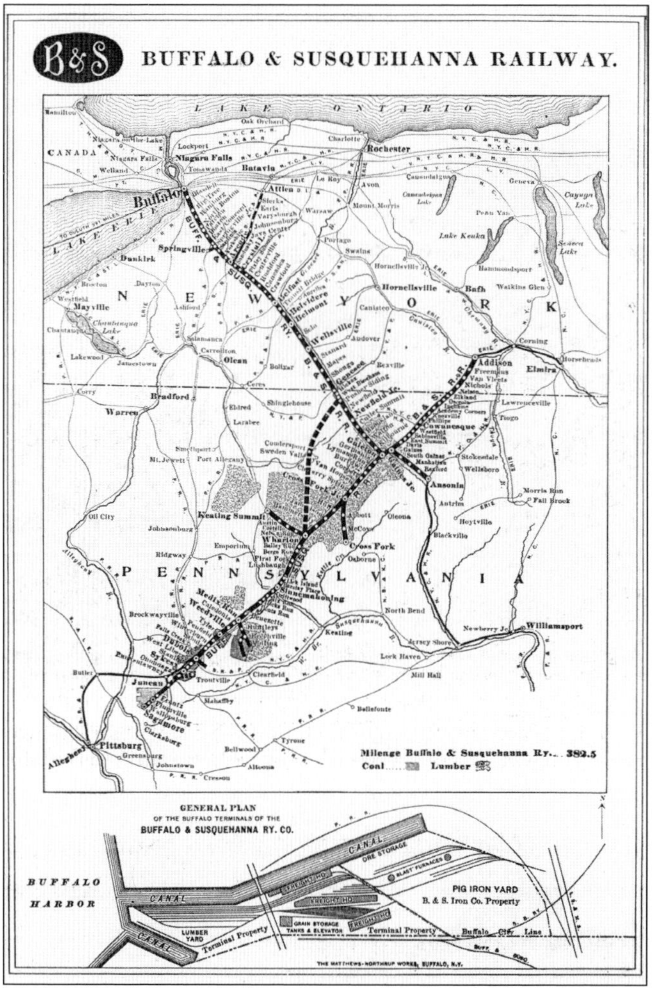


The Buffalo & Susquehanna Railway formally opened a 90-mile line from Wellsville to Blasdell on June 29, 1907. Unfortunately this occurred soon after the death of Frank H. Goodyear, the railroad's president and cofounder. This and the incomplete state of the railway resulted in bankruptcy in 1910 and ultimate abandonment in 1916. (Michael J. Connor Collection.)

The Buffalo & Susquehanna connected Buffalo with no major metropolitan areas. As such its otherwise well-appointed passenger trains never carried Pullman sleepers or dining cars, though trains 342 and 343 usually carried a buffet-observation car serving light refreshments. In 1907, train 342, powered by Atlantic-type No. 278, awaits departure from Galeton for a 127-mile and 5-hour run to Exchange Street Station in Buffalo. (Michael J. Connor Collection.)

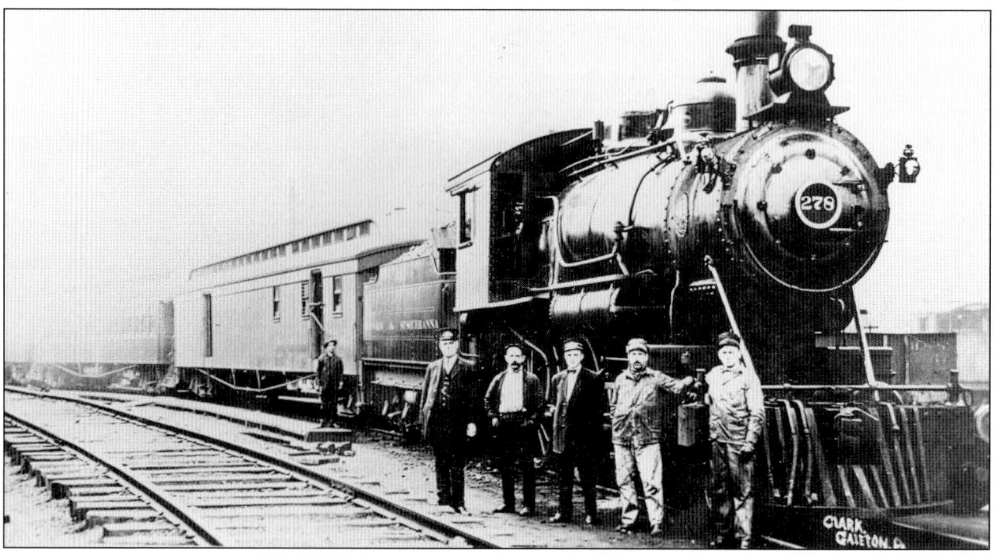

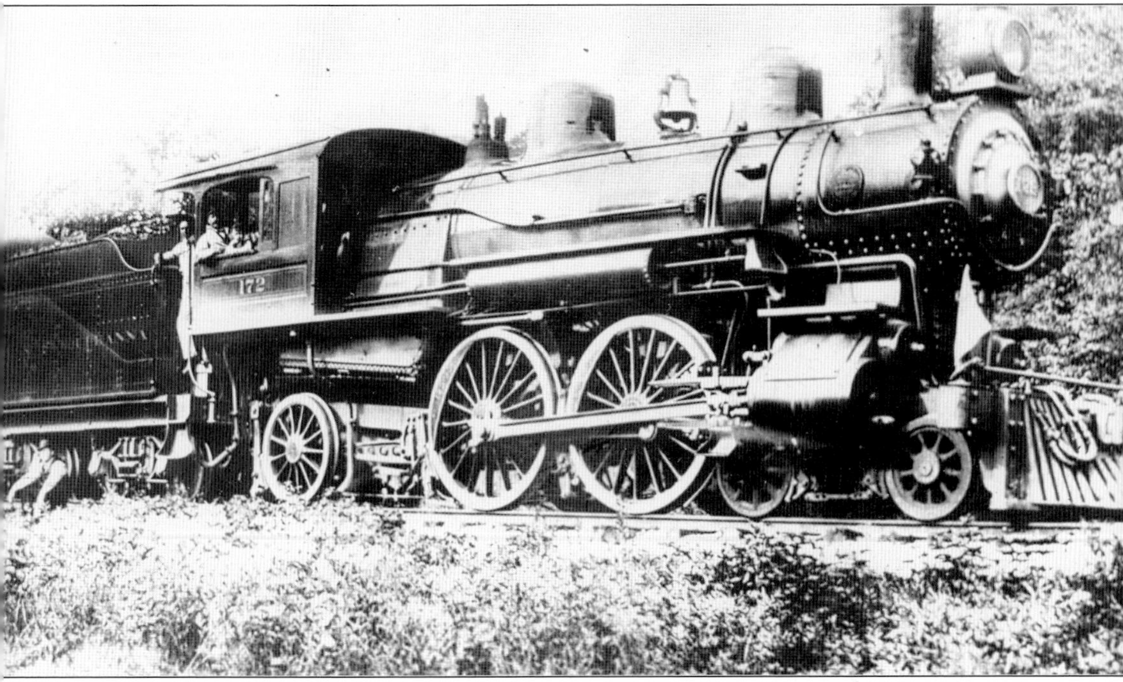

The Buffalo & Susquehanna had one of the youngest locomotive fleets of any Buffalo railroad. No. 172 was an Atlantic type with a 4-4-2 wheel arrangement and was only four years old when pictured on this special excursion train about the time of the railroad's 1907 opening to Buffalo. (Michael J. Connor Collection.)

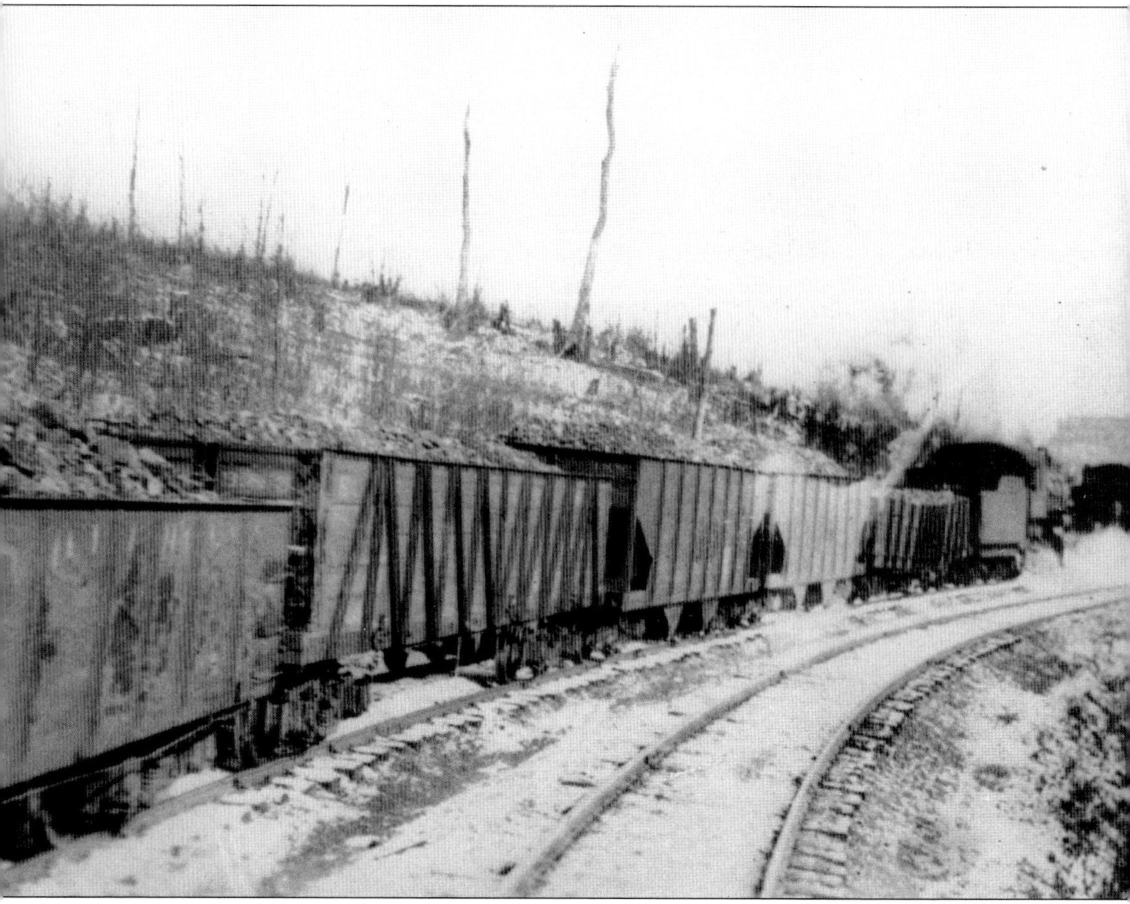

The curse of the Buffalo & Susquehanna was a set of switchback tracks on its main line over the Hogback. This was a mountainous barrier near Galeton, Pennsylvania, 135 miles south of Buffalo. Here at Cherry Springs, Pennsylvania, a Buffalo-bound coal train prepares for its next move. Four switchback tracks were encountered crossing the Hogback. No other Buffalo railroad had such a challenging alignment. (Michael J. Connor collection.)

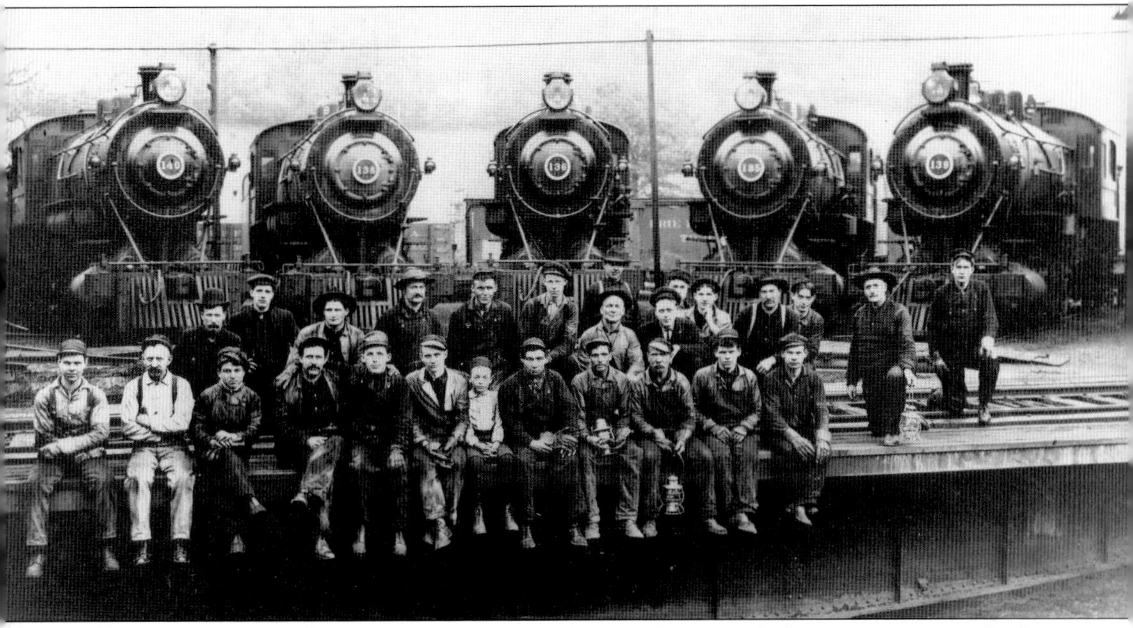

In 1906, the Buffalo & Susquehanna took delivery of eight Consolidation-type 2-8-0 wheel arrangement locomotives from The American Locomotive Company. Five engines are spotted at the Galeton, Pennsylvania, roundhouse soon after arrival. These engines and others would be needed when the Buffalo extension opened shortly after. (Michael J. Connor collection.)

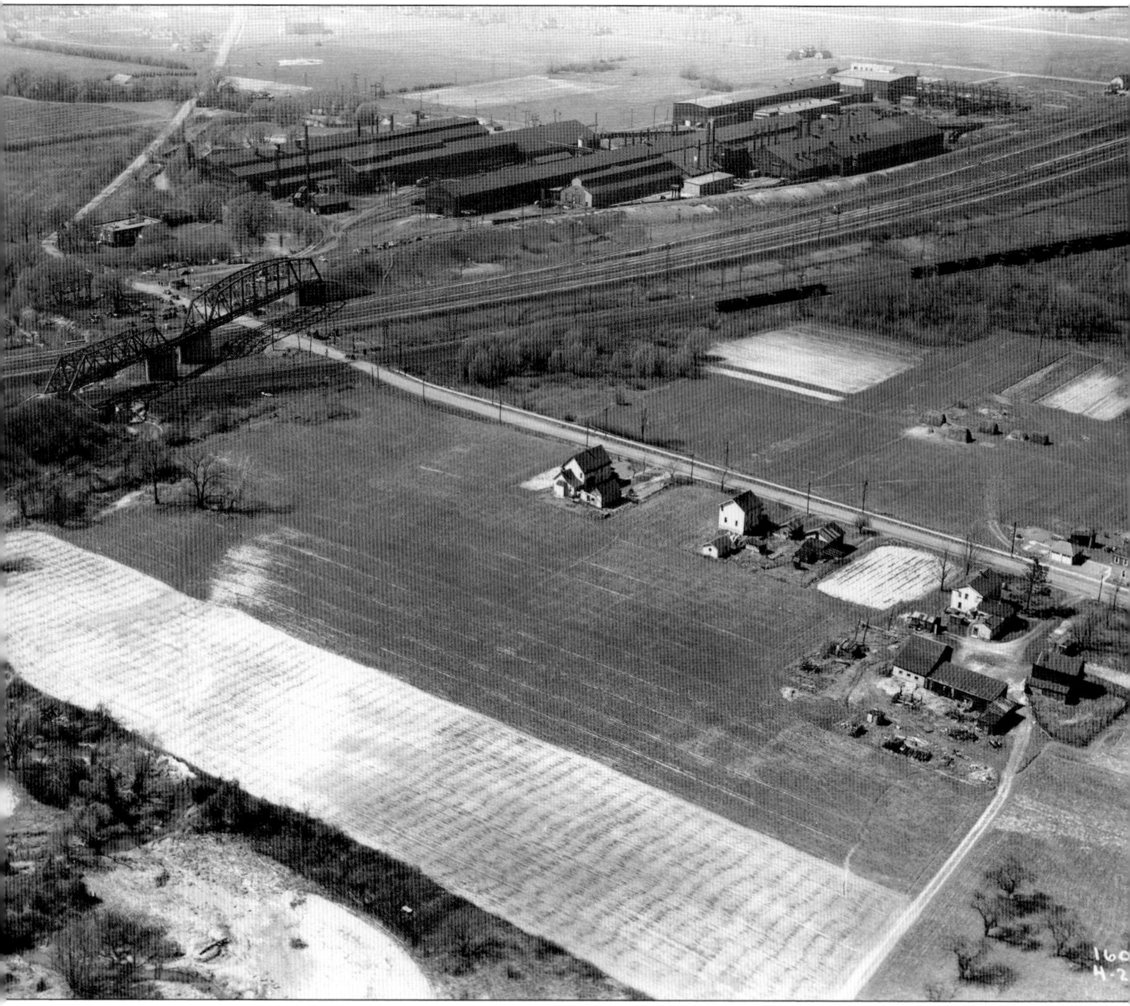

This aerial view was taken April 26, 1941, almost a quarter-century after the Wellsville & Buffalo Railroad, the Buffalo & Susquehanna's (B&S) short-lived successor, ceased operation. Mile Strip Road in Blasdell crosses the Pennsylvania, Nickel Plate, and New York Central railroads at grade. The B&S's approach grades and massive skewed bridges over the same railroads stand stripped of rails. (Paul V. Pietrak collection.)

# *Six*

# Norfolk Western and Prior Mergers

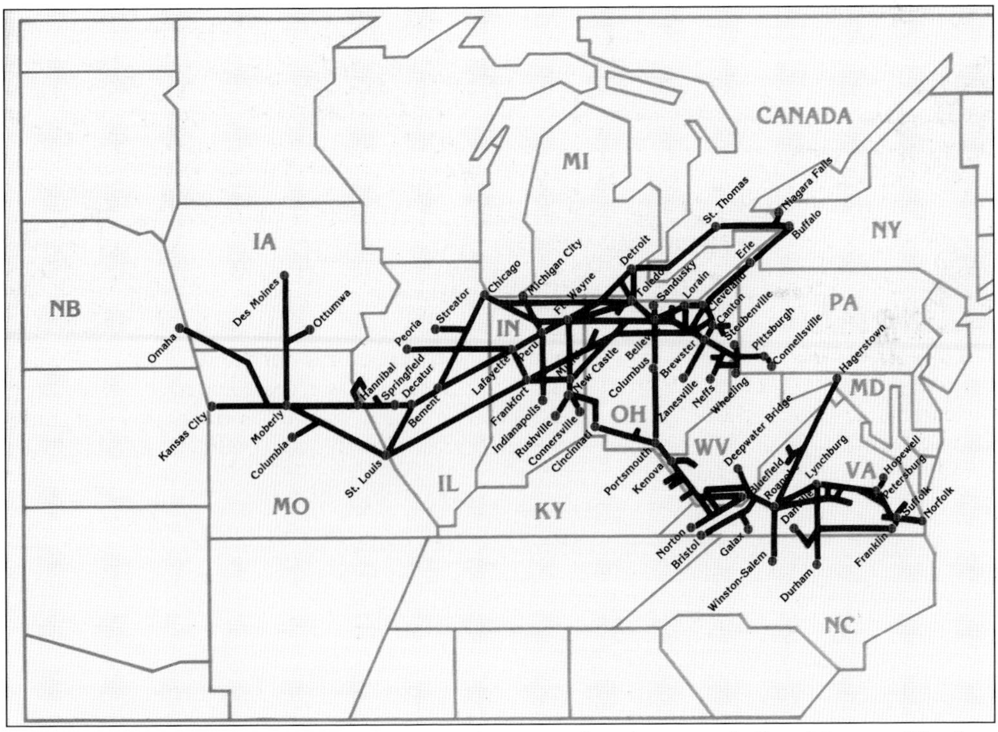


The Norfolk & Western Railway and its predecessors date from antebellum Virginia. The late 19th century saw it tap into its prime traffic, coal from western Virginia and West Virginia, to tidewater at Norfolk, Virginia. In a strategy to expand from its coal base, the N&W acquired two railroads serving Buffalo, the Nickel Plate Road and the Wabash, on October 16, 1964. (Michael J. Connor collection.)

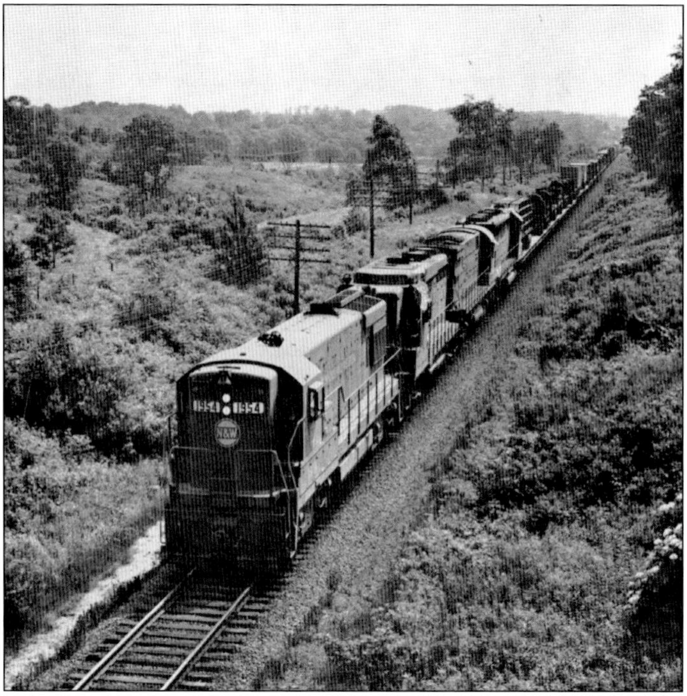


Norfolk & Western diesel-electric locomotive No. 1954 leads a four-unit consist pulling a mixed freight west from Buffalo in 1968. The post-merger N&W had two routes available from the west but the preferred route was the former Nickel Plate Road line, which skirted the south side of Lake Erie, versus the former Wabash Railroad, which ran through Ontario. (Michael J. Connor collection.)

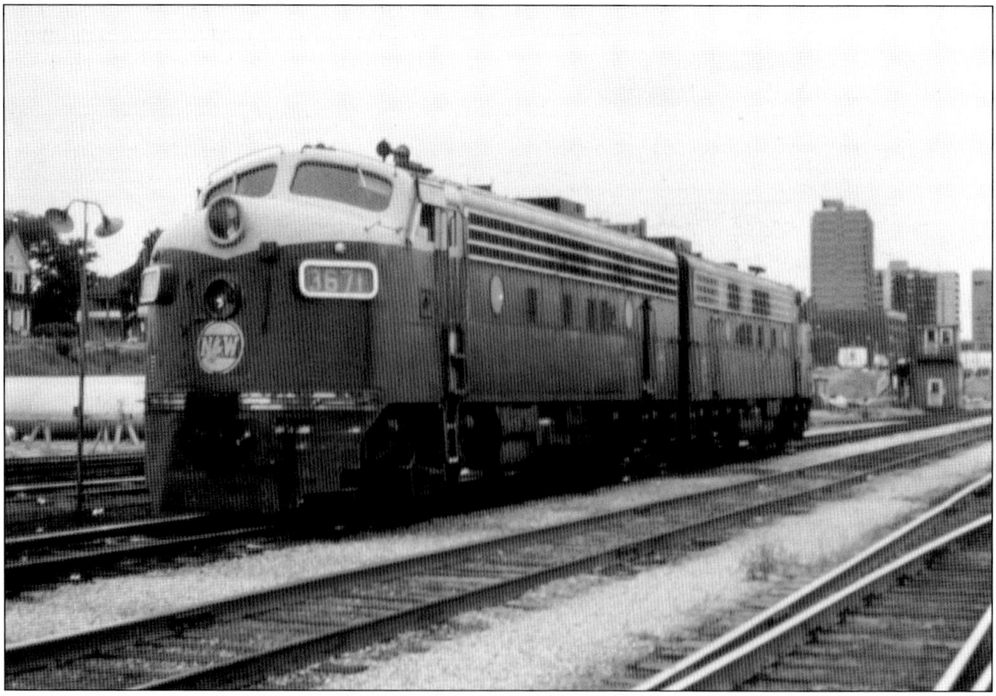


The Norfolk & Western leased the property of the Wabash Railroad Company effective October 16, 1964. Traffic to and from Buffalo formerly handled by the Wabash was increasingly routed over the N&W's former Nickel Plate Road line, which lacked the Wabash's handicap of extensive operation over other railroads and even a car float operation. N&W 3671, formerly Wabash 1162, waits in Windsor, Ontario, for a train to Buffalo in May 1976. (Joseph Schveder collection.)

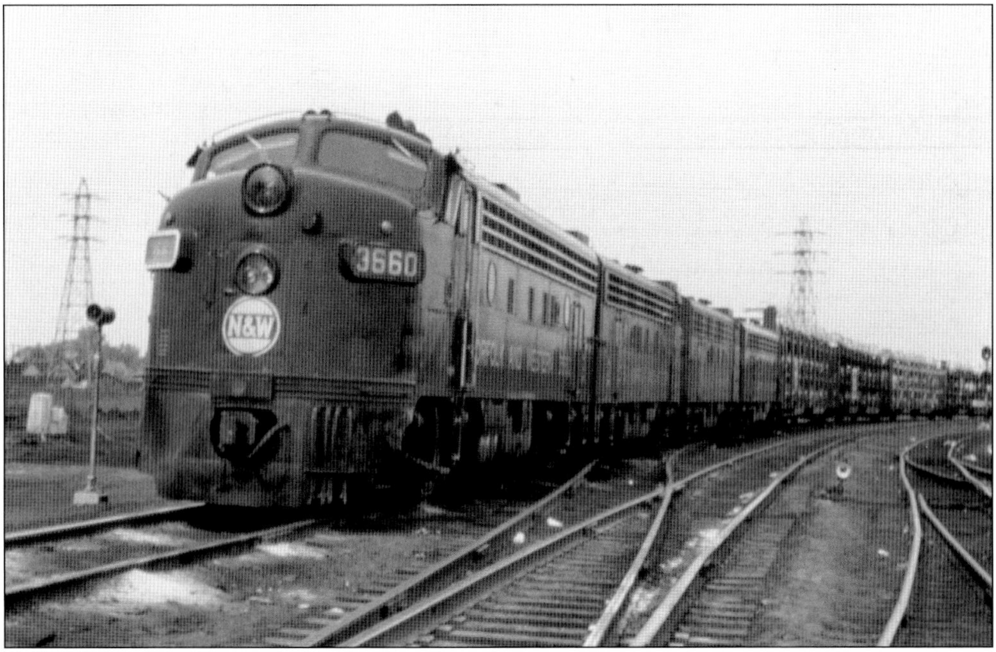

In 1960, the Erie Lackawanna Railroad envisioned major savings from the construction of a modern electronic classification yard. EL's perilous financial status eventually induced the Nickel Plate Road and successor Norfolk & Western Railway to join in Bison Yard as a one-half owner and joint operator. N&W 3660, formerly Wabash 1156A, arrives in Bison Yard May 11, 1968. (Joseph Schveder collection.)

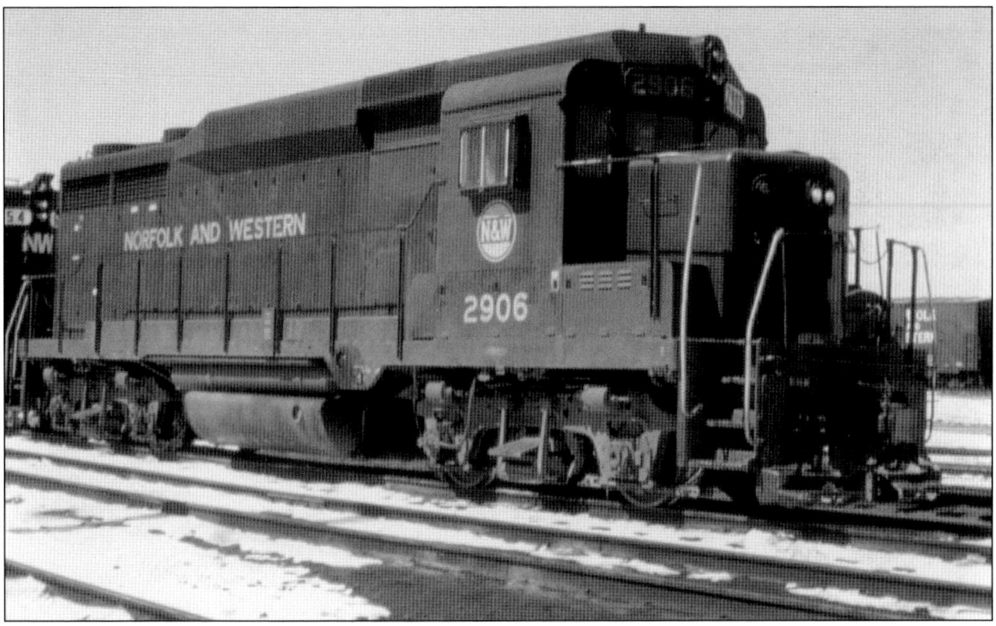

Nickel Plate had a reputation of operating relatively short, frequent, and fast merchandise trains. N&W was primarily a coal-hauling railroad. NKP's sidings and yards weren't equipped for long trains and delays were common. Seen in this photograph, N&W locomotive 2906 is the former NKP 906. (Joseph Schveder collection.)

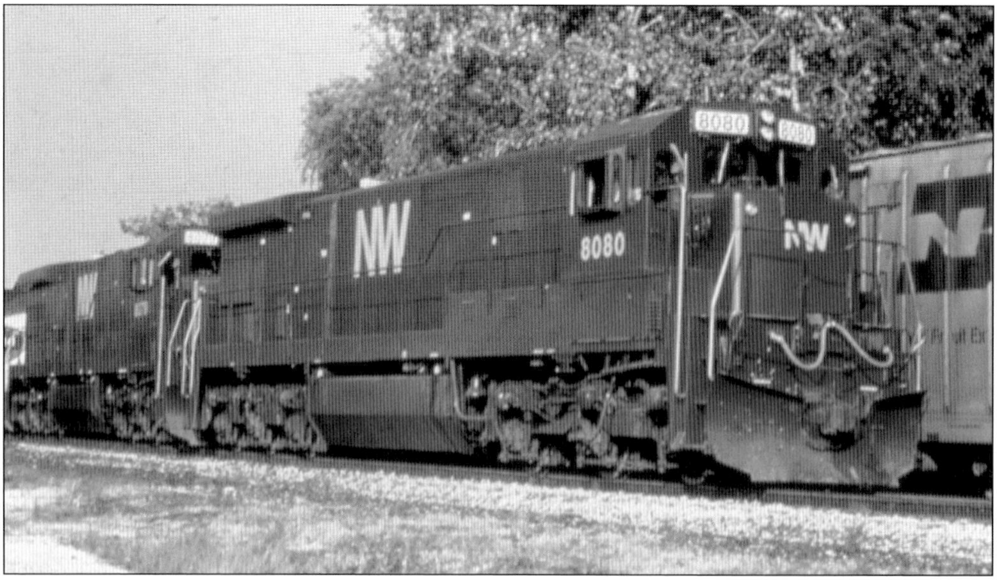


While the majority of Buffalo's two largest railroads entered bankruptcy in the 1970s, the Norfolk & Western Railway stayed solvent. While its bankrupt neighbors labored with tired and increasingly obsolete locomotives, N&W was constantly upgrading its motive power. N&W 8080 pulls a train towards Buffalo in Ohio in 1980. Bought new in 1979, N&W 8080 is a 3,000-horsepower General Electric model C30-7 built in Erie, Pennsylvania. (Joseph Schveder collection.)

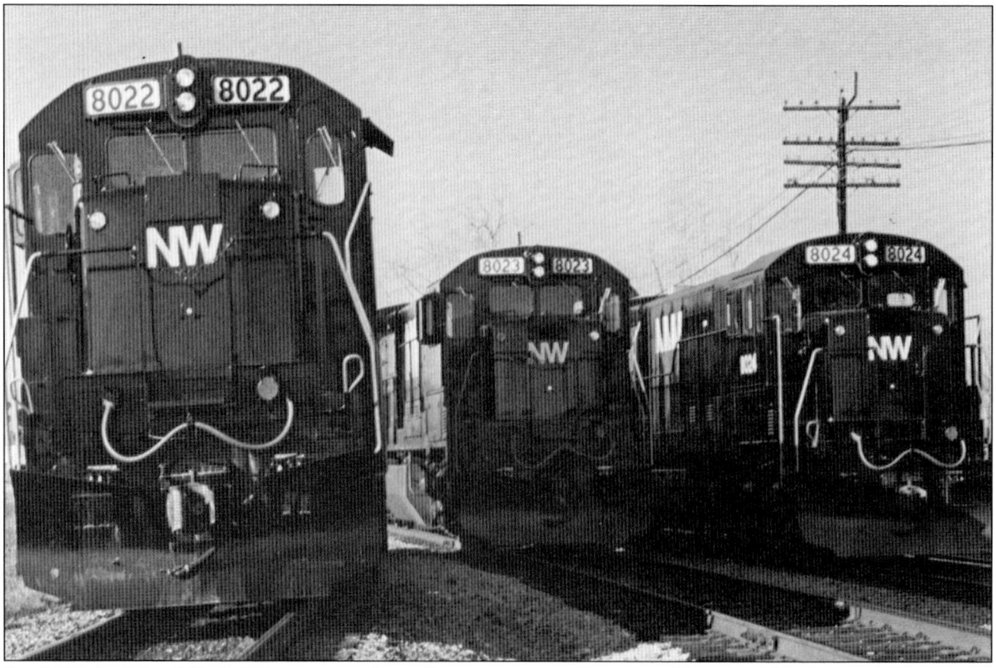


In 1982 the Norfolk & Western Railway became an operating affiliate of the Norfolk Southern Corporation (NS). One of the last locomotive liveries, black with a block "NW," of the pre-NS Norfolk and Western is seen on locomotives 8022, 8023, and 8024 fresh from their builder, General Electric, in Erie, Pennsylvania. These model C30-7 six-axle 3,000-horsepower diesel-electric locomotives were built in 1976. (Norfolk & Western Railway Company)

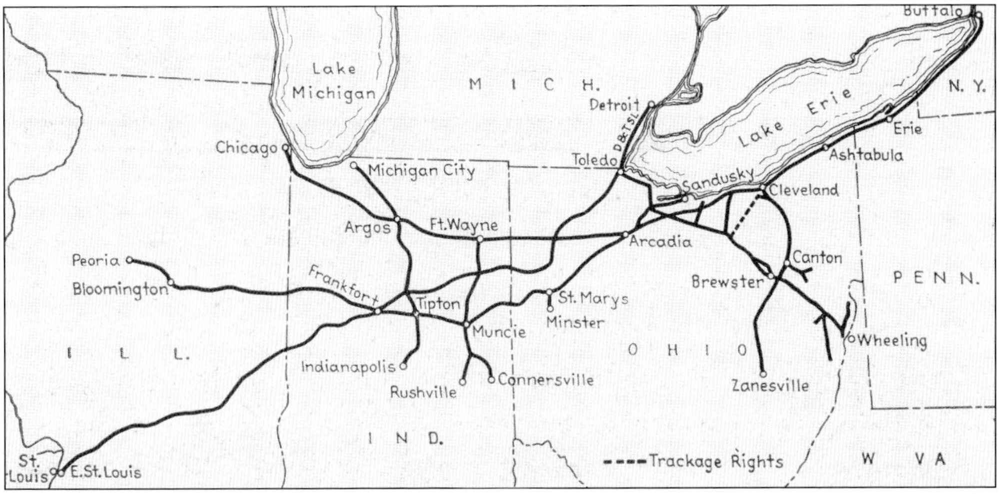


The Nickel Plate Road opened its 524-mile Buffalo-to-Chicago line on October 22, 1882. The NKP had minimal facilities in Buffalo and operations were at a small yard near South Park Avenue and Smith Street. Passenger trains used the New York Central's Exchange Street station until 1917 when the NKP moved its trains to the Lackawanna Railroad's new terminal on Main Street. (Michael J. Connor collection.)

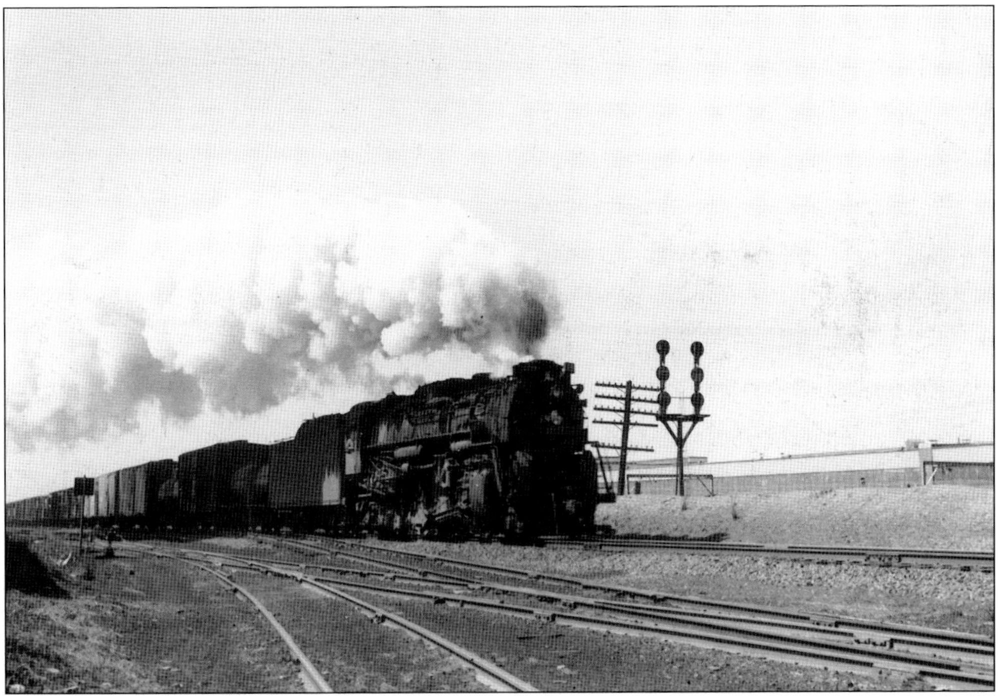

The Nickel Plate Road was the last railroad operating steam locomotives into Buffalo; here in 1949 one of its 700-series Class S Berkshires with a 2-8-4 wheel arrangement races through Wanakah towards Buffalo. In the distance signals of the neighboring New York Central are visible. The NKP ended steam operation into Buffalo on July 1, 1958, when Berkshire 719 departed with a westbound freight. (Photograph by James Van Brocklin.)

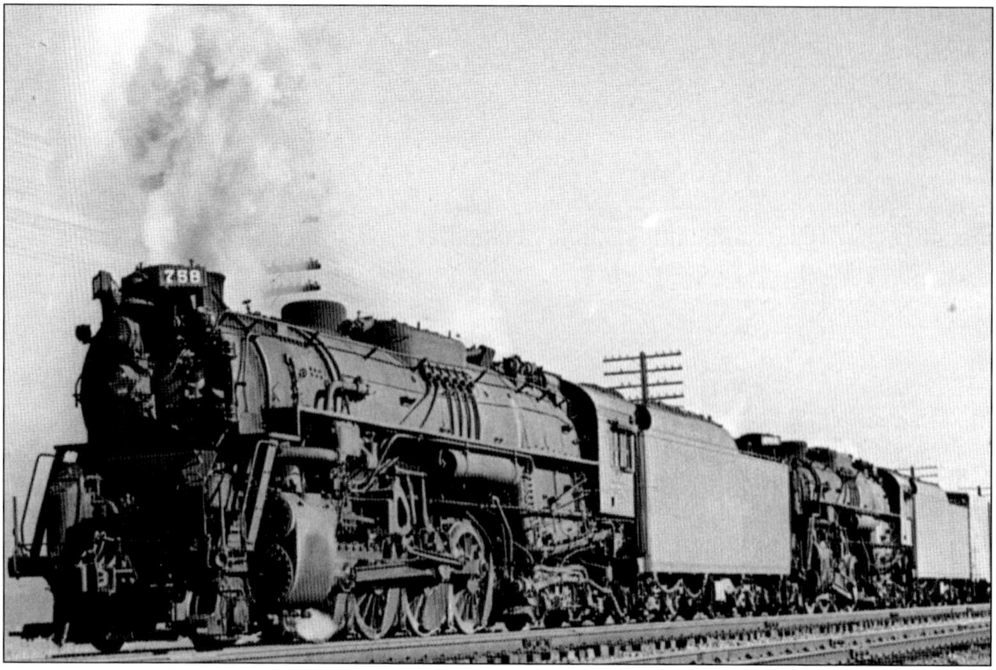


The Nickel Plate Road was one of the few railroads in the steam locomotive era that permitted freight trains to operate at 60 miles per hour. Double-headed steam locomotives, here shown by No. 758 and No. 754 westbound in Summer 1958, the last summer of steam on the NKP, enabled the Road to take full advantage of its excellent track and modern motive power. (William C. Kessel collection.)

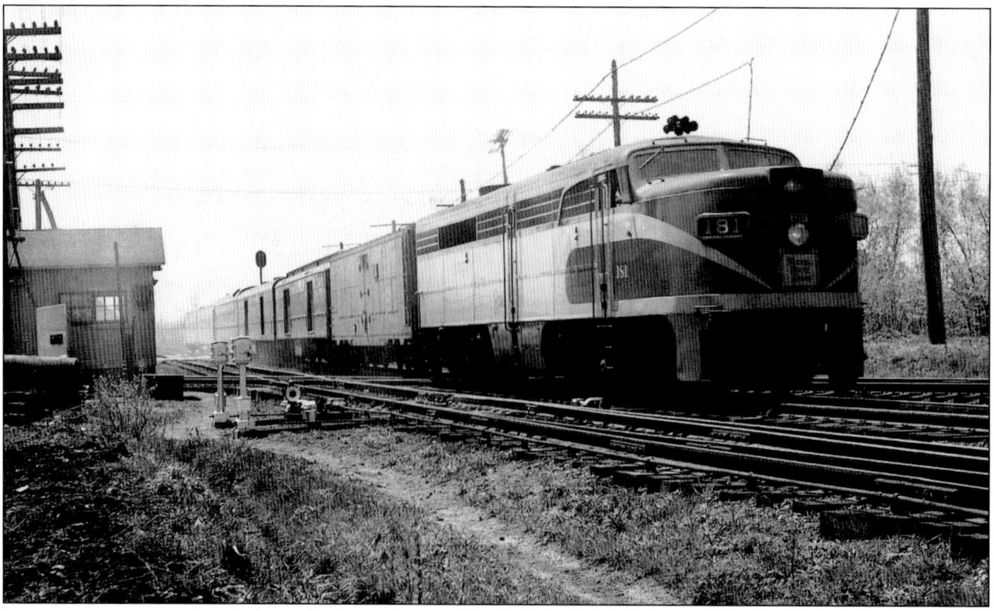


Increases in train size and track speeds motivated the Nickel Plate to dieselize its passenger service in 1948. American Locomotive built 11 model PA-1 1,200-horsepower locomotives to replace steam passenger service. In its striking blue-and-white livery, NKP Bluebird No. 181 crosses the Erie Railroad's B&SW line in Blasdell with train No. 6 in the late 1950s. (Phil Soyring collection.)

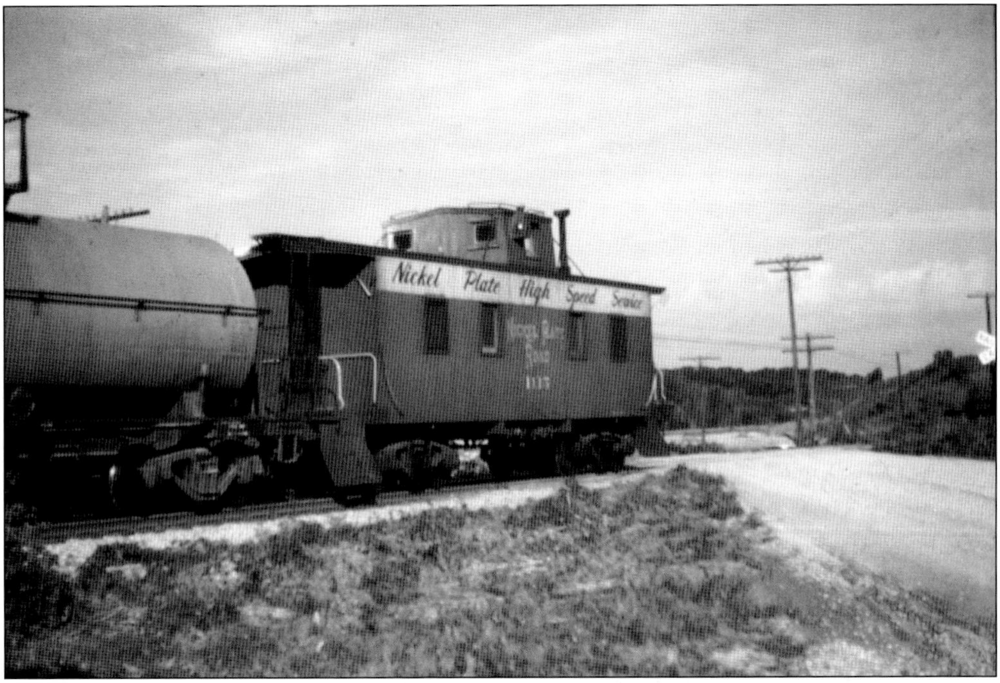


The Nickel Plate was the second or third railroad built through many of the communities it served. Industrial development tended to focus on the older railroads and for its life the NKP's forté was fast freight service bridging one railroad to another. Unlike any other major railroad, the NKP advertised itself and its service with "Nickel Plate High Speed Service" emblazoned on its cabooses. (Ronald R. Dukarm collection.)

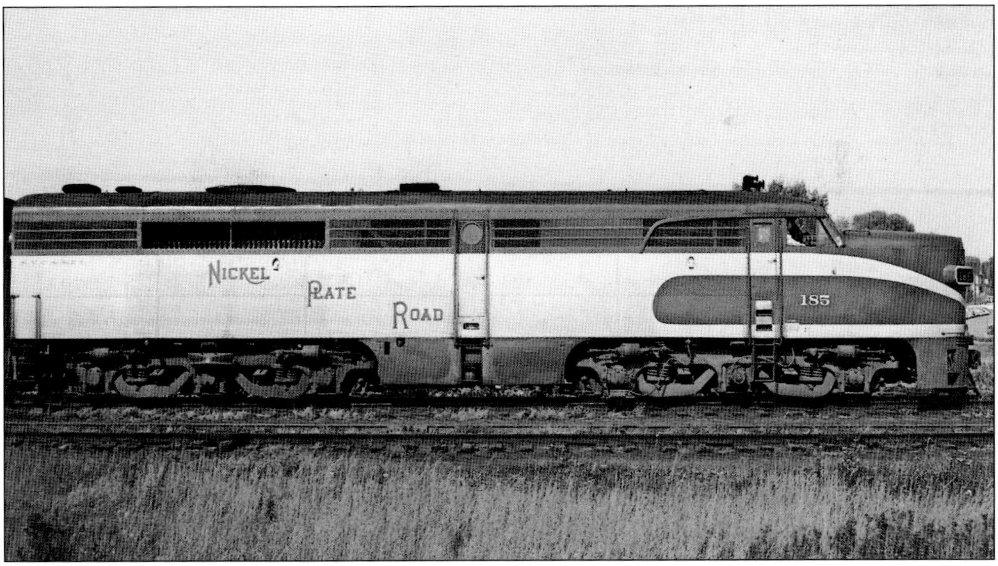


The Nickel Plate Road's passenger service connected Buffalo with Cleveland, Chicago, and St. Louis. The New York, Chicago & St. Louis Railway ordered 11 American Locomotive Company PA units in 1947 and named them bluebirds. Here is a builder's photograph of ALCO PA-1 No. 185. The PA series passenger locomotives are probably the most handsome diesel locomotives ever built. (Michael J. Connor collection.)

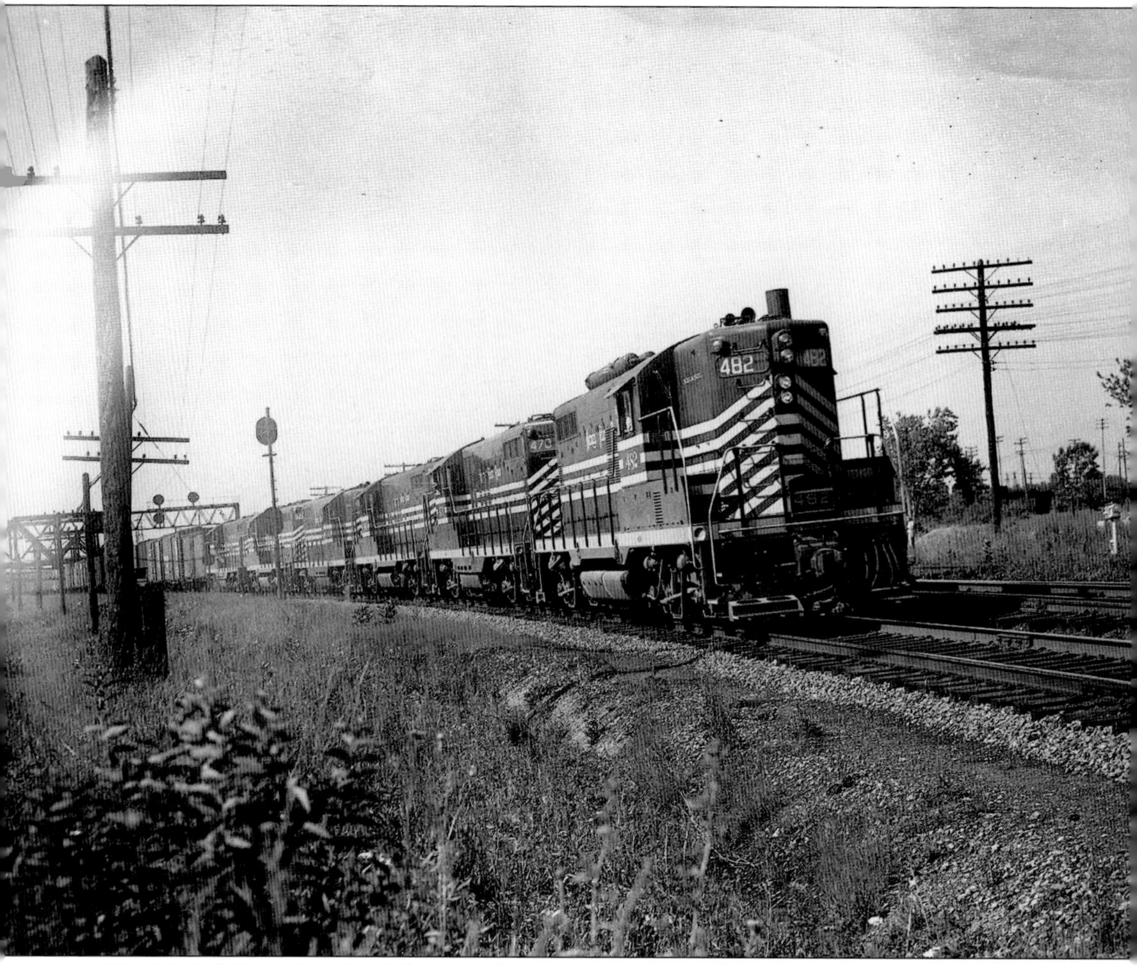


The Nickel Plate bought 272 general-purpose road switcher diesels after 1950, completing dieselization. In 1962, No. 482 leads five sisters westbound through Blasdell. The train has just passed under the bridge carrying Track 5 of NYC's Gardenville cut-off and will cross the Erie's B&SW line in seconds. (Phil Soyring collection.)

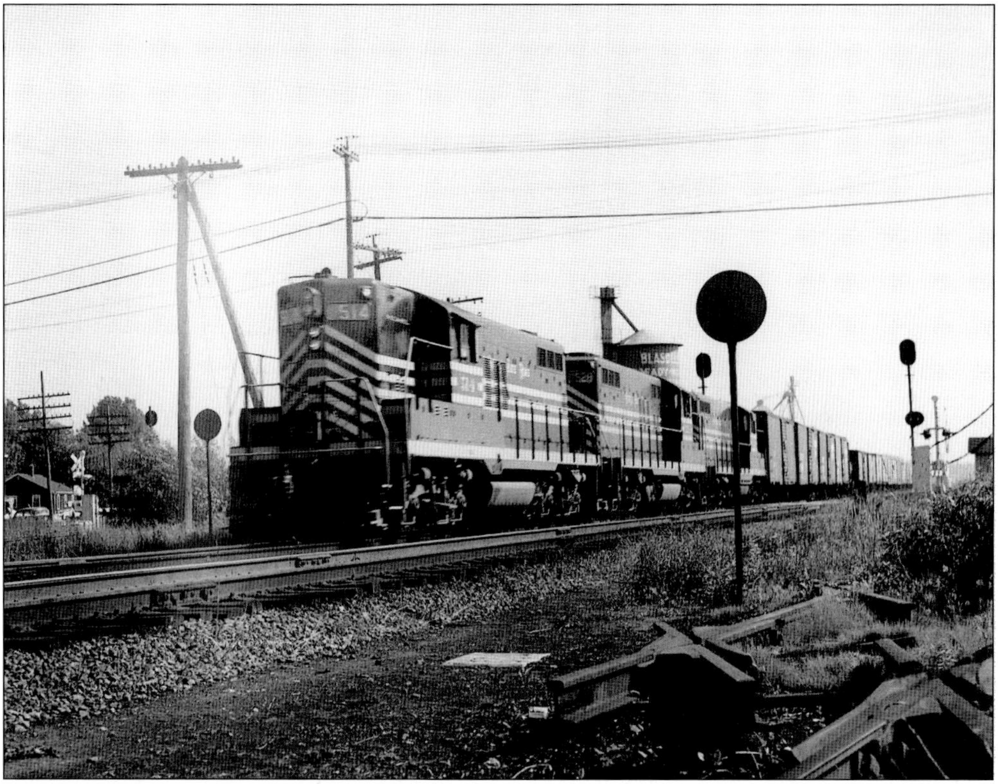

Prior to moving its Buffalo terminal operations into Bison Yard, the Nickel Plate had very few yard tracks in the area. Most switching of traffic destined for other railroads was done at Conneaut, Ohio or Bellevue, Ohio where adequate NKP yard facilities existed. Diesel-electric locomotive 514, a 1,500-horsepower GP-7 model locomotive, and two sisters race through Blasdell in 1961 for Buffalo and connections. (Phil Soyring collection.)

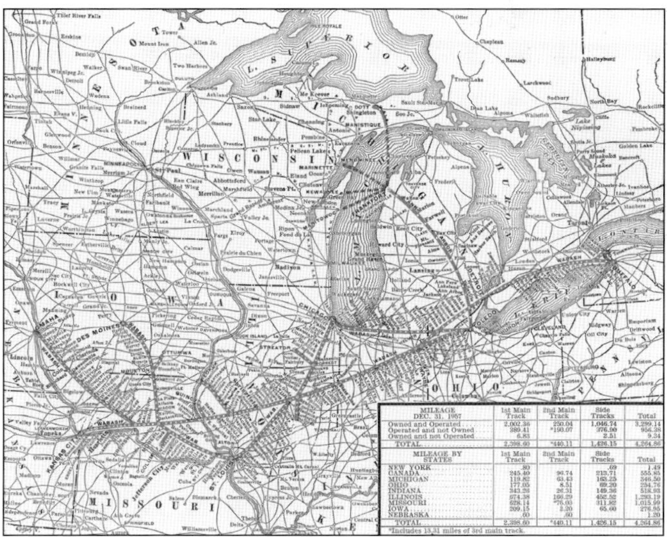

| MILEAGE DEC. 31, 1957 | 1st Main Track | 2nd Main Track | Side Tracks | Total |
|---|---|---|---|---|
| Owned and Operated | 2,002.36 | 250.04 | 1,046.74 | 3,299.14 |
| Operated and not Owned | 389.41 | *190.07 | 376.90 | 956.38 |
| Owned and not Operated | 6.83 | | 2.51 | 9.34 |
| TOTAL | 2,398.60 | *440.11 | 1,426.15 | 4,264.86 |

| MILEAGE BY STATES | 1st Main Track | 2nd Main Track | Side Tracks | Total |
|---|---|---|---|---|
| NEW YORK | .80 | | .69 | 1.49 |
| CANADA | 245.40 | 96.74 | 213.71 | 555.85 |
| MICHIGAN | 119.82 | 63.43 | 163.25 | 346.50 |
| OHIO | 177.05 | 8.51 | 69.20 | 254.76 |
| INDIANA | 343.26 | 26.31 | 149.36 | 518.93 |
| ILLINOIS | 674.38 | 166.29 | 452.52 | 1,293.19 |
| MISSOURI | 628.14 | *76.03 | 311.82 | 1,015.99 |
| IOWA | 209.15 | 2.20 | 65.60 | 276.95 |
| NEBRASKA | .60 | .60 | | 1.20 |
| TOTAL | 2,398.60 | *440.11 | 1,426.15 | 4,264.86 |

*Includes 13.31 miles of 3rd main track.

The Wabash Railroad resembled the Erie in its multiple bankruptcies and its having been under the influence of legendary railroad financier Jay Gould. The Wabash arrived in Buffalo in 1898 having extended its main line across southern Ontario through a combination of construction and trackage rights. The 2,542-mile Wabash was leased by the Norfolk & Western effective October 16, 1964. (Michael J. Connor collection.)

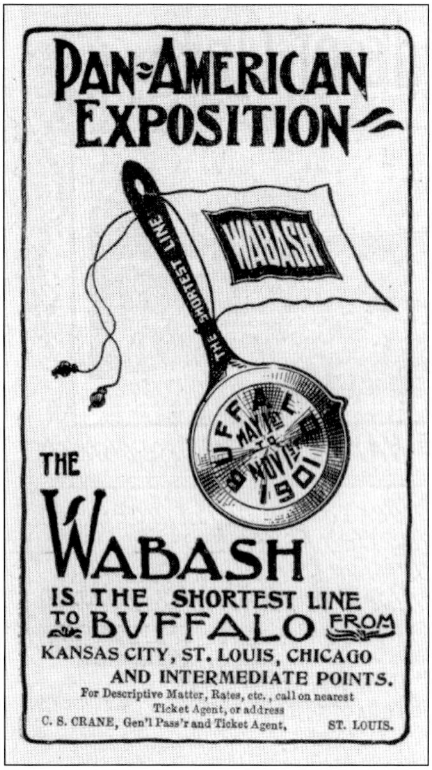


In this 1901 Wabash advertisement for the Pan-American Exposition held in Buffalo, New York, the Wabash is emphasizing that it has the shortest route from Kansas City and Chicago. The Pan Am Expo was a forerunner to modern world's fairs and was held in Buffalo in 1901, due to the importance and growth of the area. (Stephen G. Myers collection.)

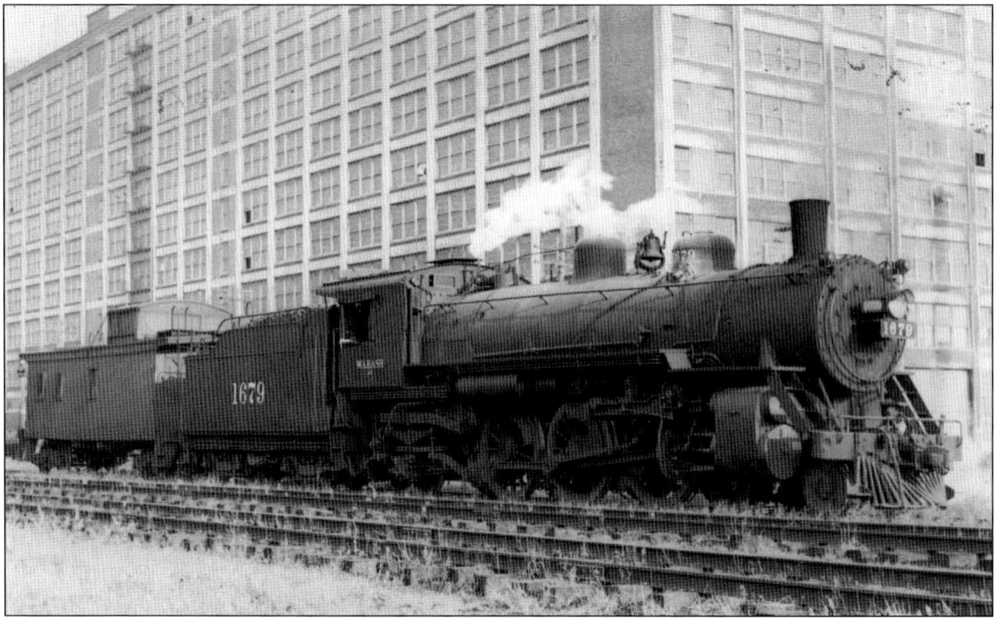


Having reached Buffalo over a car float and 246.2 miles of trackage rights, the Wabash used the Delaware, Lackawanna & Western Railroad's East Buffalo Yard and Buffalo passenger terminal. Wabash operated freight houses at Black Rock and in Buffalo at Exchange and Larkin Streets. Wabash 1679, a J-2 Pacific, stands by on Erie Railroad tracks to switch the Wabash's Buffalo freight house on June 10, 1940. (Phil Soyring collection.)

*Seven*

# The Creek and the South Buffalo

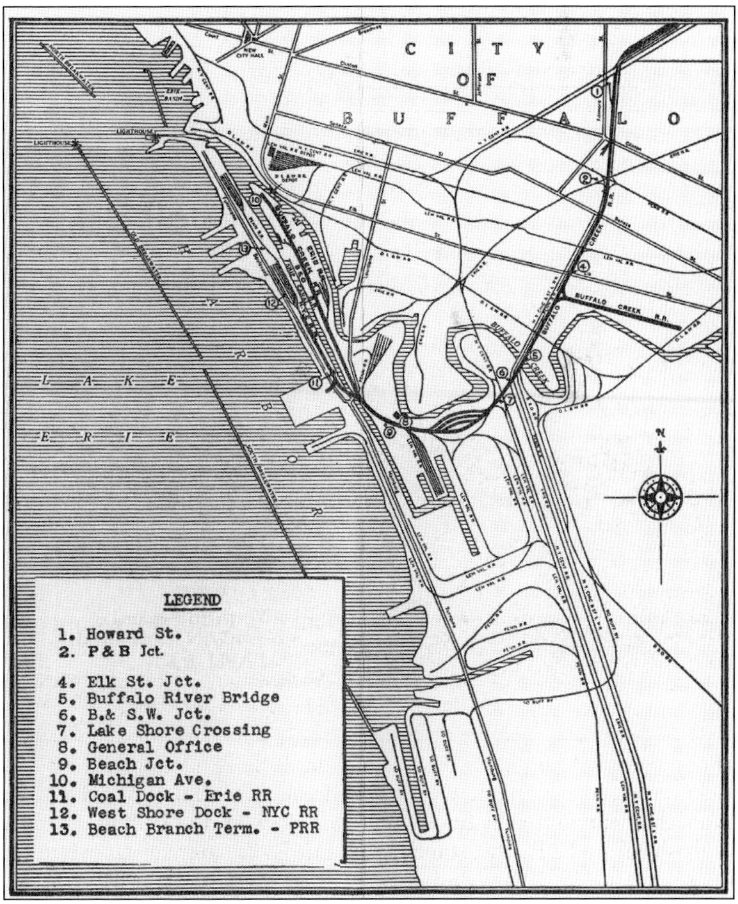


Located entirely within Buffalo's city limits, the Buffalo Creek Railroad was Buffalo's longest-lived railroad. Founded on January 26, 1869, it survived until merged into Conrail on December 31, 1983. Controlled by the Erie Railroad and the Lehigh Valley Railroad from 1889 to 1976 and Conrail thereafter, the BCK, or Creek, as it was familiarly known, provided all Buffalo railroads access to waterfront industries. (Michael J. Connor collection.)

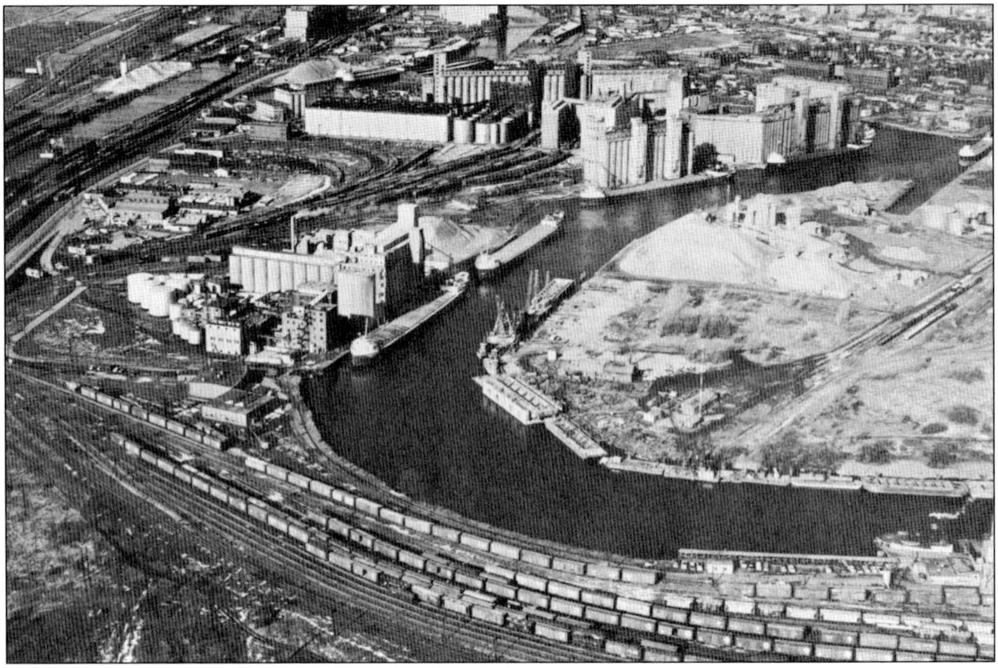

The core of the Buffalo Creek's freight traffic was in Buffalo's waterfront industries. This aerial view looks north towards downtown. In the immediate foreground is the BCK's principal freight yard and above is the railroad's engine house and general office. At least six elevators and numerous other industries are visible in this look at industrial Buffalo. (Michael J. Connor collection.)

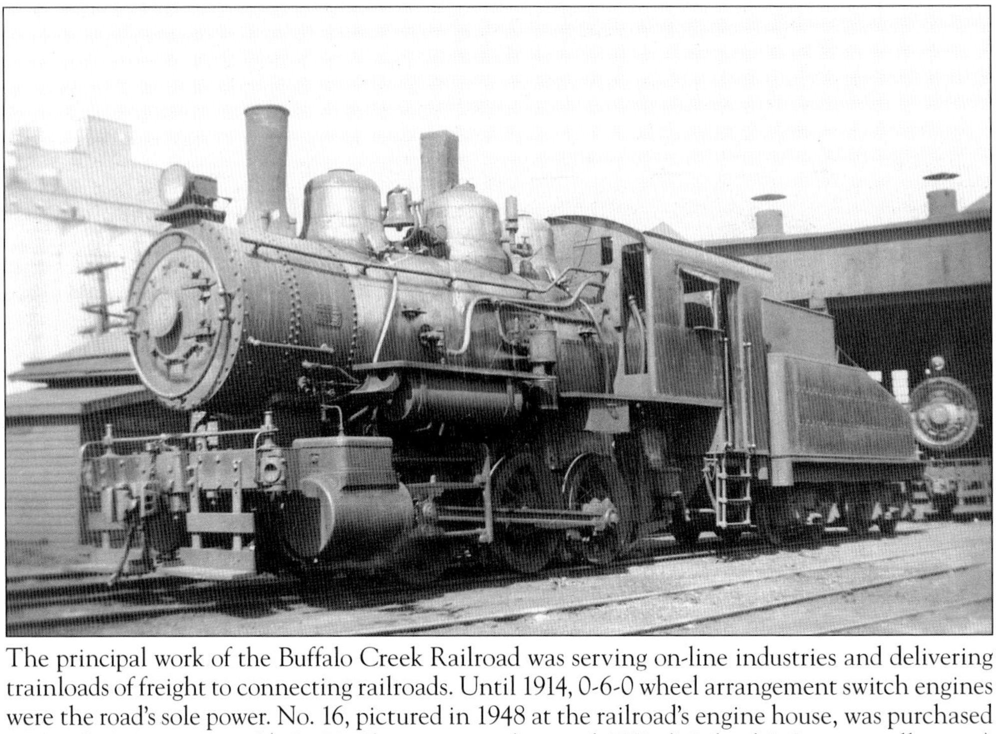

The principal work of the Buffalo Creek Railroad was serving on-line industries and delivering trainloads of freight to connecting railroads. Until 1914, 0-6-0 wheel arrangement switch engines were the road's sole power. No. 16, pictured in 1948 at the railroad's engine house, was purchased in April 1912 at a cost of $12,400. She was retired around 1952. (Michael J. Connor collection.)

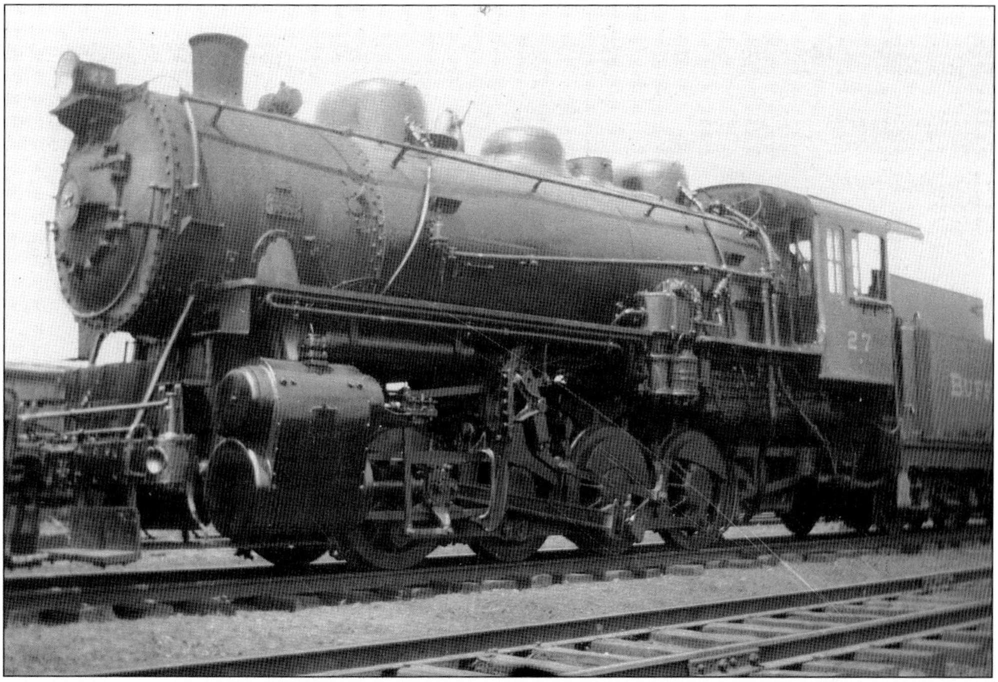

The increasing number and weight of freight cars being handled on the Buffalo Creek Railroad resulted in the acquisition of large 0-8-0 wheel arrangement locomotives such as No. 27, pictured in 1948. She was acquired new in 1923 at cost of about $25,000. Sold to the Canadian National Railway in 1949, she was scrapped in March 1960. (Michael J. Connor collection.)

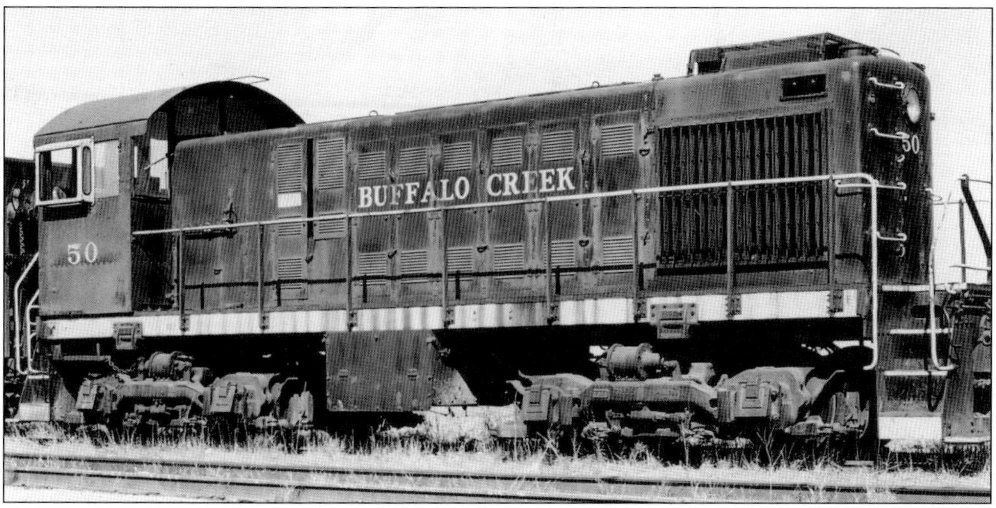


The Buffalo Creek's locomotives were all ALCO products built in Schenectady, New York, except for three General Motors EMC products built between 1938 and 1940. No. 50 was an ALCO S-2 locomotive and could put out 1,000 horsepower. BCK No. 50 was built in September of 1945 and served in the Buffalo area for many years. (Stephan M. Koenig collection.)

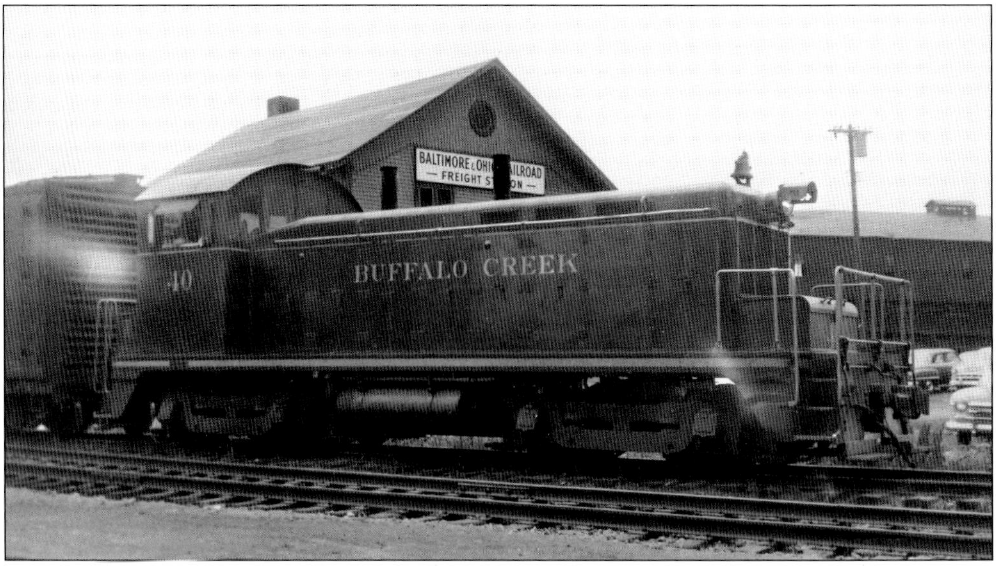


The Buffalo Creek had a total of 13 locomotives on her roster; the first was an HH660 from American Locomotive and the next three were from General Motors Electro-Motive Corporation. This photograph shows No. 40, which was an SW locomotive, built in December of 1938. The Creek was a profitable and busy little railroad. (Stephan M. Koenig collection.)

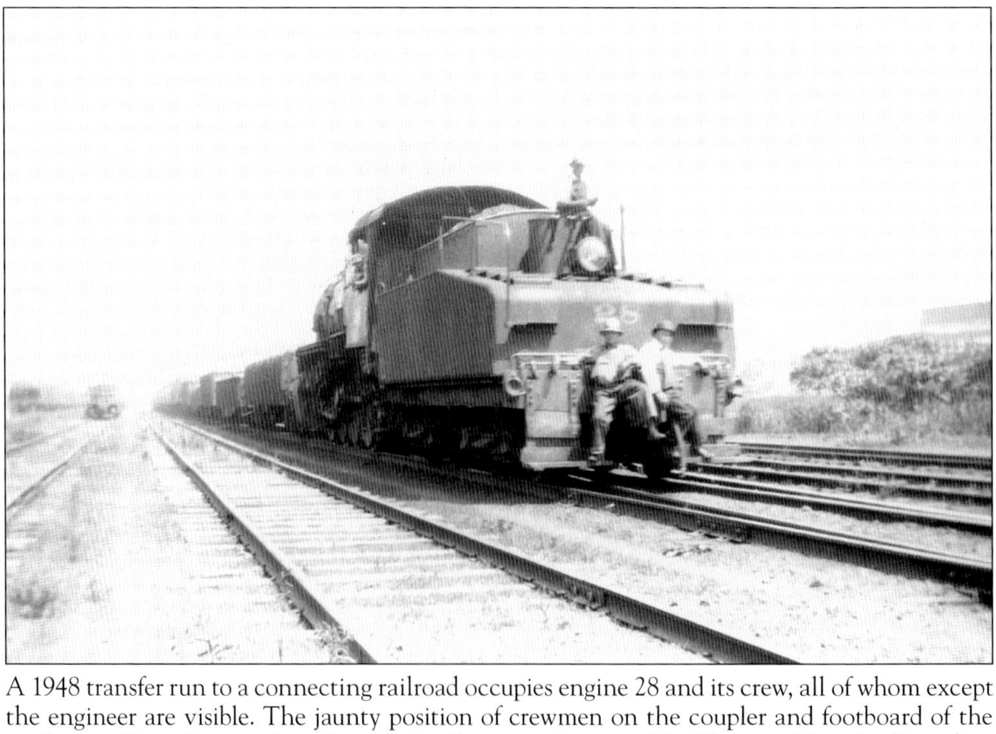

A 1948 transfer run to a connecting railroad occupies engine 28 and its crew, all of whom except the engineer are visible. The jaunty position of crewmen on the coupler and footboard of the tender would not be permitted in today's safety conscious era. No. 28 was sold to the Canadian National Railway shortly after this picture was taken and ultimately scrapped in December 1955. (Michael J. Connor Collection.)

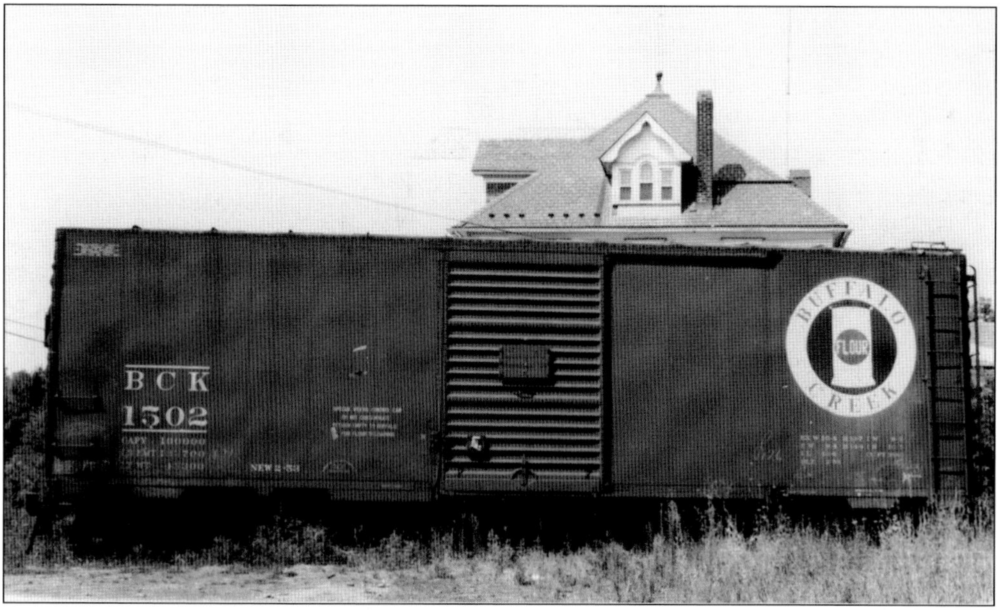

The Buffalo Creek was overwhelmingly a grain-handling railroad, and until the 1970s, this freight moved in boxcars. To alleviate car shortages on the road, Superintendent William M. Sporleder purchased 2,000 high-quality boxcars in the 1950s. With their Buffalo Creek "Flour" insignia, the cars brought recognition to the BCK and Buffalo as they traveled throughout the nation carrying grain products from Buffalo. (Clinton T. Andrews collection.)

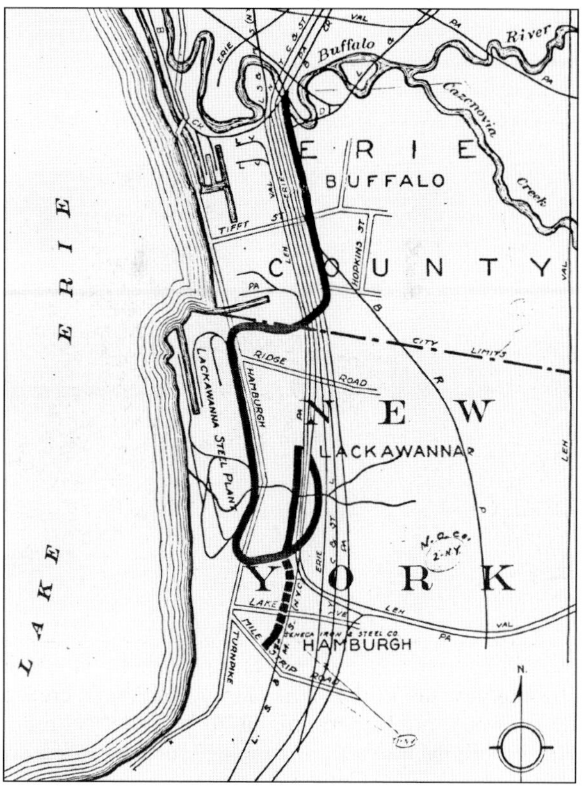

The South Buffalo Railway was incorporated on April 25, 1899, and its 8-mile line opened in 1902. It was owned for its first 102 years by the Lackawanna Steel Company and its successor, Bethlehem Steel. In October 2001, its bankrupt parent sold the SB to Genesee and Wyoming Industries, which has integrated operation of the SB into its Buffalo & Pittsburgh Railroad. (Michael J. Connor collection.)

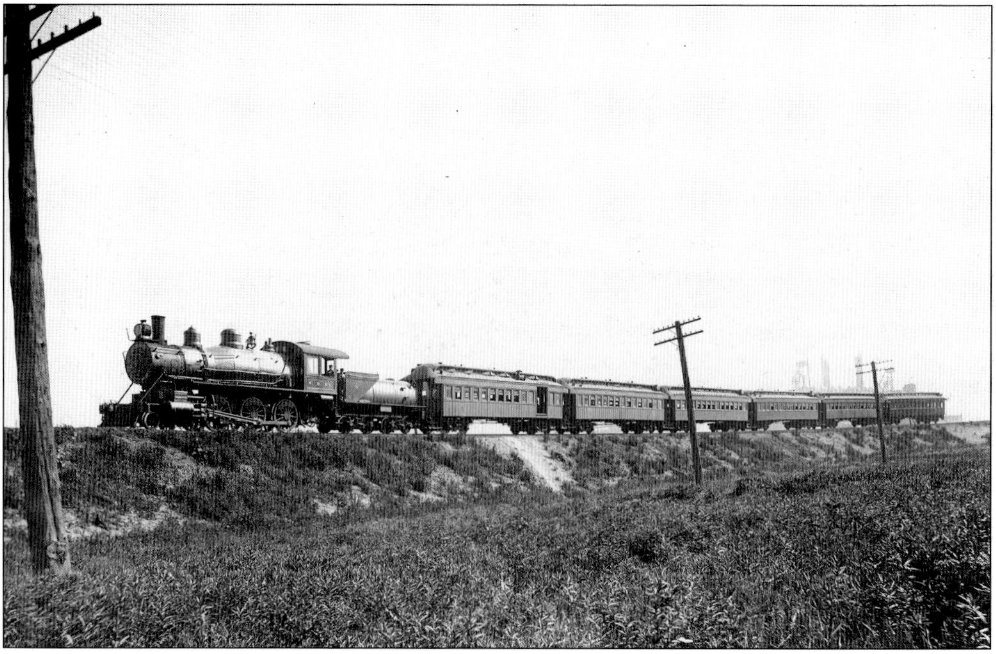

Prior to the construction of street and interurban electric railways, the South Buffalo operated passenger trains between the Delaware, Lackawanna & Western station at the foot of Buffalo's Main Street and the Lackawanna steel plant. This train, made up of former Nickel Plate Road passenger cars and powered by No. 8, a 10-wheeler, is pictured on June 11, 1907, near the Hamburg Turnpike. (Paul Pietrak collection.)

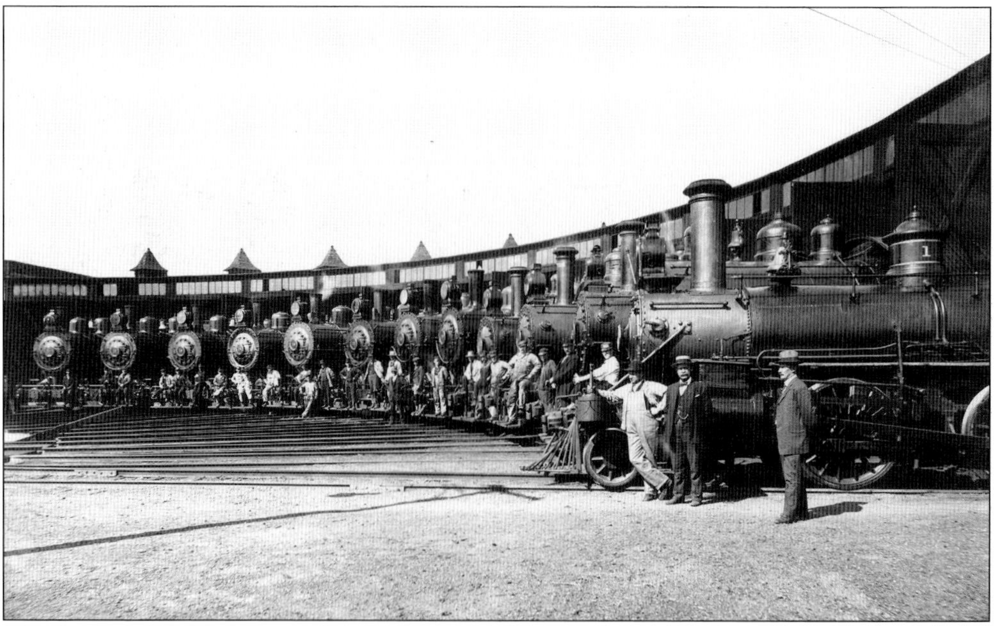

It took a lot of locomotives to serve both the South Buffalo Railway and the internal switching at the steel mill. Over its life the SB has rostered at least 48 steam locomotives. Here in 1911, 12 SB and Lackawanna Steel Company engines line up for a display of steam power at the SB engine house. (Paul Pietrak collection.)

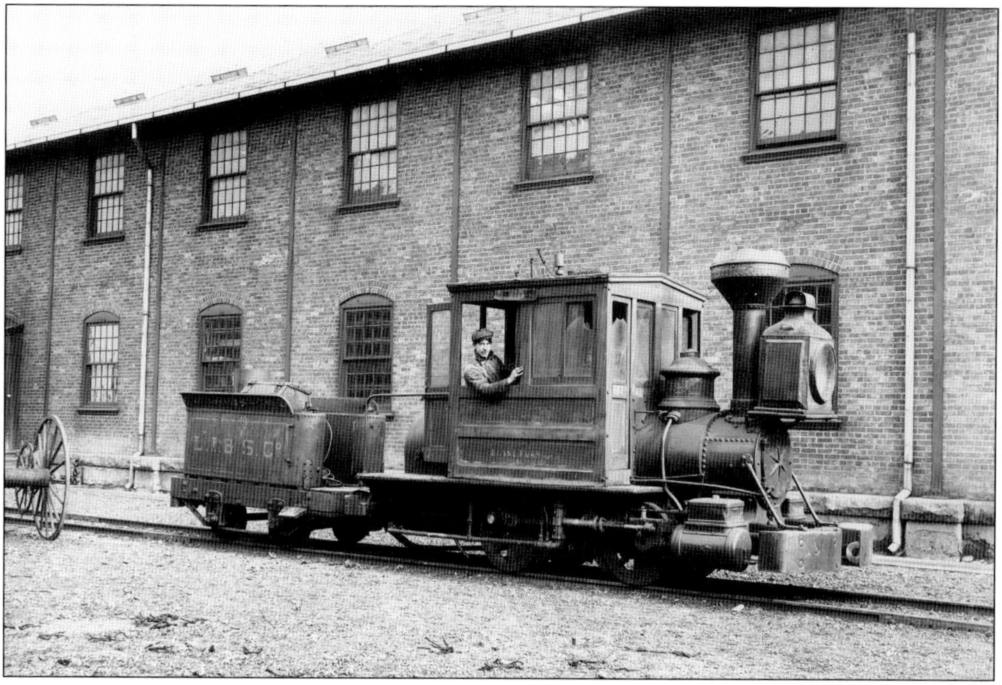

Besides the standard gauge South Buffalo Railway, the steel mill operated an extensive narrow 36-inch gauge in-plant system. One of its earliest and smallest narrow gauge locomotives is No. 4, which, like most Lackawanna Iron and Steel Company early locomotives, was named, in this case *Dewey*. *Dewey* was brought from LI&S's Scranton, Pennsylvania, operation to help build and open the Lackawanna plant. (Paul Pietrak collection.)

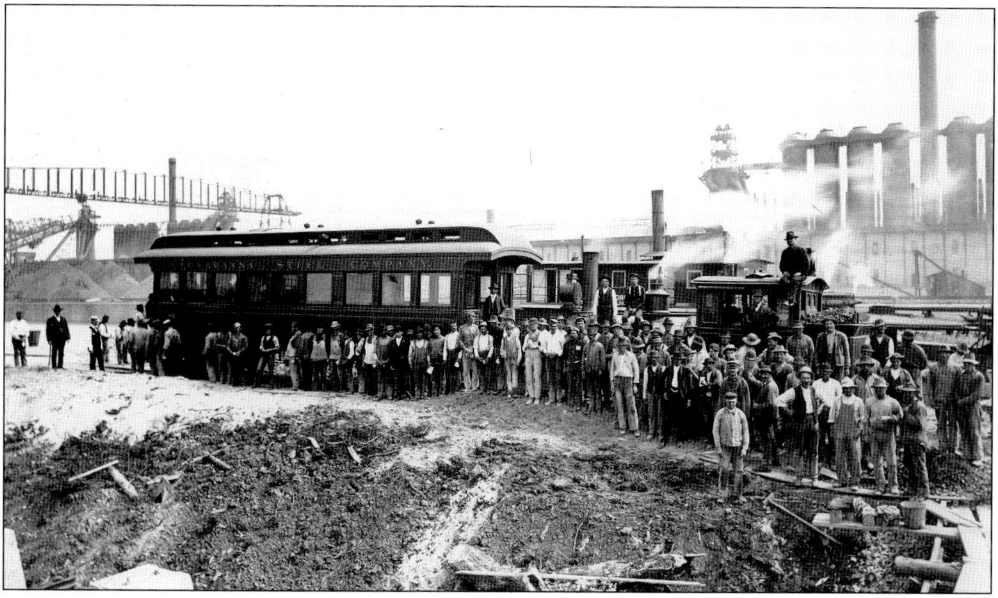

Payday was as welcome in the early 20th century as it is today. Here Lackawanna Steel Company 0-4-0 type locomotive No. 2 has spotted the pay car next to the ship canal amidst the mill's construction site. Workers entering the pay car will present brass checks to verify their identity. (Paul Pietrak collection.)

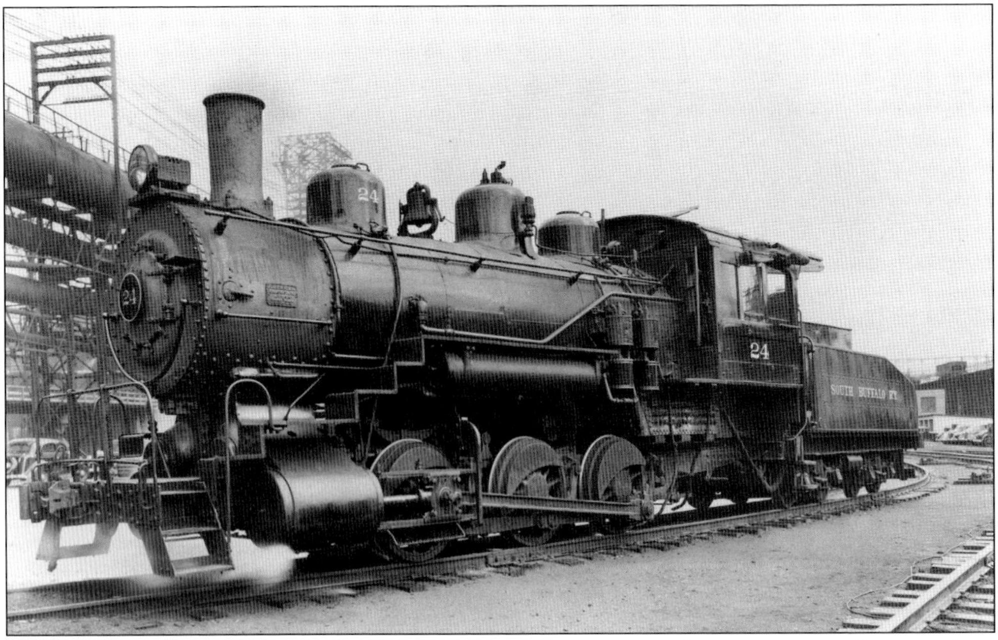


Accidents and injuries cause lost production and needless expense. In a continuing effort to reduce injuries to switchmen, the South Buffalo Railway equipped many of its steam locomotives with handrails and wide, easy to mount front steps and platforms. Here 0-6-0 type steam locomotive No. 24 illustrates its new safety features on October 7, 1937. (Paul Pietrak collection.)

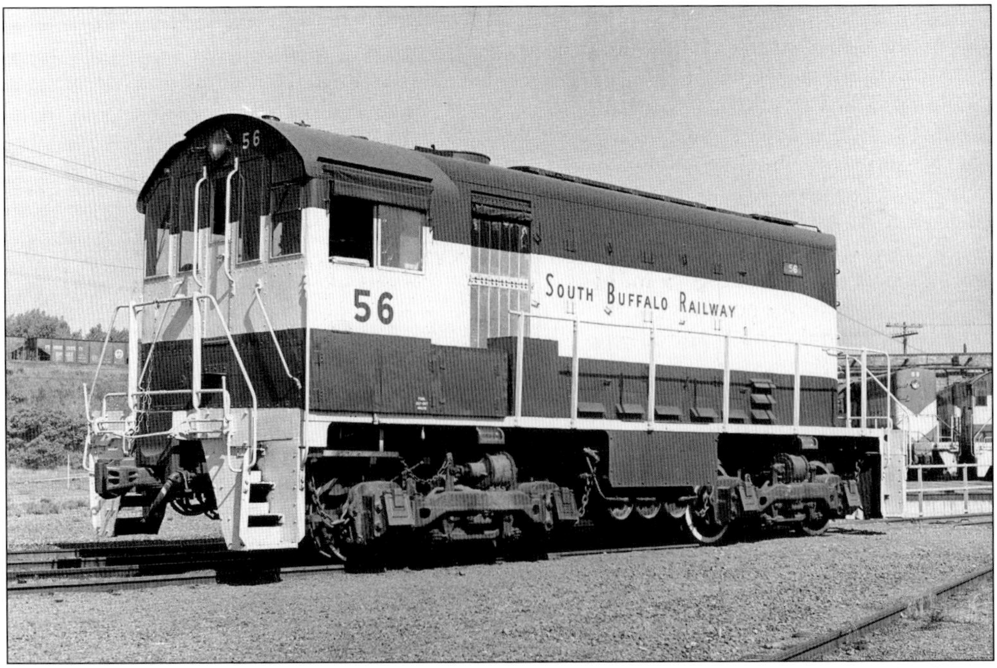


The diesel-electric locomotive was especially well suited for improving the efficiency and reducing the cost of industrial switching railroads such as the South Buffalo Railway. Despite her high number, SB No. 56 was one of the road's first diesels, arriving from builder Alco in June 1937. She is one of at least 102 diesel electric locomotives owned by the SB. (Paul Pietrak collection.)

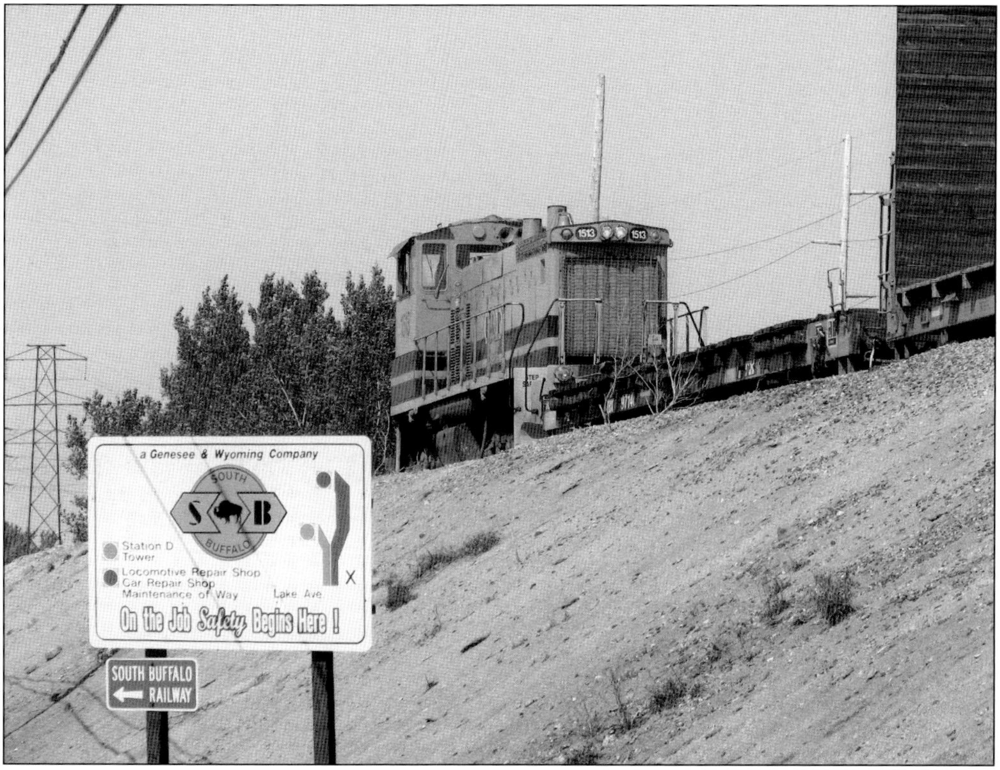


On September 9, 2006, five years after joining the Genesee & Wyoming Industries family, a South Buffalo yard job shows its new ties through the use of Buffalo and Pittsburgh No. 1513. The SB, unlike its one-time parent, Bethlehem Steel, adapted to Buffalo's diminished industrial landscape through new marketing initiatives, including large transloading operations. Some of its former locomotives now serve the neighboring Buffalo Southern Railway. (Photograph by Stephen M. Koenig.)

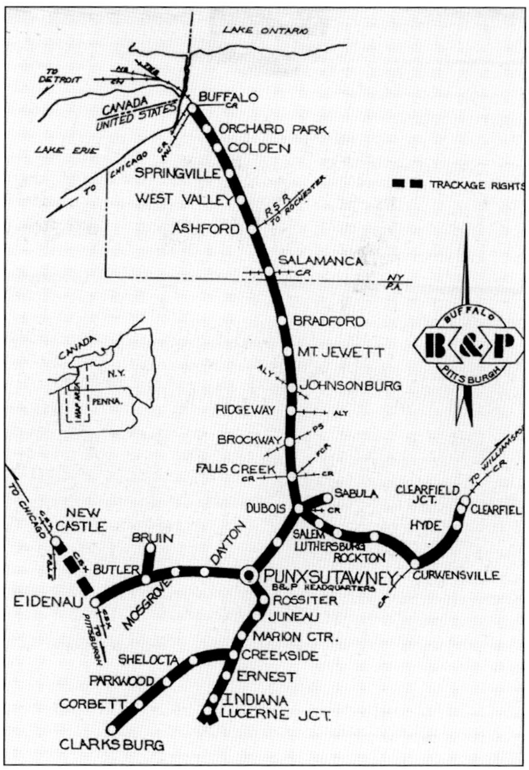


The Staggers Rail Act of 1980 brought 80 years of heavy-handed federal economic regulation of the railroad industry to an end. A key provision of the act encouraged major railroads to sell to new smaller railroads track proposed for abandonment. Using this law, the Buffalo & Pittsburgh Railroad acquired 369 miles of the former Baltimore & Ohio Railroad's lines between Buffalo and Eidenau, Pennsylvania, on July 19, 1988. (Buffalo and Pittsburgh Railroad Company.)

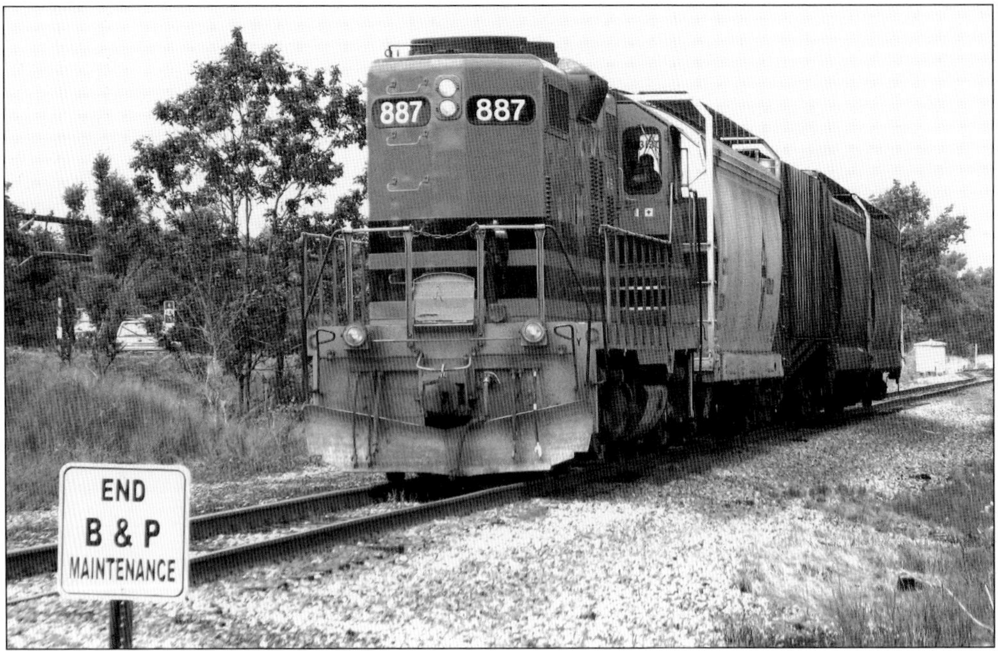


Buffalo & Pittsburgh (B&P) freight BF-3 is southbound at Gravity in August 2008. Its operation on the former Pennsylvania Railroad reflects changes in Buffalo's railscape. After acquiring the former Buffalo to Harrisburg, Pennsylvania, line in the 1999 split of Conrail, Norfolk Southern decided in 2007 to substitute a more circuitous route. The B&P leased the line from Gravity to Machias, thereby abandoning its line through Springville. (Photograph by Stephen M. Koenig.)

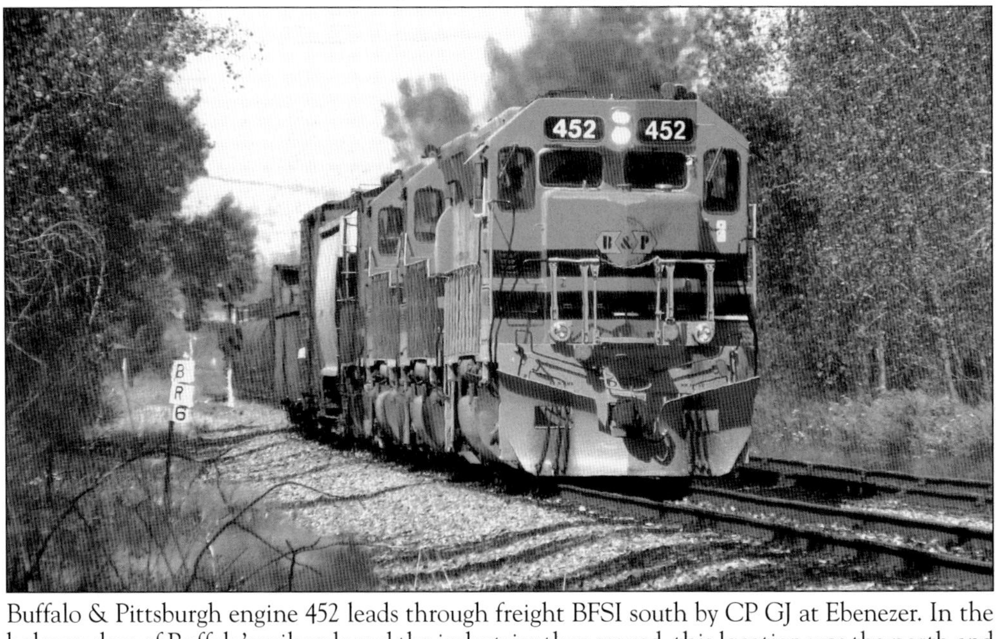


Buffalo & Pittsburgh engine 452 leads through freight BFSI south by CP GJ at Ebenezer. In the halcyon days of Buffalo's railroads and the industries they served, this location was the north end of Ebenezer Yard, the location of GJ Interlocking tower, the crossing of the New York Central's double-track Gardenville cut-off, and the junction of the Pennsylvania's West Seneca Branch. (Photograph by Stephen M. Koenig.)

## *Eight*

# Chessie System and Relatives

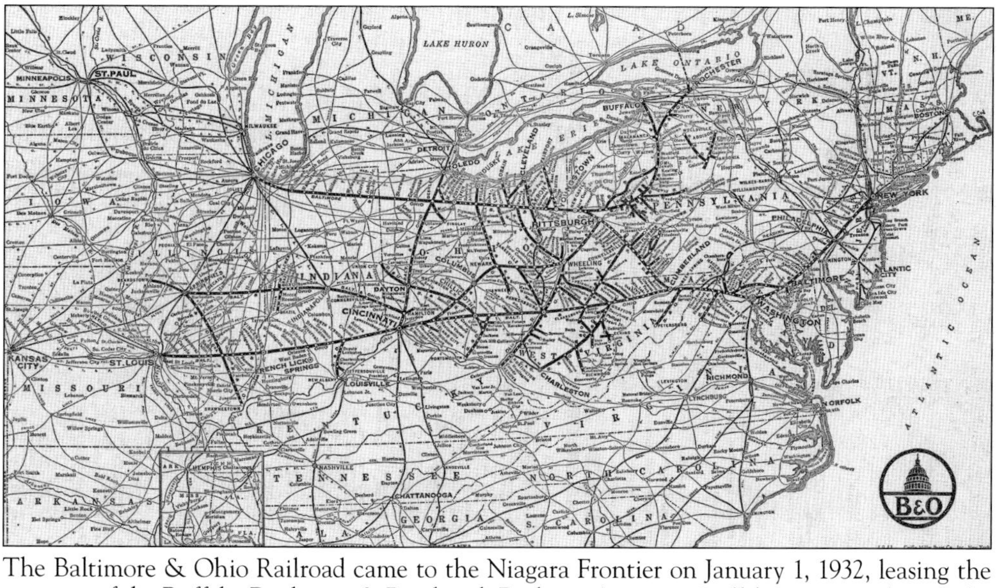


The Baltimore & Ohio Railroad came to the Niagara Frontier on January 1, 1932, leasing the property of the Buffalo, Rochester & Pittsburgh Railway. Access to Buffalo was secondary to the B&O's primary goal in acquiring the BR&P with creation of a short cut to New York City across Pennsylvania, a goal that died in the Great Depression. (Michael J. Connor collection.)

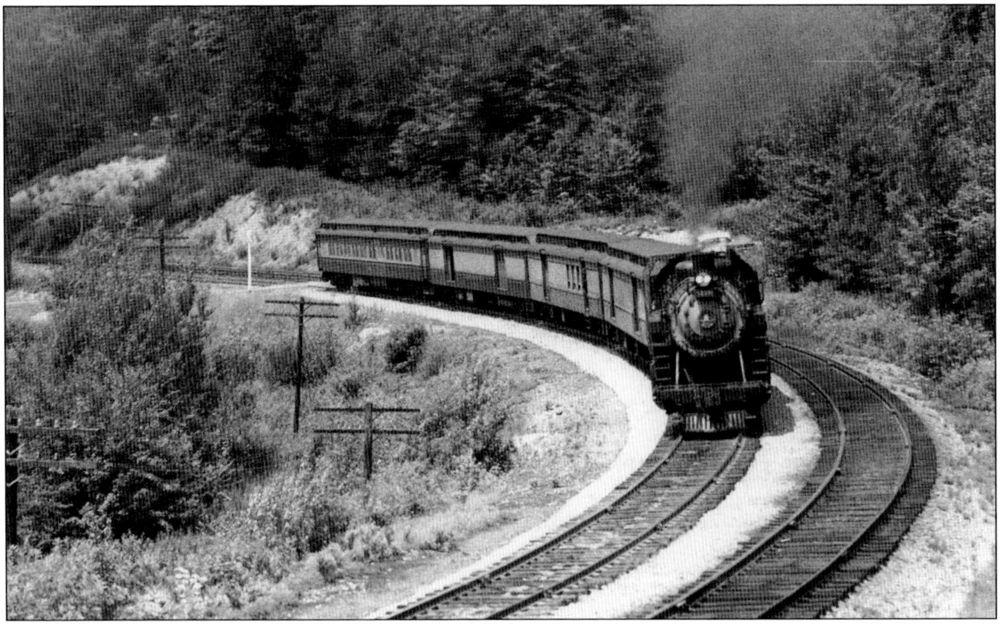

Baltimore & Ohio Pacific-type 4-6-2 wheel arrangement locomotive No. 5220 leads four-car train No. 52 near Johnsonburg, Pennsylvania, in 1950. The train will terminate in the Delaware, Lackawanna & Western's Buffalo passenger station, 118 miles and 3 hours and 15 minutes from here. Locomotive 5220 was retired in October 1956, soon after the end of B&O passenger service to Buffalo. (William C. Kessel collection.)

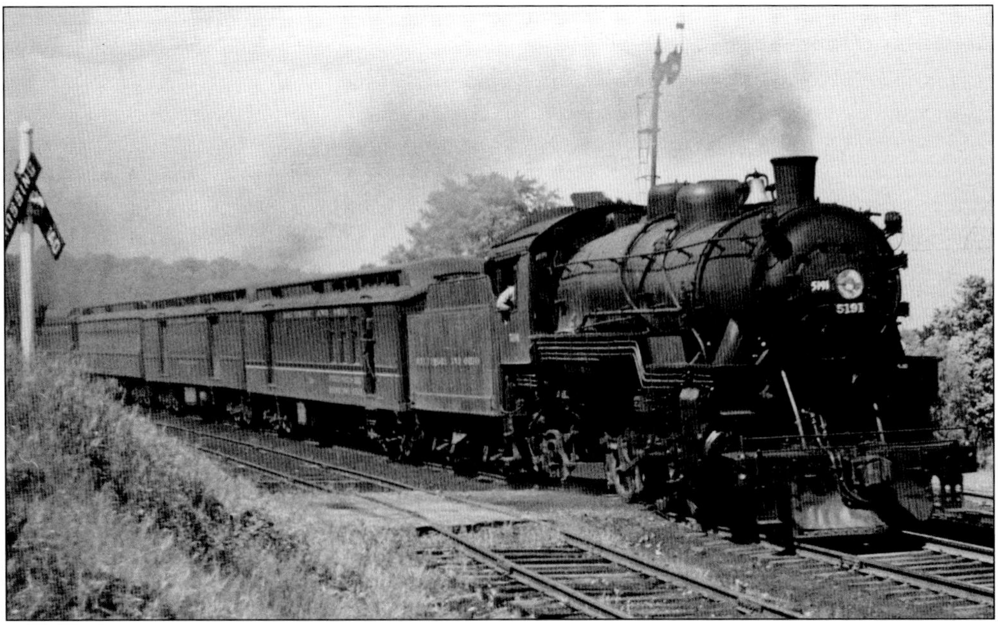


Train 52's consist includes a working Railway Post Office car, a baggage and express car, and two coaches on this 1950 day as Pacific type locomotive 5191 traverses the "Big Level" plateau in northwestern Pennsylvania en route to Buffalo. Eighteen years after the Baltimore & Ohio leased the Buffalo, Rochester & Pittsburgh Railway, little has changed other than train numbers and equipment. (George W. Thornton photograph, courtesy Erie Lackawanna Historical Society.)

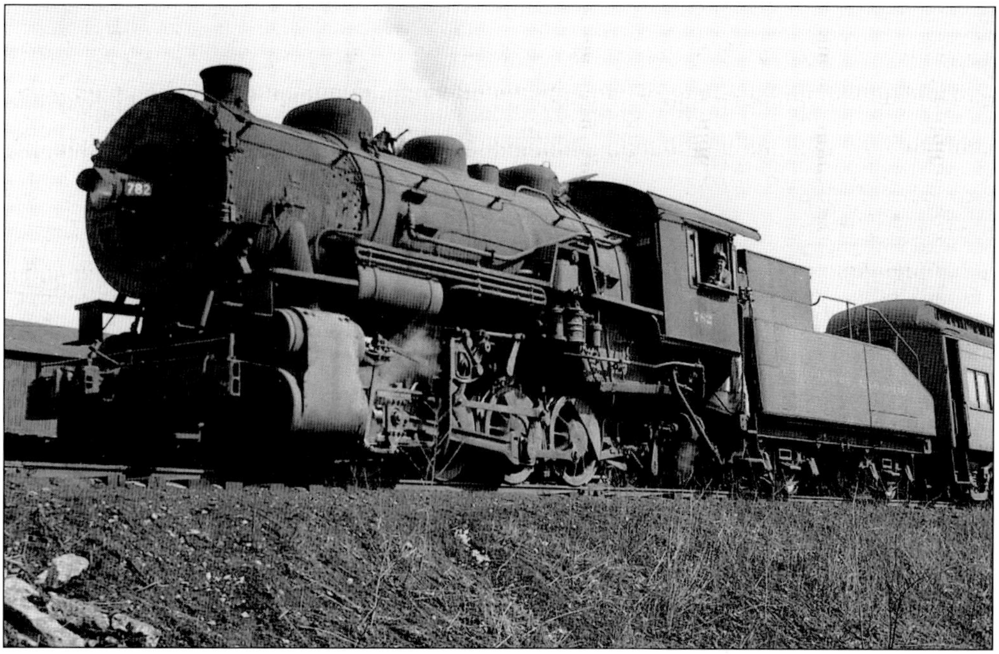

At its January 1, 1932, lease to the Baltimore & Ohio, the Buffalo, Rochester & Pittsburgh Railway owned about 270 steam locomotives. The B&O kept many in service on the former BR&P. No. 782, here switching at Buffalo in 1946, was a BR&P F4 Class, an 0-8-0 wheel arrangement locomotive built in July 1923 as BR&P No. 530. Renumbered to 782 in 1932, she was retired in 1955. (Phil Soyring collection.)

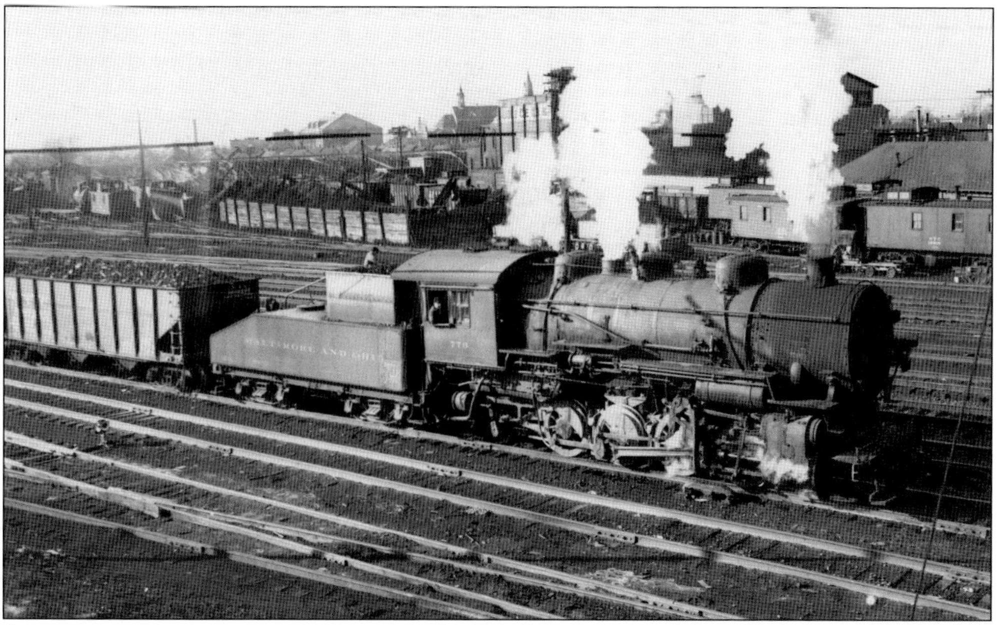

Baltimore & Ohio Class F4 with an 0-8-0 wheel arrangement No. 776 leads a transfer run of cars to the New York Central's Buffalo yard for interchange in this 1944 picture. As was the common practice, she will return to home rails without any cars. No. 776 was built in March 1918 as Buffalo, Rochester & Pittsburgh 534 and retired in 1958. (R. Ganger photograph courtesy Phil Soyring collection.)

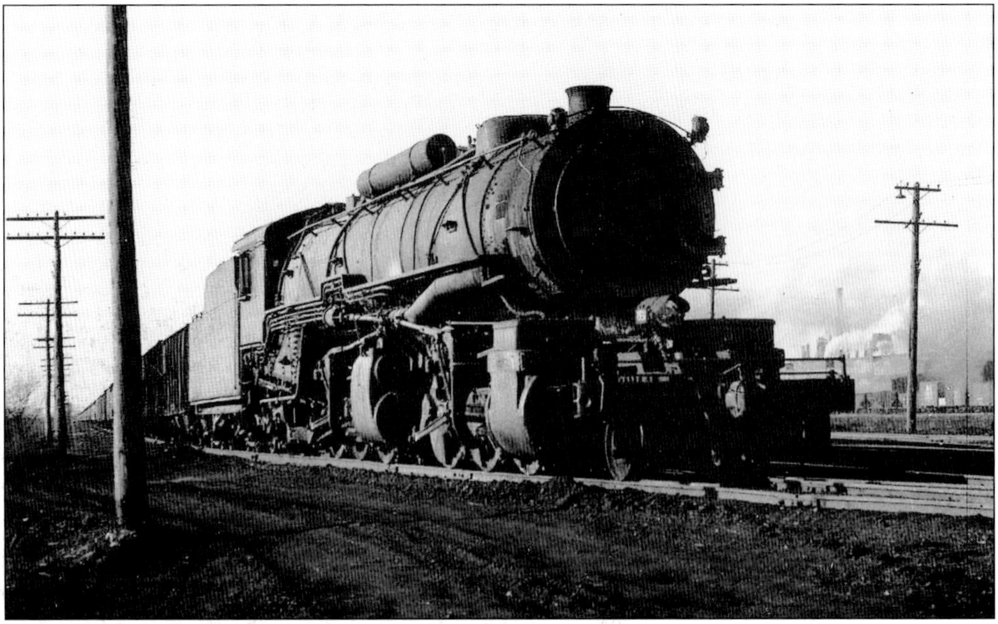

The Buffalo, Rochester & Pittsburgh Railway articulated locomotive, a Class KK-4 with a 2-6-6-2 wheel arrangement, was built in July 1914. In 1947, a Baltimore & Ohio Class LL articulated, as the former BR&P KK-Class engines were reclassified in 1932, pulls into the B&O's Buffalo Creek Yard in south Buffalo with a train of bituminous coal. (Phil Soyring collection.)

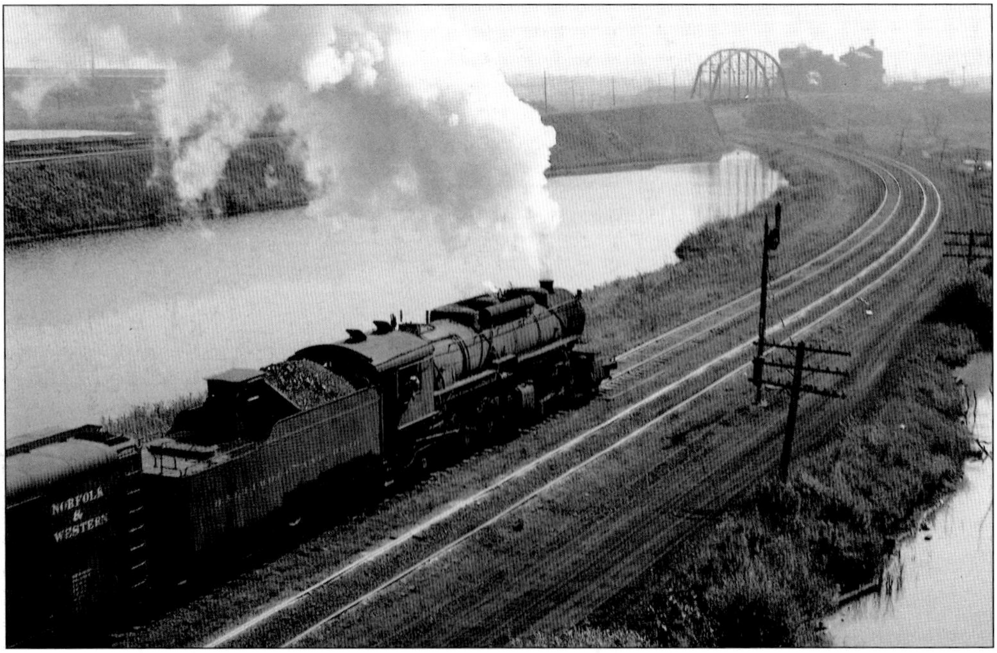


Most of the railroads that served Buffalo in the age of steam owned articulated locomotives. Only the Buffalo, Rochester & Pittsburgh Railway and its successor, the Baltimore & Ohio Railroad, regularly operated them into Buffalo. A freshly serviced former BR&P KK-Class 2-6-6-2 wheel arrangement articulated departs Buffalo Creek Yard in 1944. The bridge carrying the South Buffalo Railway over the B&O looms in the distance. (Phil Soyring collection.)

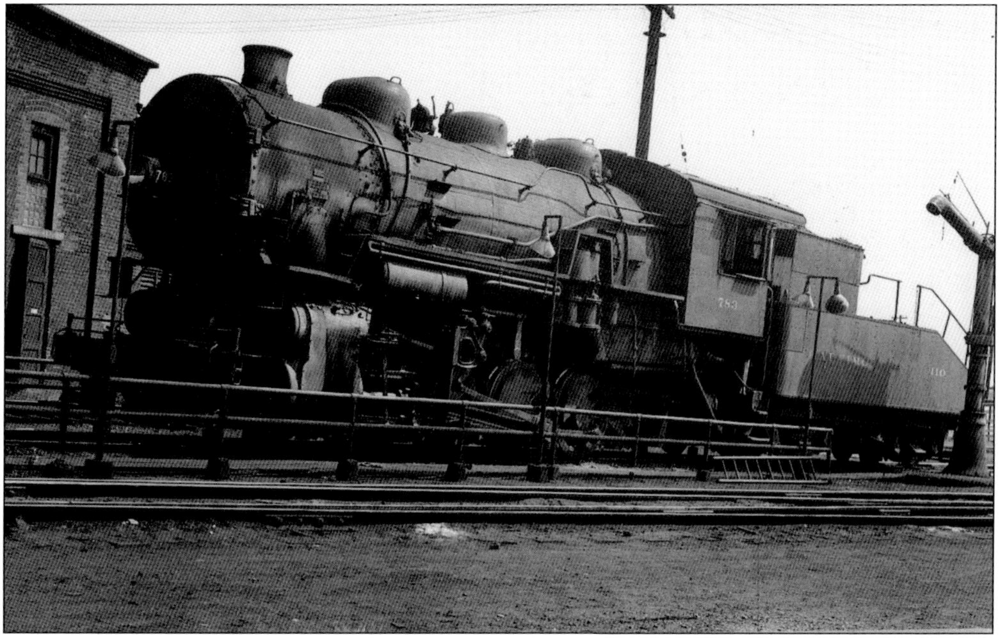

Baltimore & Ohio Railroad locomotive No. 783 sits by the water plug in South Buffalo on a brisk October day in 1949. She is a Buffalo, Rochester & Pittsburgh veteran who was adopted into the B&O family in 1932. At this time Buffalo was the second largest railroad hub and a growing city that railroads fought to get tracks to. (Phil Soyring collection.)

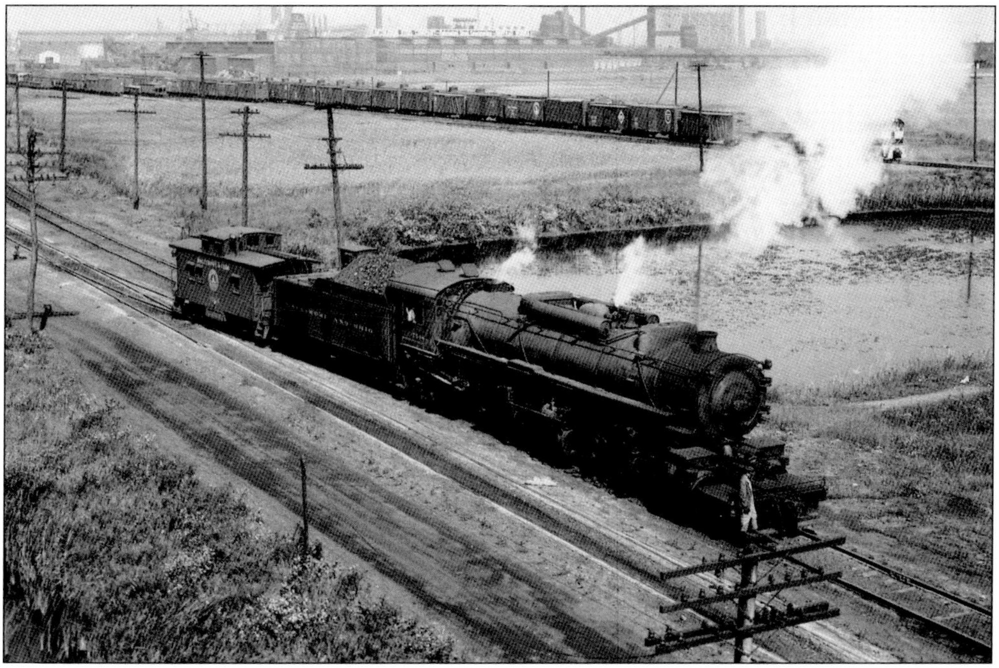

It is June of 1944 and Buffalo's steel mills are churning out more than any other mill in the world for the war effort. Baltimore & Ohio No. 7548, with only a caboose, makes its way slowly down the tracks. The brakeman is on the front step of the locomotive and ready to line the track. (Phil Soyring collection.)

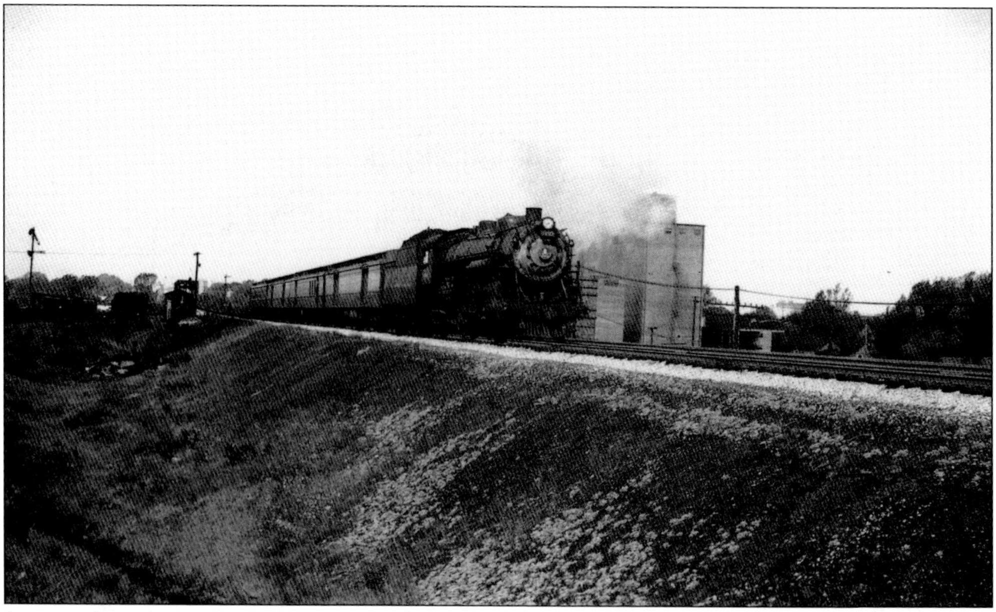

In a timeless scene, this Baltimore & Ohio train scurries along the track to deliver her passengers to their destination. This day, October 15, 1955, is the final train from Buffalo to Pittsburgh. The automobile has come of age and the airplanes' speed leaves passenger service on railroads no longer the first choice of travel. (R. Ganger photograph, Phil Soyring collection.)

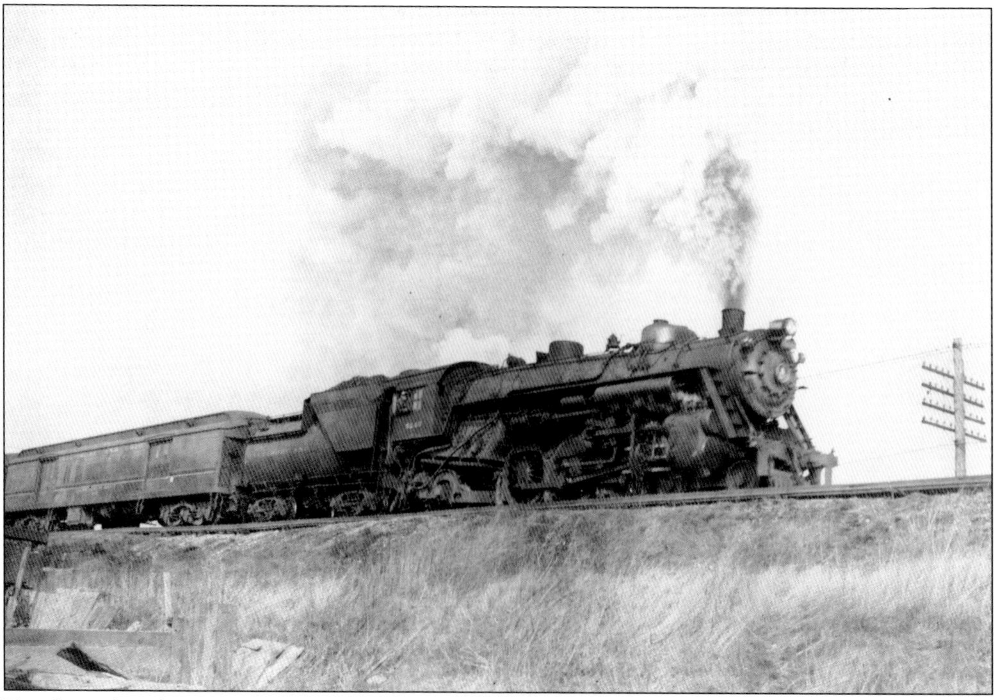

For the railroader, it was an age of soot and filth to work with steam, but for those who watched, there was nothing better. Another Baltimore & Ohio passenger train rushes through Buffalo with mail, baggage, and people eager to get to their destination. Like Doris Day's sentimental journey, only this 1948 photograph remains. (R. Ganger photograph, Phil Soyring collection.)

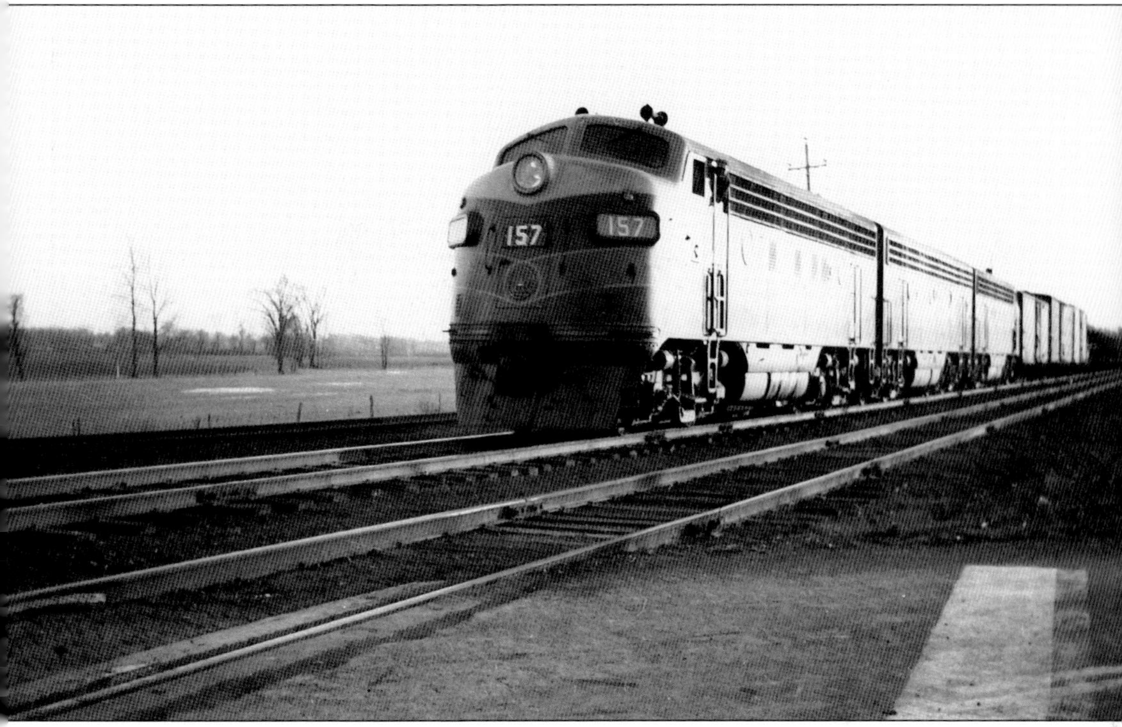

Baltimore & Ohio diesel-electric No. 157 leads a freight near Rochester on November 5, 1950, in this look at early diesel use on the Buffalo Division. A major advantage of diesels was the ability to build multiple horsepower consists without additional crewmen. Here three 1,500-horsepower units provide the 4,500 horsepower needed to move the entire train. (William C. Kessel photograph, Michael J. Connor collection.)

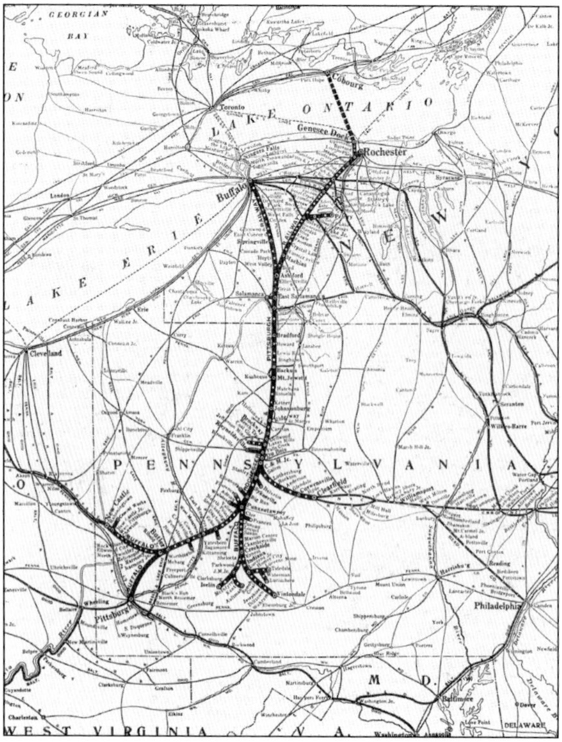


The Buffalo, Rochester & Pittsburgh Railway entered Buffalo on September 15, 1883. In its nearly 50 years as an independent railroad, it became, next to the Delaware, Lackawanna & Western, Buffalo's most financially successful railroad. Like the DL&W, it built that success on coal and a commitment to engineering and operational excellence. The BR&P operated a 602-mile system. (Michael J. Connor collection.)

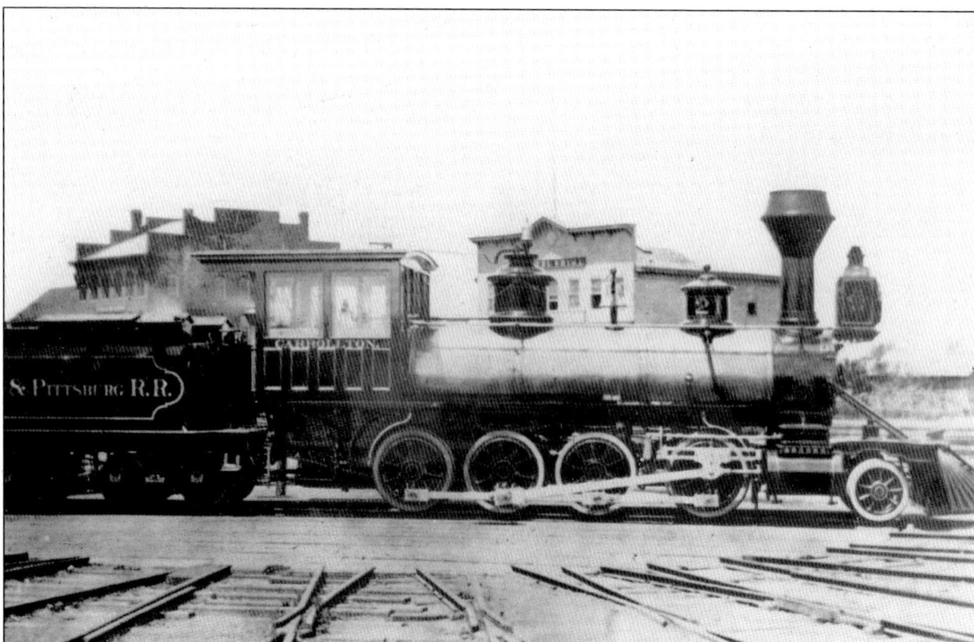


Until October 1885, the Buffalo, Rochester & Pittsburgh Railway was known as the Rochester & Pittsburgh Railroad. One of the first R&P locomotives into Buffalo at its 1883 opening was this BR&P-R&P Class H Consolidation-type bearing the name "Carrollton" and the No. 21. She served primarily in freight service from her June 1882 construction in Dunkirk, New York, until retired around 1897–1899. (Michael J. Connor collection.)

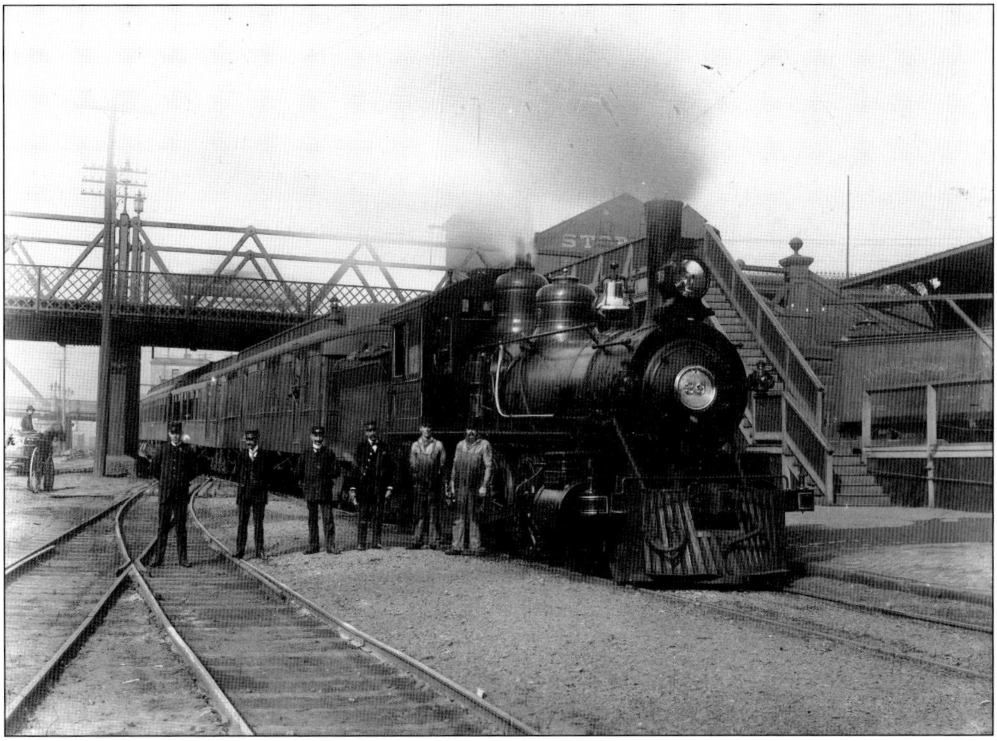

The Buffalo, Rochester & Pittsburgh Railway reached Pittsburgh in 1899 over the Baltimore & Ohio Railroad from near Butler, Pennsylvania. Here, *c.* 1910, No. 39, a Class D 10-wheeler sporting a highly polished brass number plate, poses with her crew and four-car consist at the Smithfield Street Station in Pittsburgh. Buffalo was 288 miles and 8 hours, 35 minutes away. (Michael J. Connor collection.)

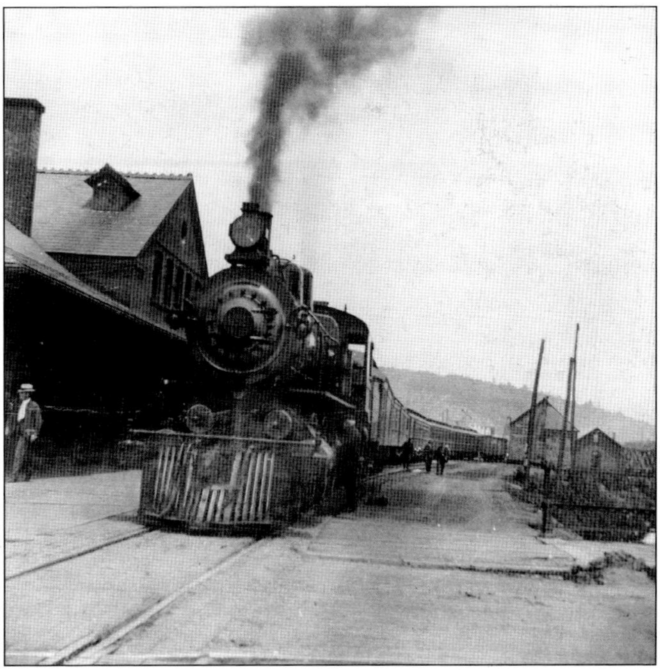

Buffalo, Rochester & Pittsburgh Railway Class W Atlantic type No. 168 has arrived at Bradford, Pennsylvania, 78 miles from Buffalo's Exchange Street Station with Train No. 3 in this 1912 view. The engineer is seen oiling before departure. No. 168 and her six cars were a regular in and out of Buffalo. (Michael J. Connor collection.)

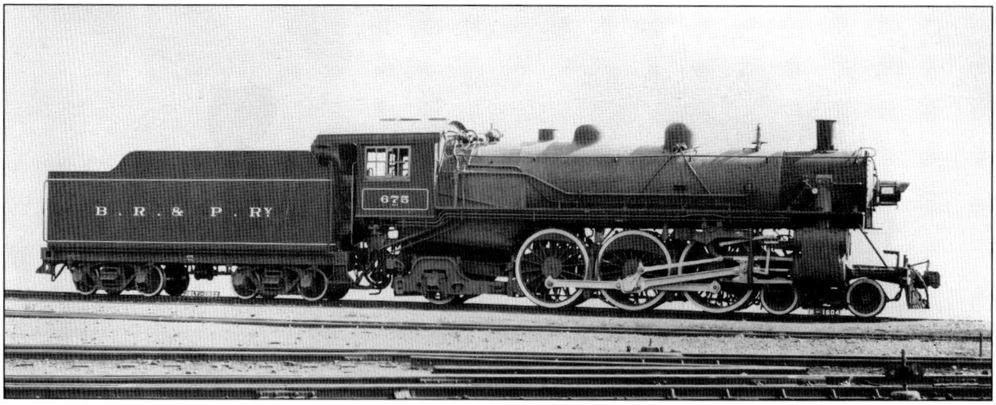

As passenger trains increased in weight due to heavier steel cars and longer consists, the Buffalo, Rochester & Pittsburgh Railway purchased 22 Class WW Pacific type locomotives between 1911 and 1924. No. 675, at her Dunkirk, New York, builder in August 1923, was renumbered 5260 by the Baltimore & Ohio in 1932 and worked passenger trains on the former BR&P until scrapped in May 1952. (Michael J. Connor collection.)

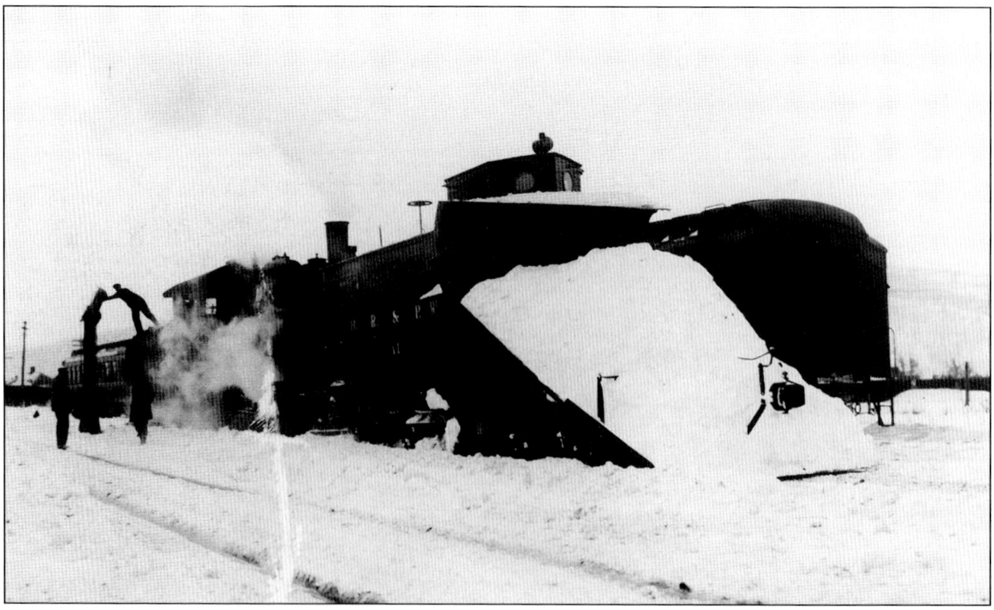

Much of the Buffalo, Rochester & Pittsburgh Railway lies in the Lake Erie snow belt and keeping tracks clear of drifting snow was a constant wintertime task. Here in 1917 a locomotive is being serviced from a water plug so that it can continue pushing snowplow No. A1 towards Buffalo. These rugged plows were situated at many strategic locations across the railroad. (Michael J. Connor collection.)

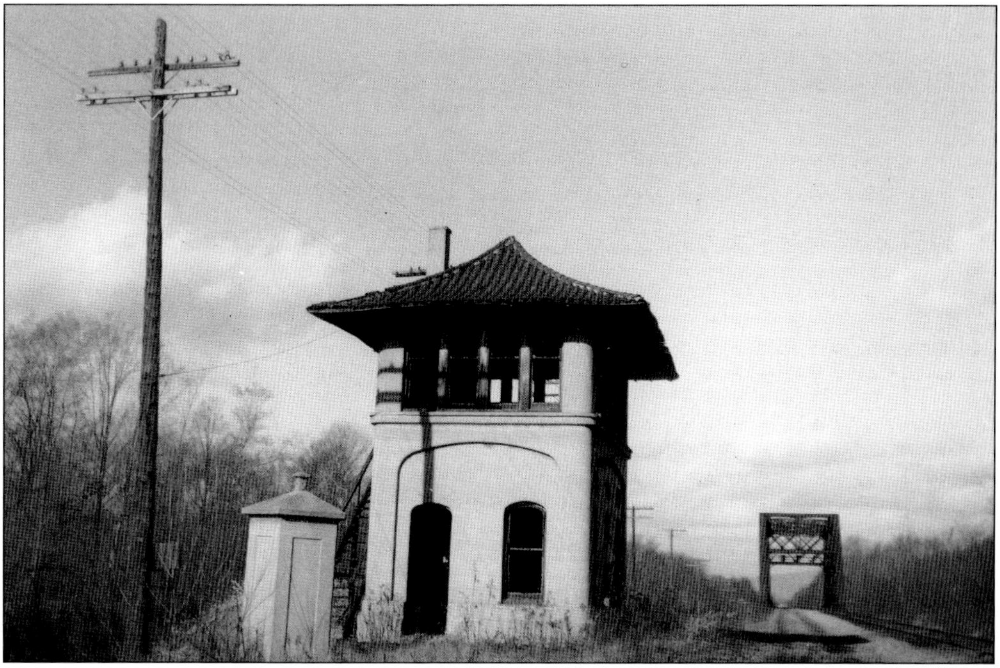

The Buffalo, Rochester & Pittsburgh Railway was a leader in concrete construction, which it combined with a unique style of architecture. Here in January 1973 is the Riverside Junction Tower, which formerly protected the grade crossing of the Buffalo to Pittsburgh main line with the now abandoned Olean-Salamanca-Warren, Pennsylvania, line of the Pennsylvania Railroad. (L. W. Kilmer photograph, William C. Kessel collection.)

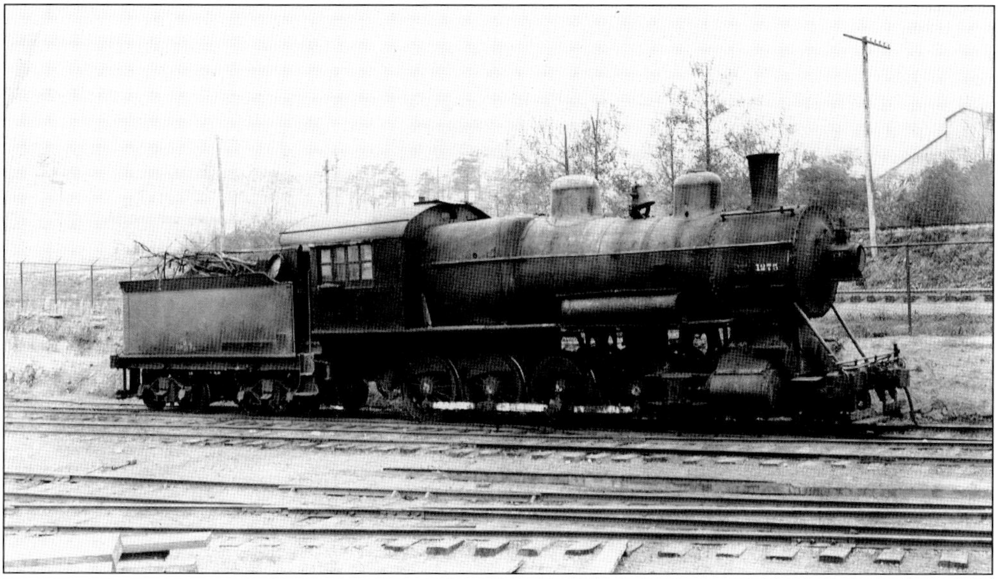


Southern Iron and Equipment Company in Birmingham, Alabama, was for decades the used car dealer of steam locomotives. Here Buffalo, Rochester & Pittsburgh Railway Class S-3 12-wheeler No. 244 rests in the SI&E yard in winter 1918 following its sale by the BR&P. SI&E renumbered the locomotive as 1275 and sold it in April 1918 to Dupont Engineering Company as their No. 6. (Michael J. Connor collection.)

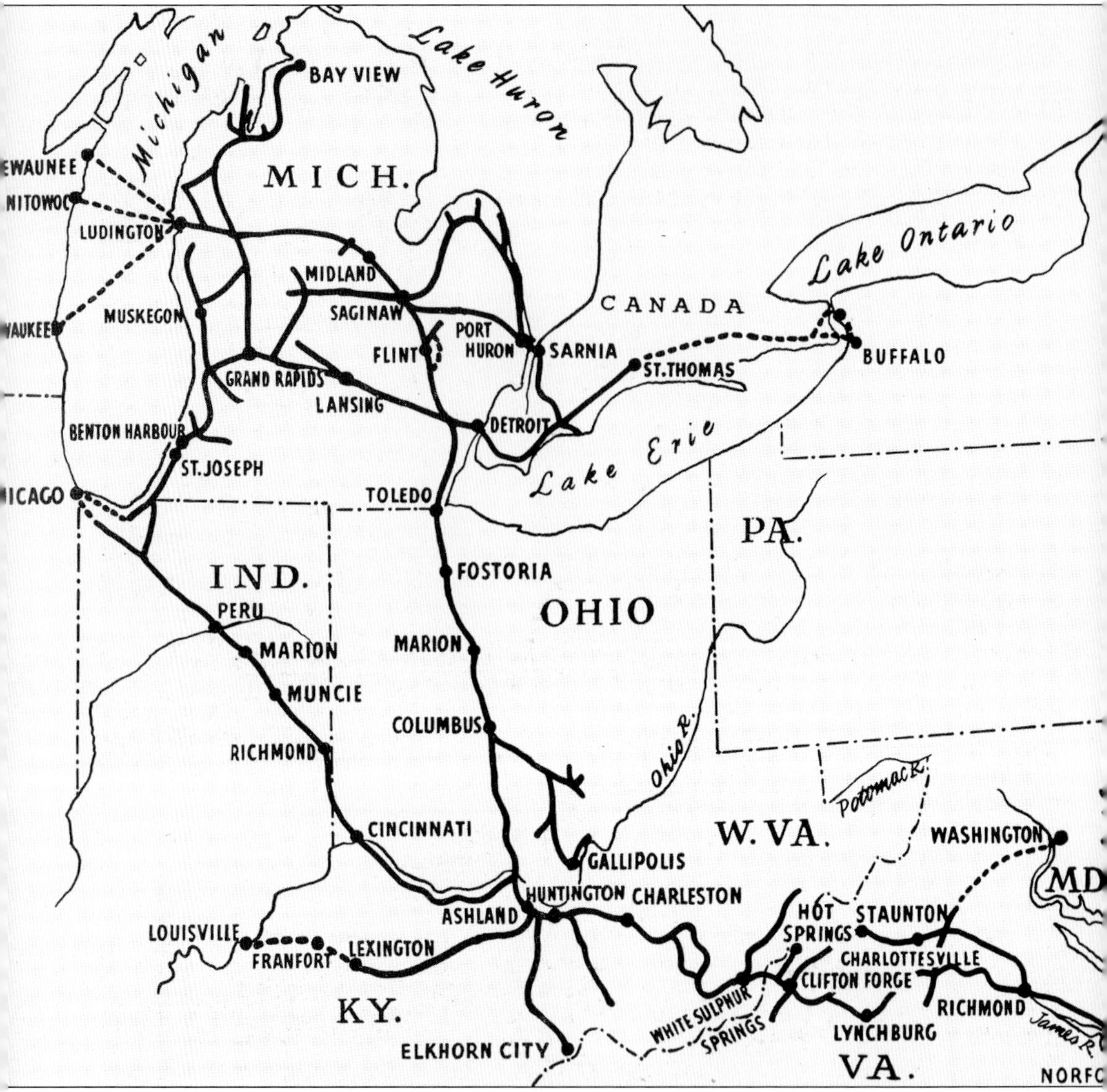


The Chesapeake & Ohio Railway came to the Niagara Frontier on June 6, 1946, when it absorbed the Pere Marquette Railway Company through merger. While most of the former PM lines were organized as the Pere Marquette District of the C&O, there was little change in operation. In Buffalo and Suspension Bridge the C&O continued the PM's use of Erie Railroad yards and engine houses. (Michael J. Connor collection.)

On this 1946 Chesapeake and Ohio Railroad passenger timetable is a picture of "Chessie" the cat. Chessie became one of the most popular advertising icons of the time for her "sleep like a kitten and wake up fresh" artwork. Chessie soon had a husband named "Peake," along with two kittens, "Nip" and "Tuck," to help exemplify the comforts of C&O trains. (Stephen G. Myers collection.)

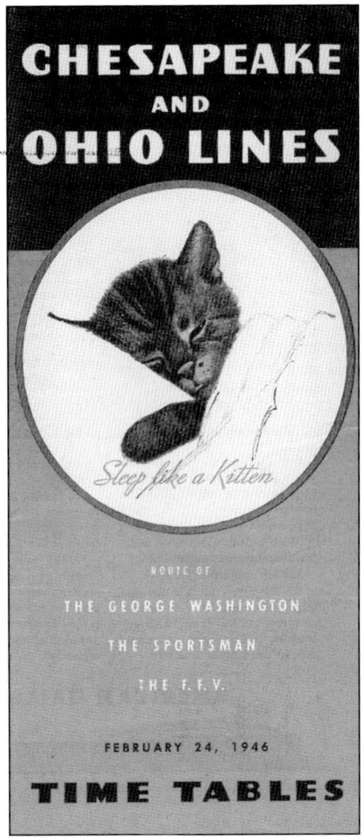


The Pere Marquette reached Buffalo on July 18, 1904, through a combination of ownership and trackage rights. While its early history was financially precarious, the PM was well located to serve the new automobile industry and typically brought twice as many carloads east as it took west. It came under the influence of the Chesapeake and Ohio in 1924 and they merged on June 6, 1946. (Michael J. Connor collection.)

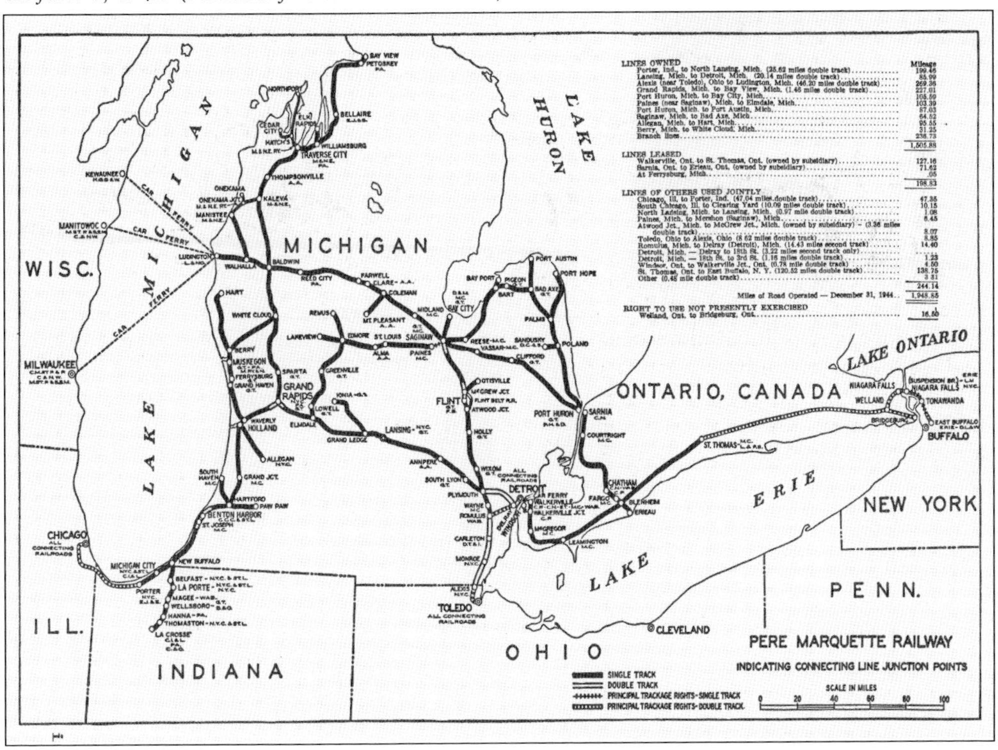

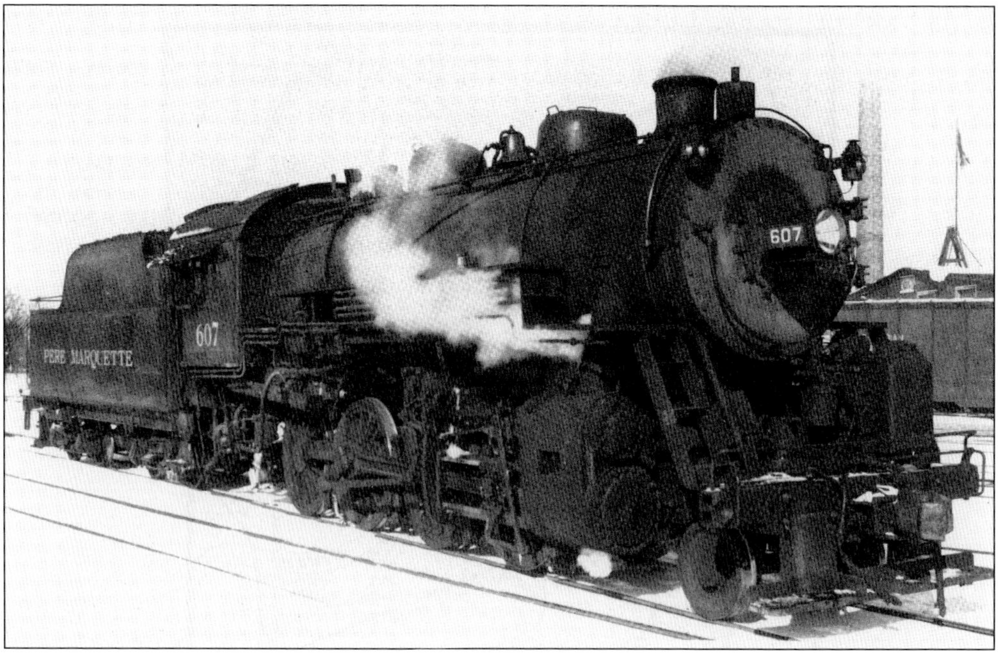


The Pere Marquette was, during its life, the only American railroad named after a real person. Pere Marquette was Father Jacques Marquette S. J., 1637–1675, who opened Michigan to settlement. Fifty-five Mikado-type locomotives with a 2-8-2 wheel arrangement joined the roster between 1913 and 1920 and were the road's primary motive power in Canada until dieselization. (Michael J. Connor collection.)

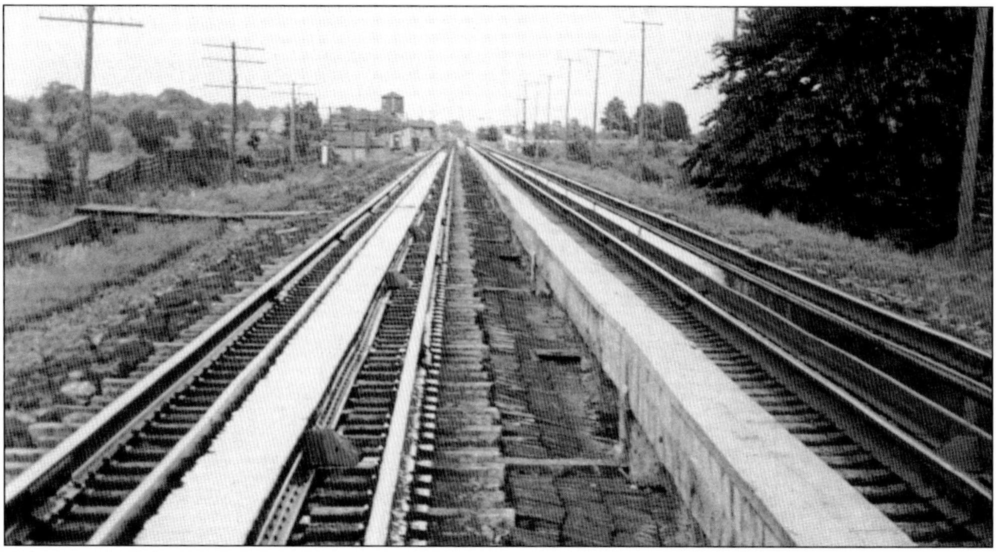

Of the railroads serving Buffalo, only the New York Central, the Michigan Central, and the Pere Marquette used tender scoops to re-water engines in motion. Here in 1934 are the track pans at Tillsonburg, Ontario. Several PM locomotive tenders were equipped with retractable scoops, which, when lowered while passing over the quarter-mile-long track pans, quickly picked up several thousand gallons of water. (Photograph by William C. Kessel.)

# *Nine*

# Gould Coupler

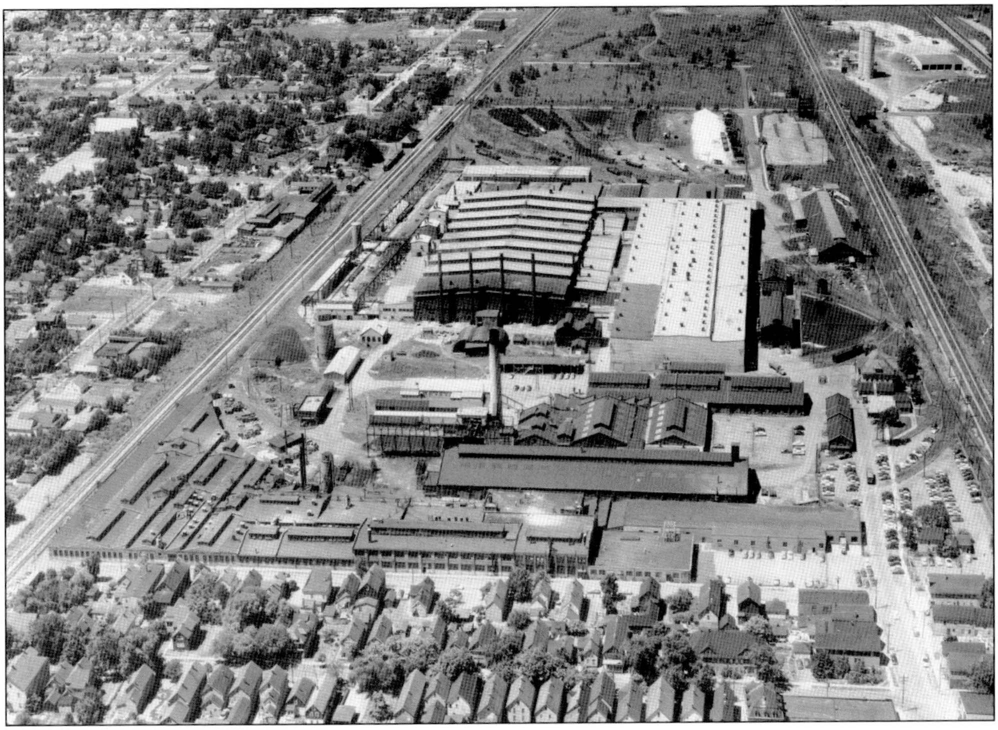

The Gould Coupler Company was founded in 1892. Chauncey Depew, the president of the New York Central & Hudson River Railroad, along with other Buffalo businessmen, purchased parcels of land east of Buffalo with the intent of building railroad related factories for the supply and maintenance of the New York Central. The area soon became known as Depew and was incorporated into a village. (Village of Depew Historian collection.)

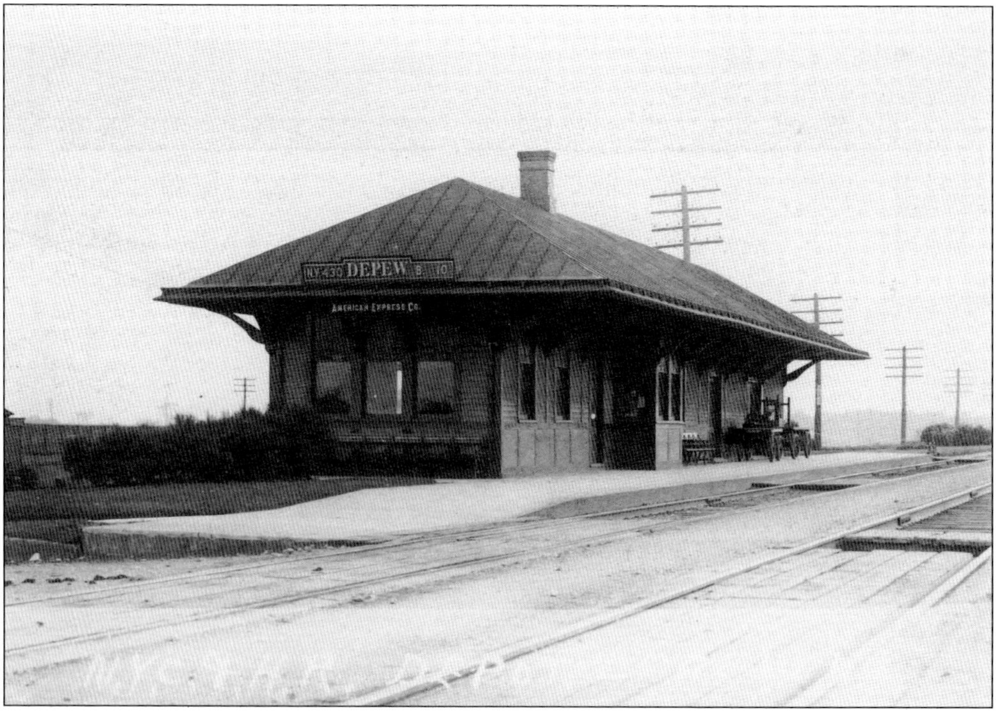


It is ironic that despite the role of New York Central & Hudson River Railroad president Chauncey M. Depew in bringing Gould Coupler to his namesake community, the plant was located between the main lines of the Erie Railroad and the Delaware, Lackawanna & Western and not the New York Central. This New York Central station was built shortly thereafter and was located 10 miles from Buffalo. (Village of Depew Historian collection.)

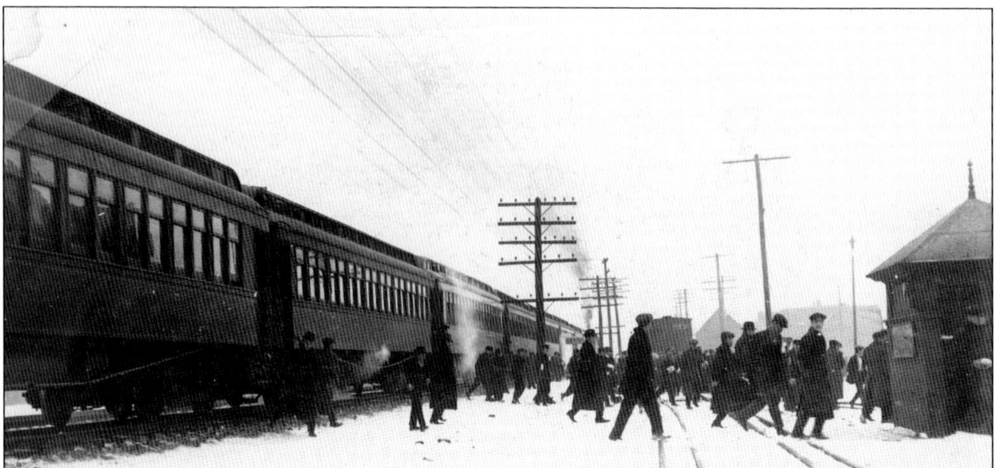

The strike of 1914 was an unforgettable event at the Gould Coupler Works. At the beginning of 1914, a new general manager was appointed at the plant. With the new promotion came changes in work rules that resulted in union employees refusing to work. Non-union workers were brought in by train from Buffalo to fill the jobs. (Village of Depew Historian collection.)

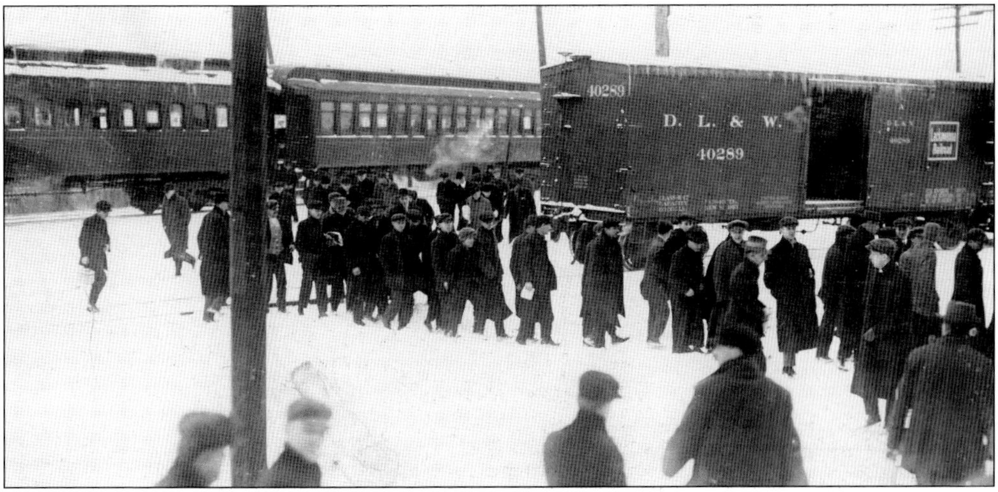


General Manager Hayden decided to lengthen the workday from 9 to 9.5 hours, cancel the 9:00 a.m. break, and allow no smoke breaks. Nine hundred International Molders Union members refused to work under these conditions. This photograph shows the men coming from the train to work at Gould. (Village of Depew Historian collection.)

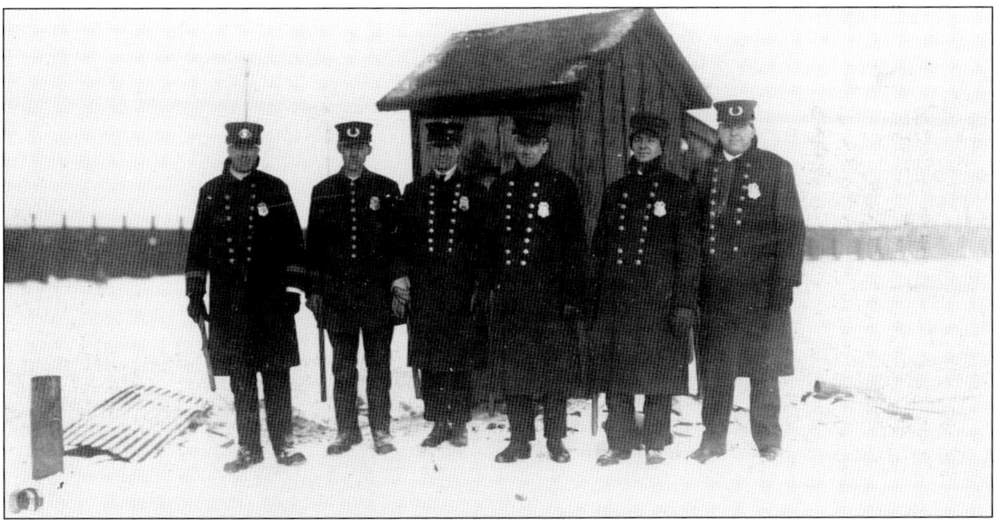

Local union officials tried to meet with management but were removed and their jobs replaced by non-union employees. The company hired 24 uniformed men carrying guns and clubs and had them sworn in as Depew police. When the citizens of Depew complained, the new police were told to stay within the confines of the Gould property. (Village of Depew Historian collection.)

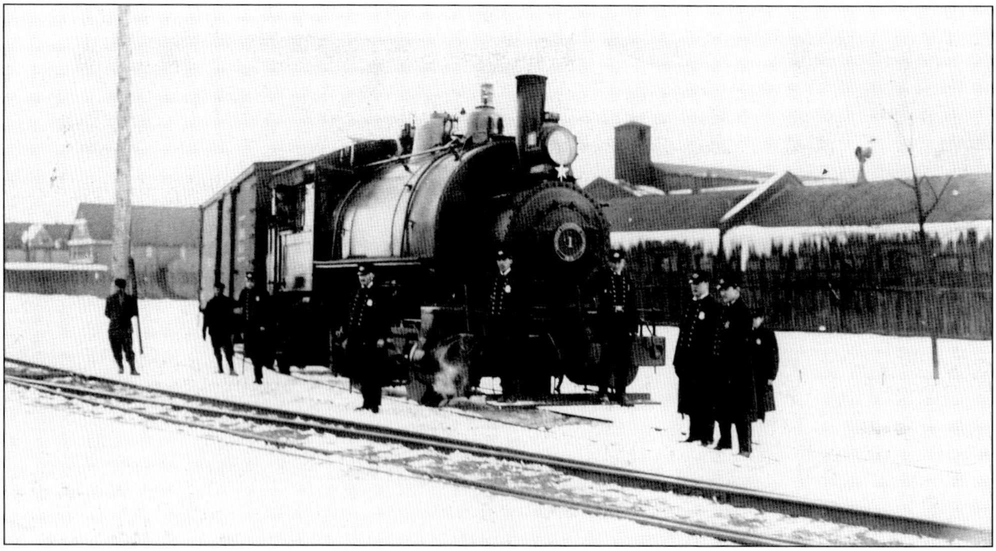

On March 23, 1914, logs were placed across the DL&W tracks, stopping the train that carried the non-union workers. A riot ensued as 300 to 400 men attacked the train firing guns and throwing rocks. Four men were shot and several injured. Stanislaus Skolonski ended up dying from his wounds and Deputy Thomas Fogarty was shot through both cheeks. (Village of Depew Historian collection.)

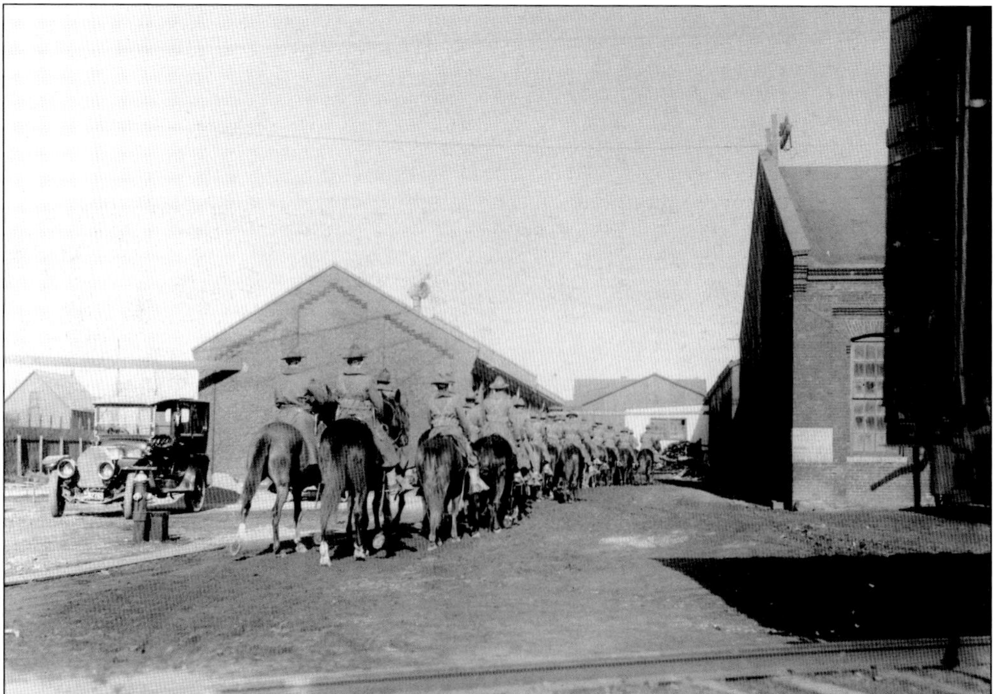

Forty deputies were on patrol in Depew, but after the riot, the 74th Regiment was brought in with 900 men and stayed for two weeks. Sixty members of Troop I First New York State Cavalry replaced the regiment. After 10 days, the military was removed and regular police resumed their duties. Within a year, the union was broken. (Village of Depew Historian collection.)

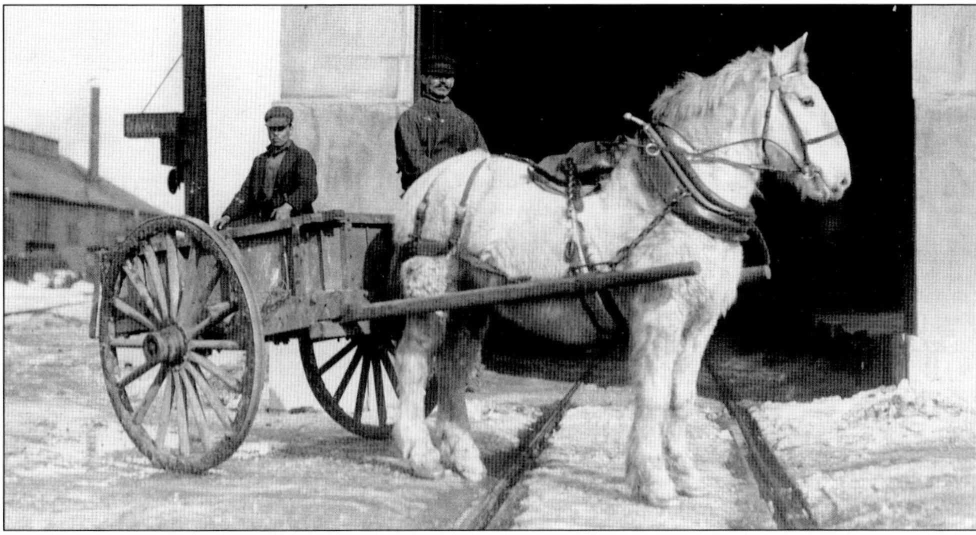

Steam power did not do all the work, as this 1914 photograph illustrates. Horses as well as the strong backs of young men were still used to carry equipment to parts of the factory. This was a period of a great influx of European immigrants. Buffalo was blessed with a large contingency of Polish and German settlers with eager young men in search of work. (Village of Depew Historian collection.)

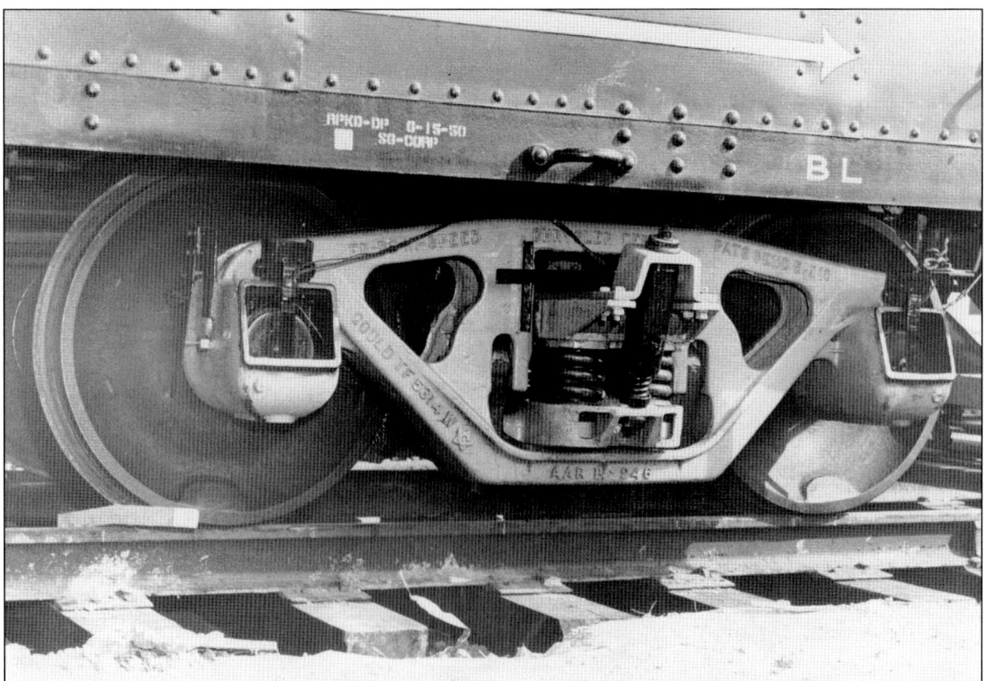


Here is a close-up of the railroad truck assembly used to hold the wheels, bearings, and springs that keep the car moving while pivoting and swaying, all the while supporting the vehicle and absorbing vibration. This particular model was a high-speed Chrysler design that was developed by Symington Wayne at the Depew plant's research department. (Village of Depew Historian collection.)

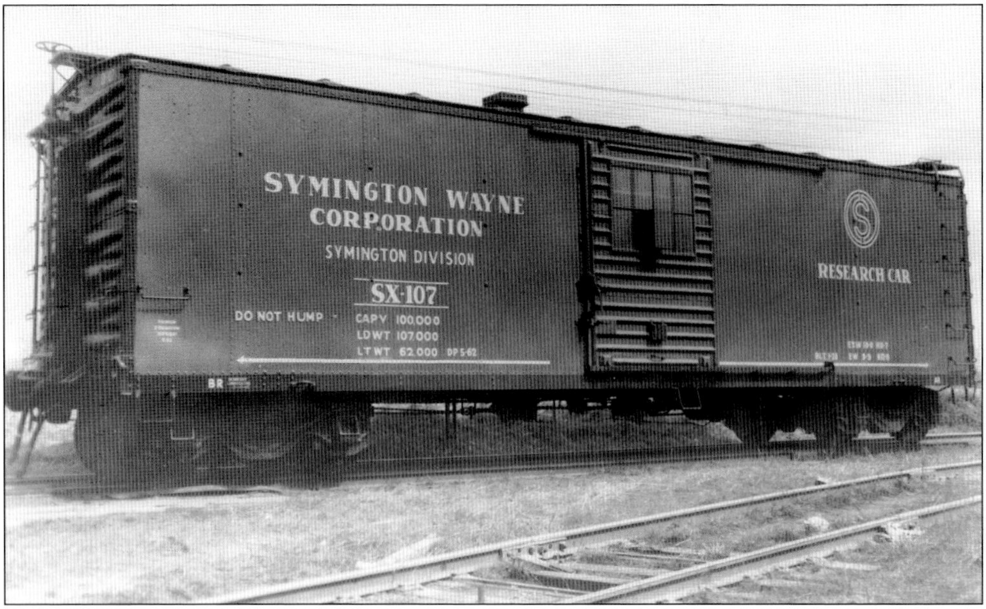


Symington Gould owned several research cars, this one built in January 1928, to monitor and collect data while a train was in motion. This test car and others owned by Symington Gould would help to make a better and safer product for the railway industry. Research by manufacturers brought benefits to both large and small railroads. (Village of Depew Historian collection.)

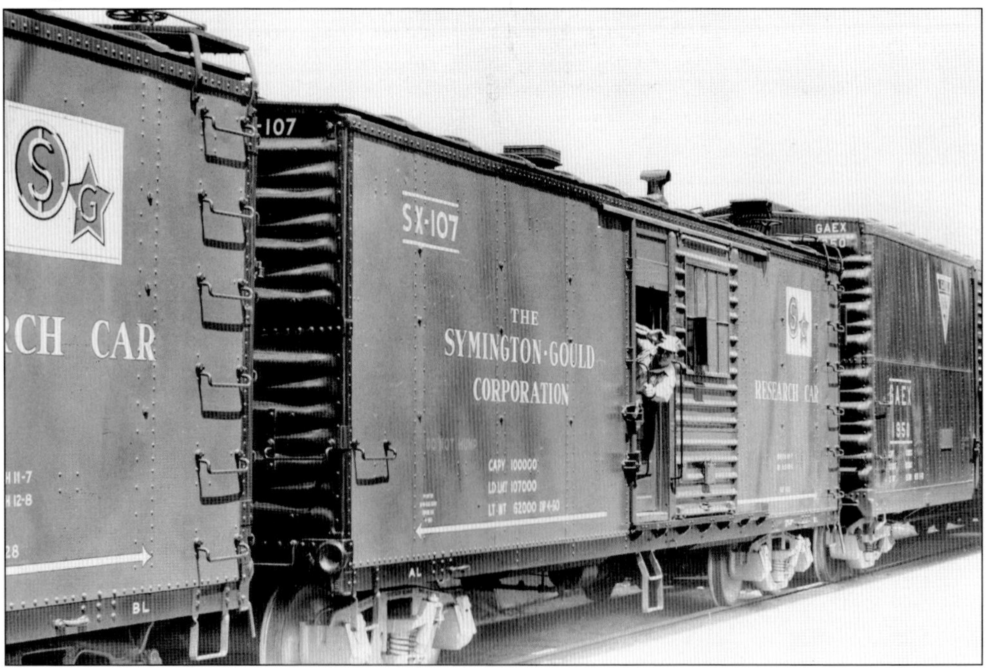


Hanging out of the side of this Symington Gould test car is an employee who would ride the train and gather information on how the trucks would perform. Gould Coupler Company had an agreement with the Delaware, Lackawanna & Western Railroad to operate test trains on their tracks. It was a nice change of pace for employees to ride the test train. (Village of Depew Historian collection.)

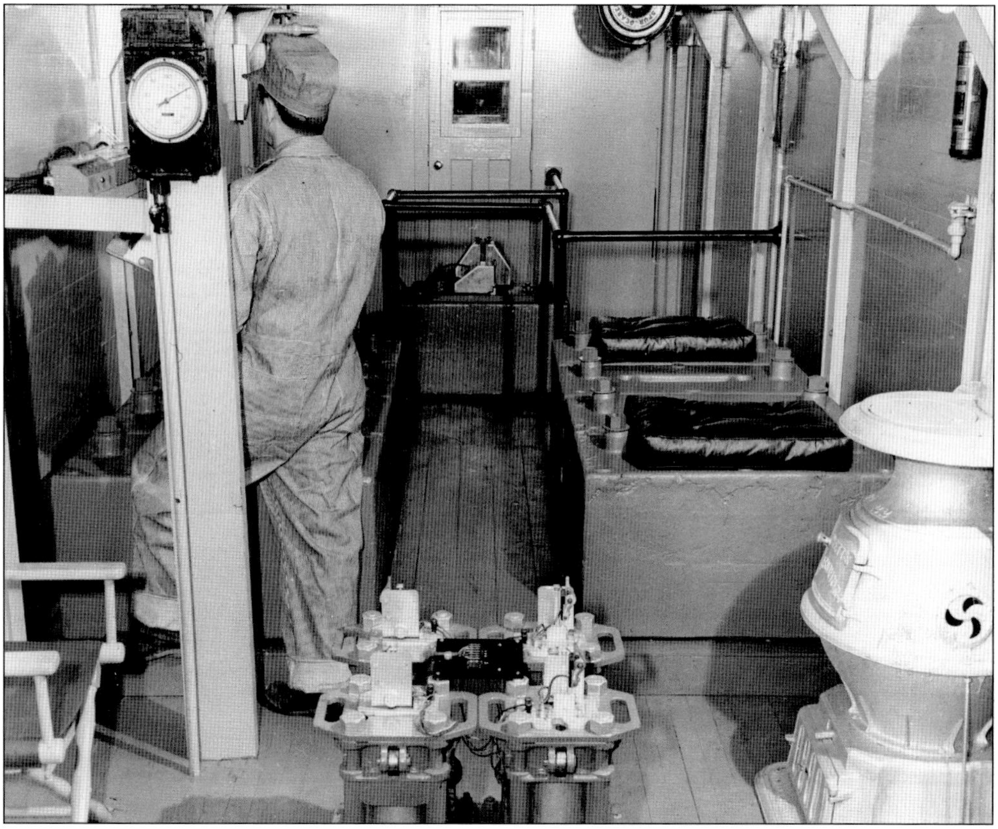

Inside the test car, this employee wears the traditional railroad garb of the day with work boots, pinstripe hat, and coveralls. Frequently checking the various gauges and instruments, he monitored the performance of the railcar's components. The car was kept warm in cold weather by the potbelly stove to the right. (Village of Depew Historian collection.)

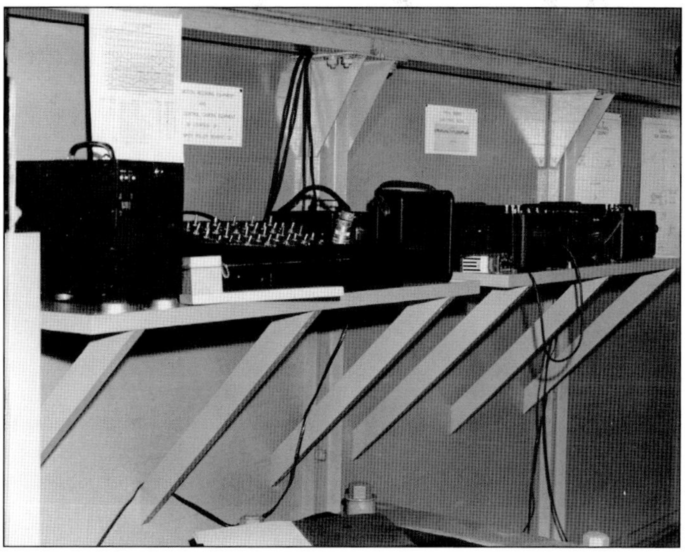

The shelves of the test cars held primitive electronic hardware to record data. The research department would later analyze the data to make repair and design changes that would help to improve speeds, prevent derailments, and extend the life of wheels and bearings. Buffalo not only had many railroads, but was also a leader in developing and manufacturing goods for railway companies. (Village of Depew Historian collection.)

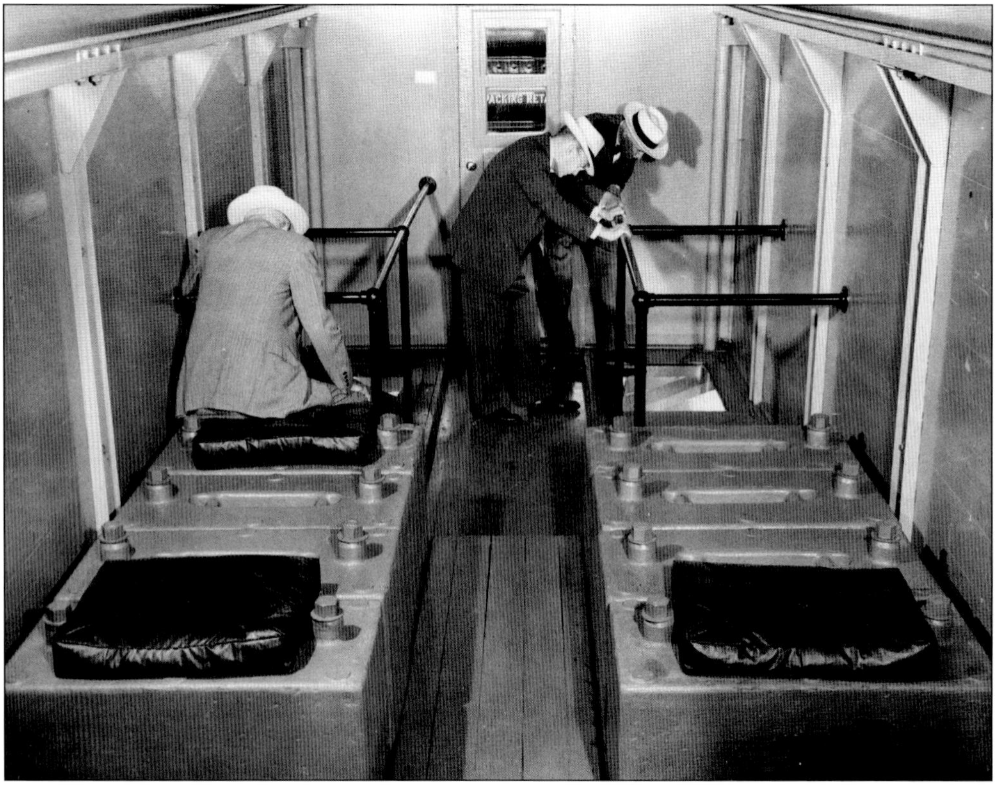

A trio of "brass hats" from the Gould factory is looking down through windows in a test car to observe the trucks and wheels in motion below them. Cameras were also mounted under the car to get a full view so that a careful study could later be made on the performance of each truck component. (Village of Depew Historian collection.)

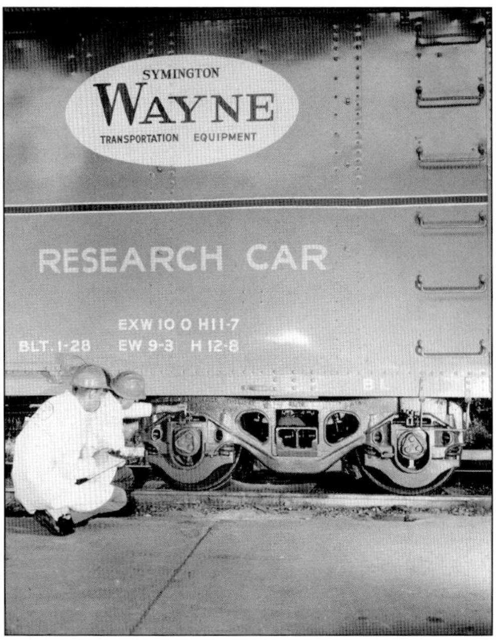


Research department personnel here take careful measurements and notes while testing this truck. On the truck side frame is stamped Gould's brand, a star with a G inside of it. Gould products can still be seen on active railroad cars today. The employee to the left is Arthur Domino, a Symington Gould retiree and currently the Depew village historian. (Village of Depew Historian collection.)

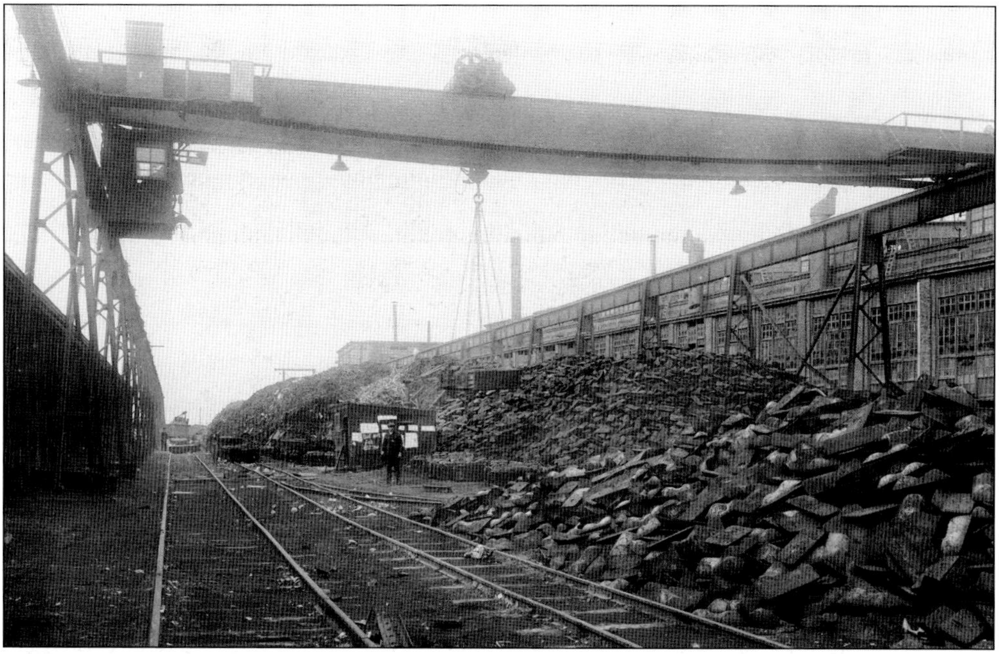

In 1930, the scene outside the factory is of mountains of steel and iron scrap, all brought in by railcars. This scrap metal would be melted in the foundry and poured into sand molds to create couplers, side frames, and other parts. Thus scrap metal, much of it generated by the railroads themselves, was recycled into useful parts. (Village of Depew Historian collection.)

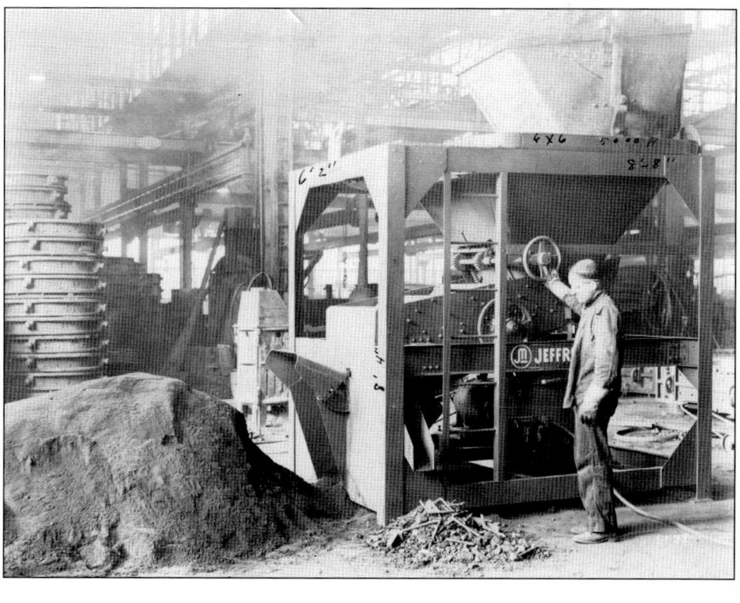

In a foundry, sand is used for making molds. In 1938, a Gould foundry man operates a sand mold machine manufactured by the Jeffrey Manufacturing Company in Columbus, Ohio. Sand arrived at the plant in railroad freight cars along with scrap iron and steel and the completed products would leave by rail. (Village of Depew Historian collection.)

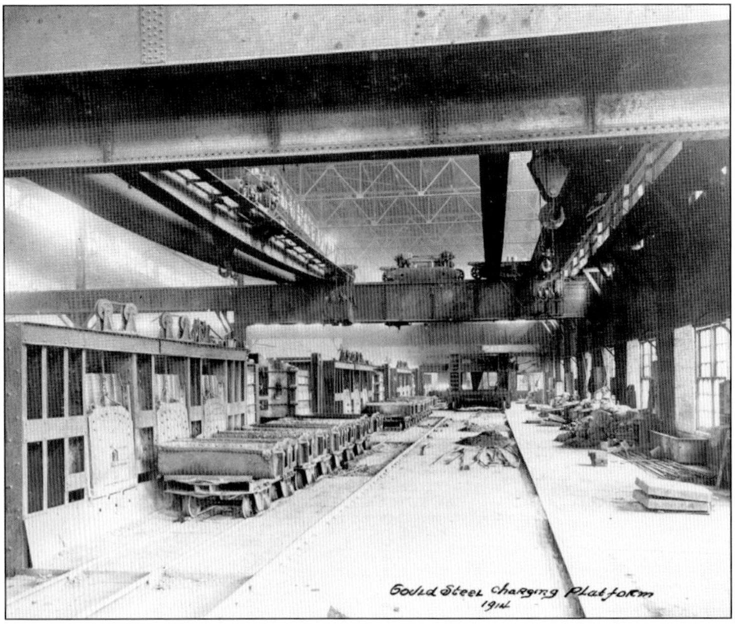


This is a charging platform where small electric railcars brought in scrap metal and dumped it into the oil-fired furnaces to heat the scrap to a temperature of around 2,800 degrees Fahrenheit. This was an absolutely essential part of the manufacturing process but inherently a dangerous operation and quality and safety were twin goals of the men who worked here. (Village of Depew Historian collection.)

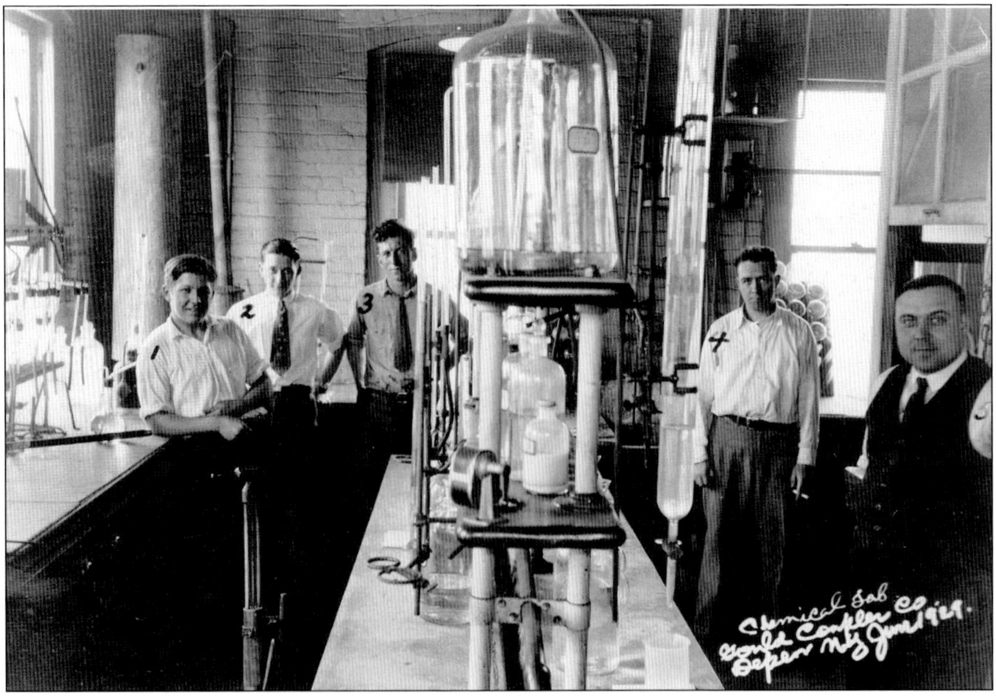


The chemical composition of the metals used in parts fabrication was a critical railroad safety factor; here in June 1929, five employees conduct the necessary analysis. Conditions in the lab are much better than for the men sweating out on the dirty work floor. The Great Depression is still four months away in an unknown future, but for now it is business as usual. (Village of Depew Historian collection.)

Here in the drop test department, a large machine could raise and drop a weight continuously to simulate the pounding, wear, and tear that a component faced while in a moving train or shifting from track to track in a freight yard. Such research helped to eliminate flaws that could cause expensive and possibly deadly train derailments. (Village of Depew Historian collection.)

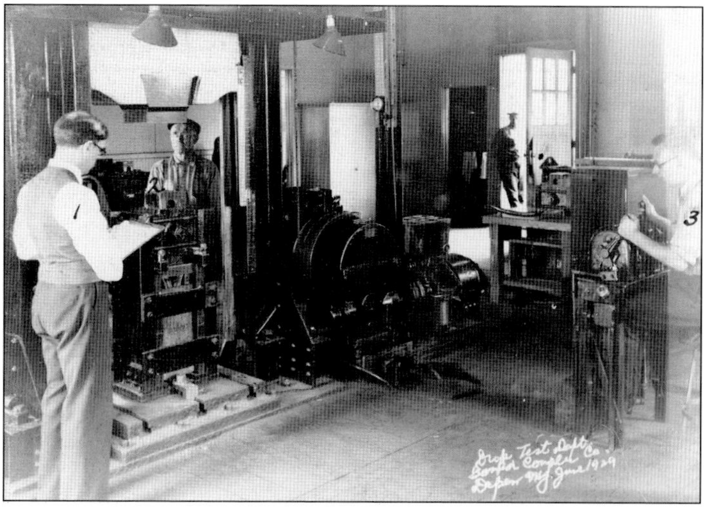

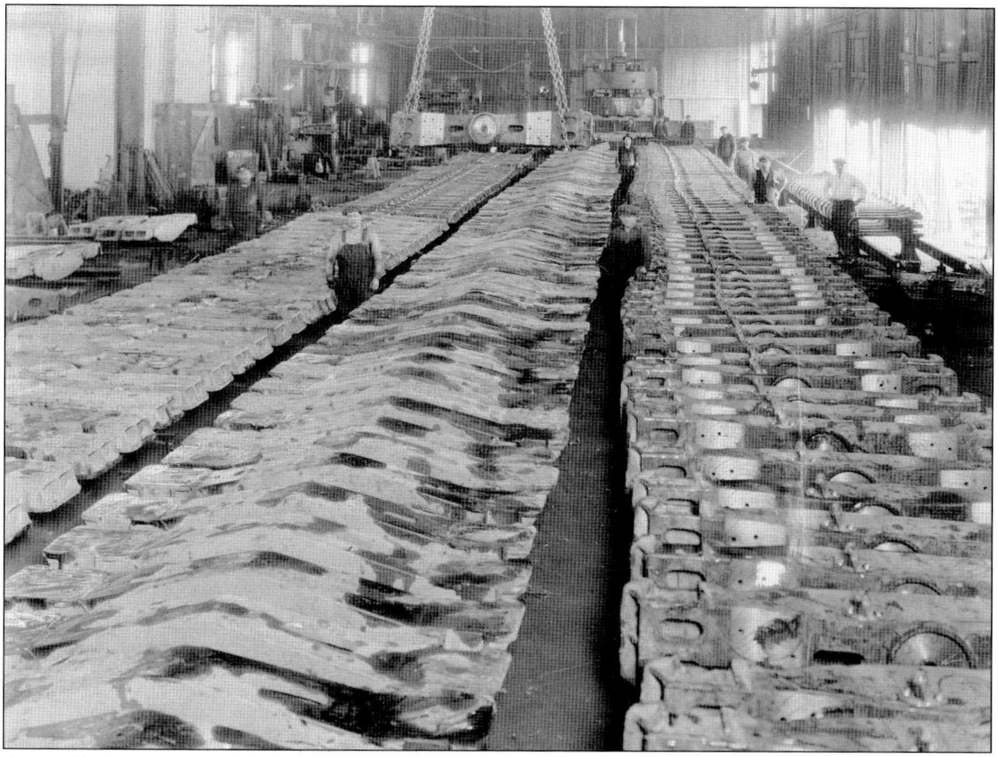

Several bolster castings are lined up and ready for shipment. A bolster is the part of the truck that sits directly under a train car at each end. It distributes the weight of the car and holds the side frames and wheels in place. The bolster is an essential element of railway truck design; they are still used today, although no longer manufactured in Buffalo. (Village of Depew Historian collection.)

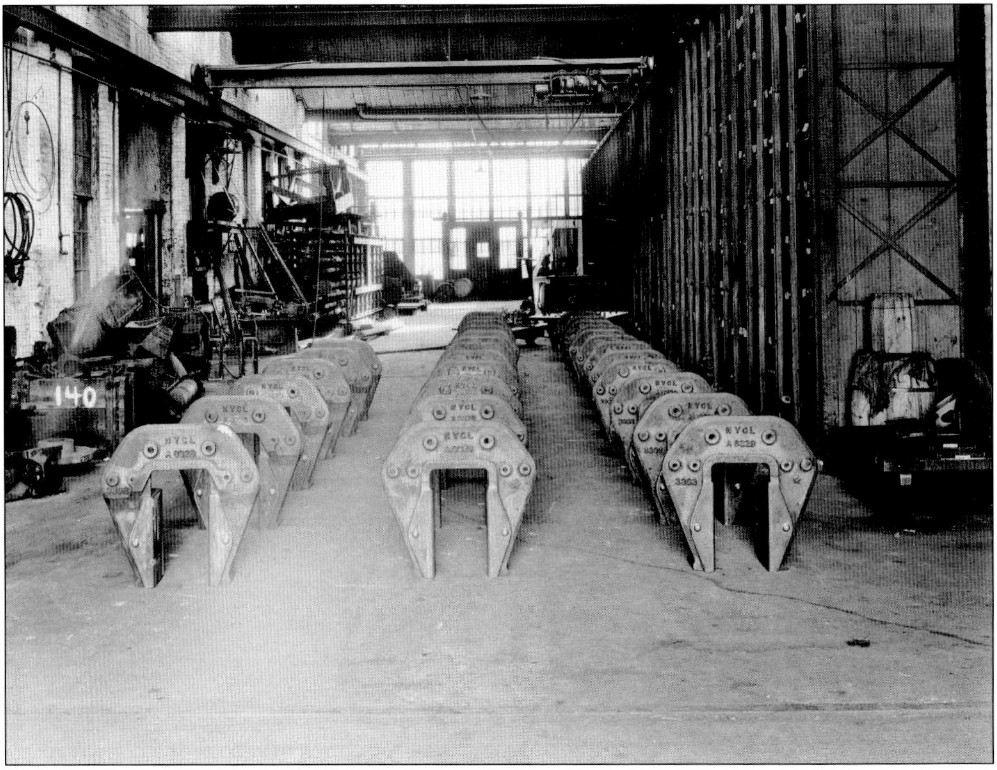


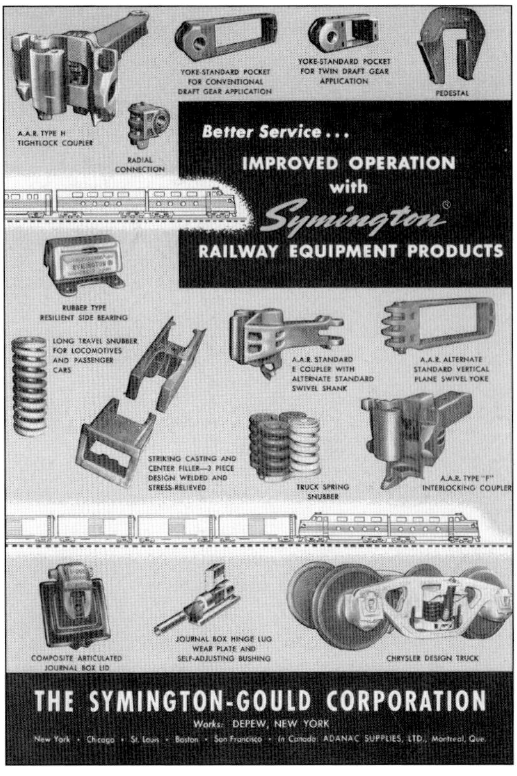


In the first three decades of the 20th century, the New York Central & Hudson River Railroad and its affiliates were collectively known as the New York Central Lines, thus "NYCL" on the rows of new pedestals in this order awaiting shipping. Gould offered the most complete line of railroad car under frame parts and was located in a strategic area to manufacture its products. (Village of Depew Historian collection.)

The factory's efforts all came together in this 1950s Symington Railway Equipment products line advertisement; it shows the several items that were manufactured at the Depew plant. The Gould Coupler Company and successors not only produced important goods to keep the railroads running, but also kept approximately 1,600 Buffalo residents employed, and in addition to the community's four railroads, it was a major taxpayer in Depew. (Village of Depew Historian collection.)

*Ten*

# Buffalo Railroads Today

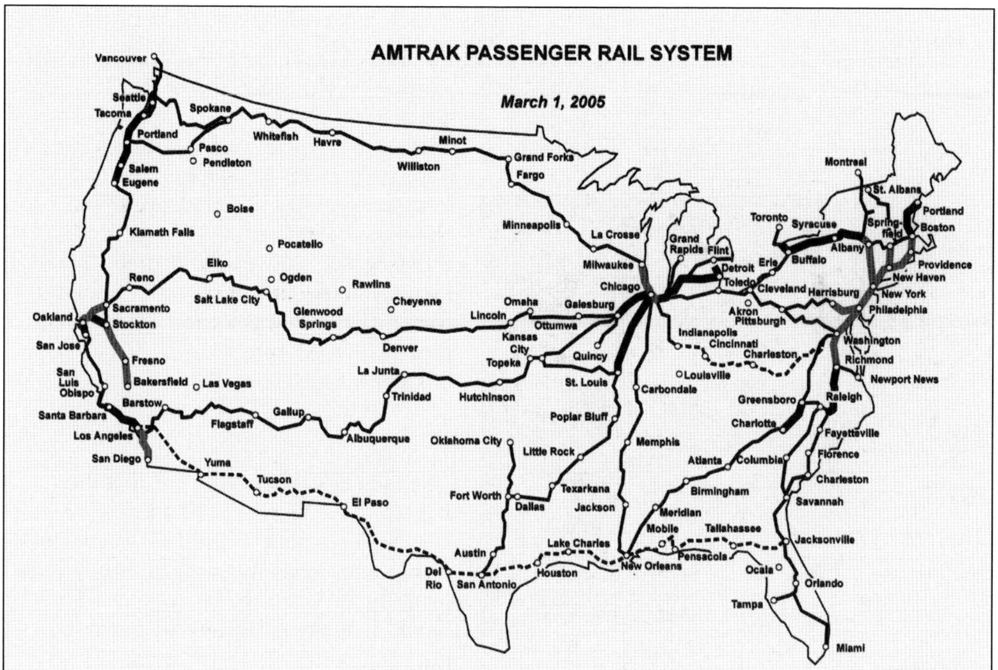


The National Railroad Passenger Corporation, otherwise known as Amtrak, serves Buffalo both at the Depew and Buffalo Exchange Street stations, as well as Niagara Falls. Amtrak is a government-owned corporation, which operates several passenger trains daily across New York State, through the United States and into Canada. Most of the daily trains serving western New York run east and west between Buffalo and Albany, New York. (National Railroad Passenger Corporation.)

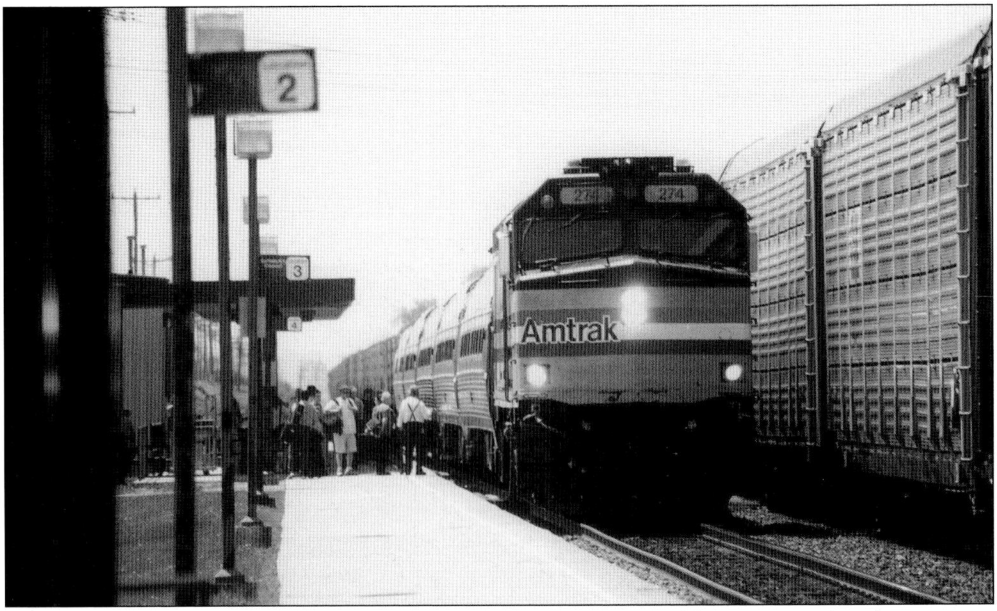


Amtrak was formed on May 1, 1971, due to the great losses incurred by private railroad companies operating passenger trains. With the inventions of the automobile and then the airplane, railroad companies continued to see a steady decline in ridership. With investment from New York state and the federal government, Amtrak upgraded the main line for speeds of up to 110 miles per hour heading to Buffalo. (Photograph by David Eagen.)

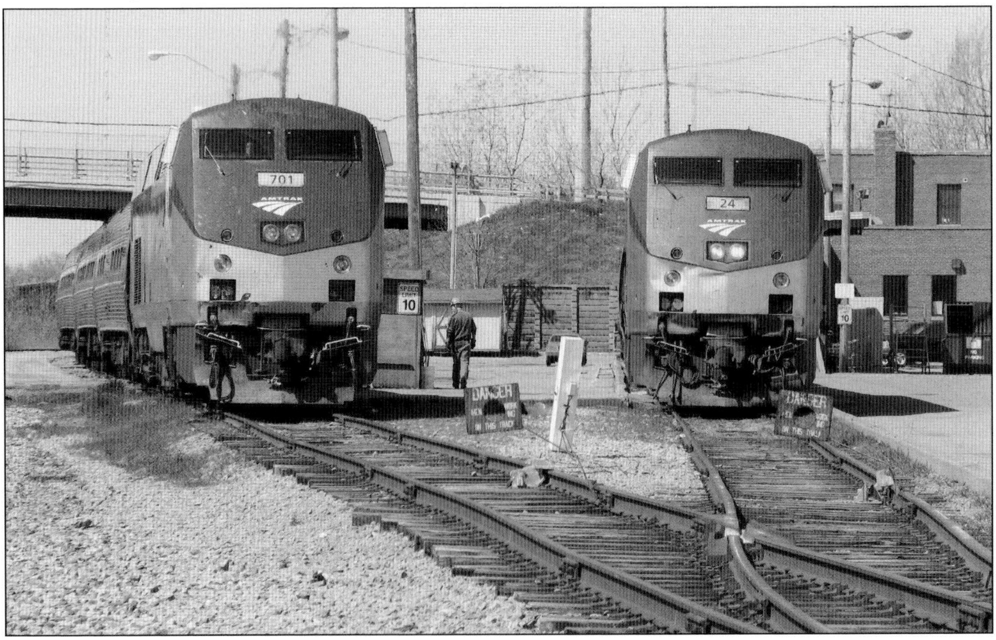


Amtrak Genesis-type locomotives No. 701 and No. 24 are being serviced in Niagara Falls on April 30, 2007, for Empire Service trains. A towering appearance belies their 14-foot-8-inch height, almost 14 inches shorter than older Amtrak locomotives. No. 701 is a 3,200-horsepower General Electric model P32AC-DM while No. 24 is a 4,250-horsepower model P42DC. Weighing 137 tons and 134 tons, respectively; both were built in Erie, Pennsylvania. (Photograph by Stephen M. Koenig.)

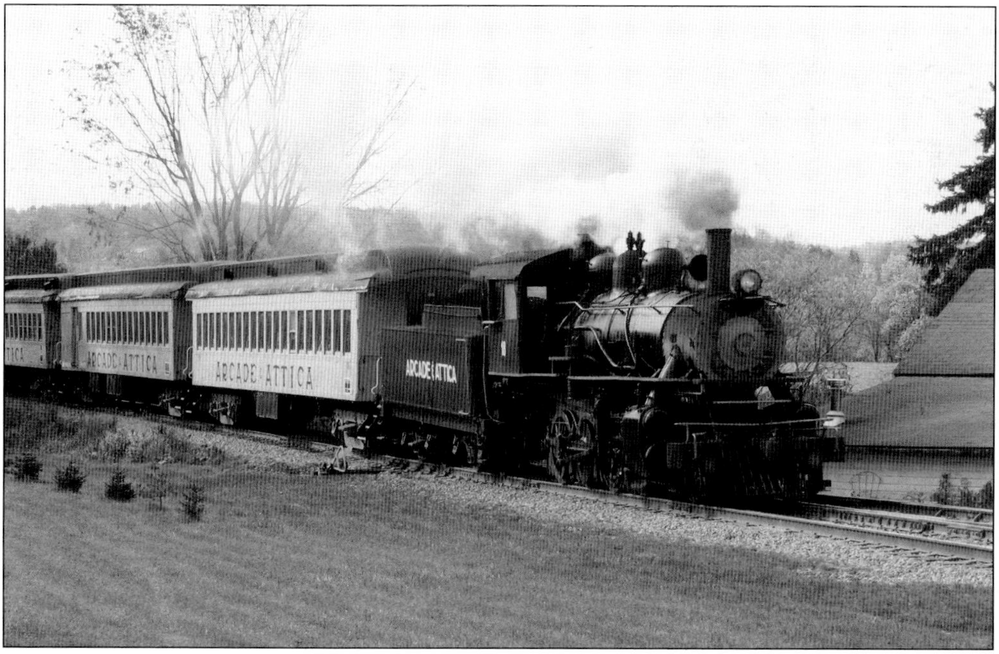

The Arcade & Attica Railroad in neighboring Wyoming County has roots back to the 1880s. The present company was formed in 1917, and by 1962, despite abandoning half its line in 1957, it was still in trouble. The A&A reinstituted steam passenger service, this time for tourists. The result became New York's most popular excursion train. In this photograph, she arrives in Curriers on October 18, 2008. (Photograph by Patrick Connors.)

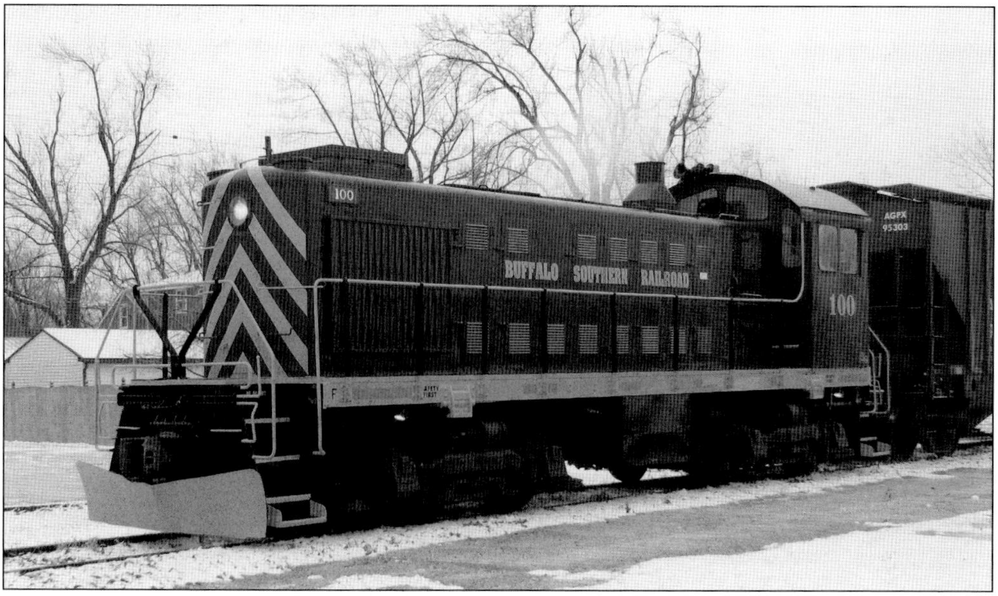

The Buffalo Southern Railway is an exclusive user of locomotives manufactured by the former American Locomotive Company, or Alco, which ceased locomotive production in January 1969. BSOR's mechanical staff has labored successfully to keep these aging engines in reliable service. BSOR 100, a 1,000-horsepower model S-2, is 63 years young here in 2008 as it waits in Blasdell to proceed north across the NS diamond at "GB" interlocking. (Photograph by Patrick Connors.)

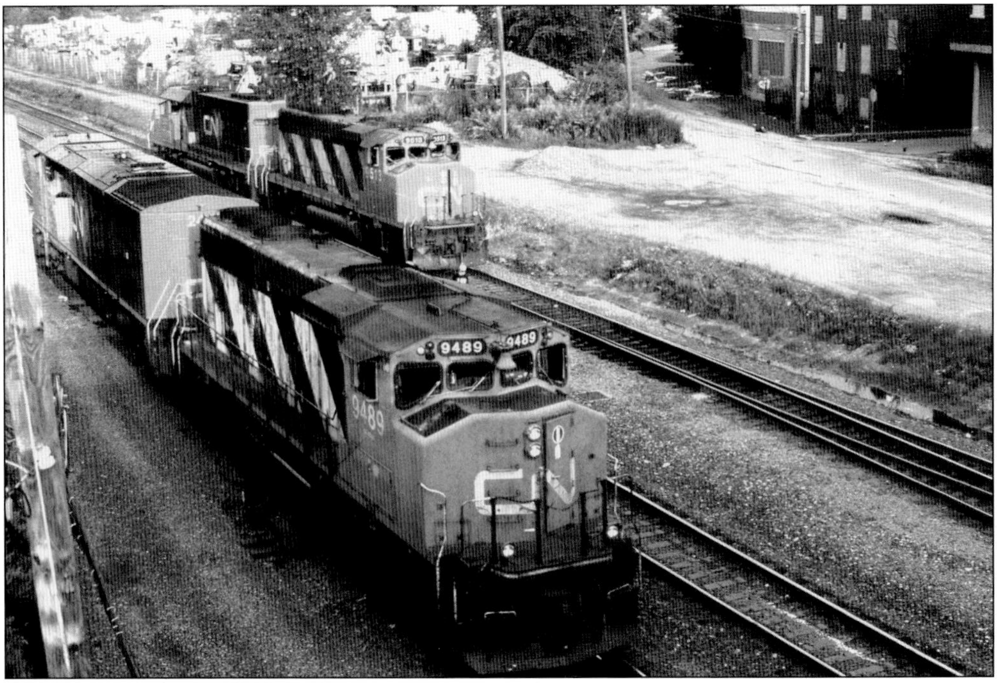

The Canadian National Railway privatized in 1985 and has expanded into the United States. Today its 20,400-mile system serves eight provinces and nine states with rails stretching from the Atlantic to the Pacific and from the Gulf of Mexico to Hudson Bay. In Buffalo, its presence is primarily to interchange freight with CSXT, Norfolk Southern, and the Buffalo & Pittsburgh. CN locomotives are ready for their assignments near Bailey Avenue in 1997. (Photograph by Stephan M. Koenig.)

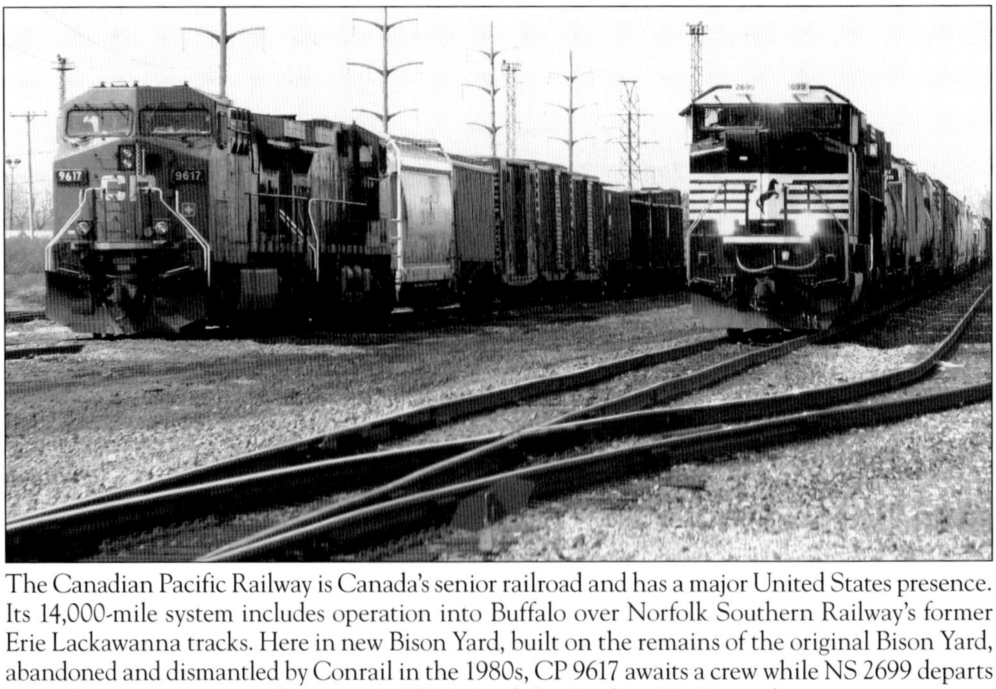

The Canadian Pacific Railway is Canada's senior railroad and has a major United States presence. Its 14,000-mile system includes operation into Buffalo over Norfolk Southern Railway's former Erie Lackawanna tracks. Here in new Bison Yard, built on the remains of the original Bison Yard, abandoned and dismantled by Conrail in the 1980s, CP 9617 awaits a crew while NS 2699 departs towards Corning, New York, in 2006. (Photograph by Stephan M. Koenig.)

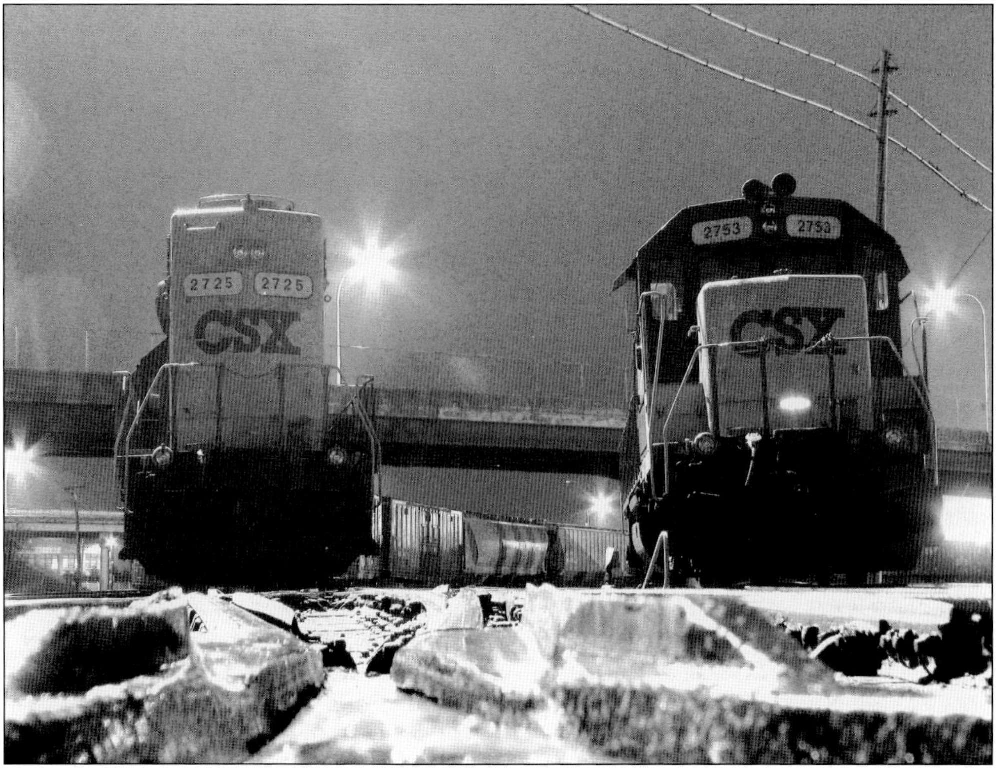


In June 1999, the split of Conrail CSXT received most of the former New York Central components and all of the Buffalo Creek Railroad. Here in 2006, CSXT locomotives 2725 and 2753 await their next assignment at Ohio Street Yard. Both are General Motors Electro-Motive Division model GP-38 2,000-horsepower locomotives manufactured for Conrail and transferred to CSXT in the 1999 division of Conrail's assets. (Photograph by Stephan M. Koenig.)

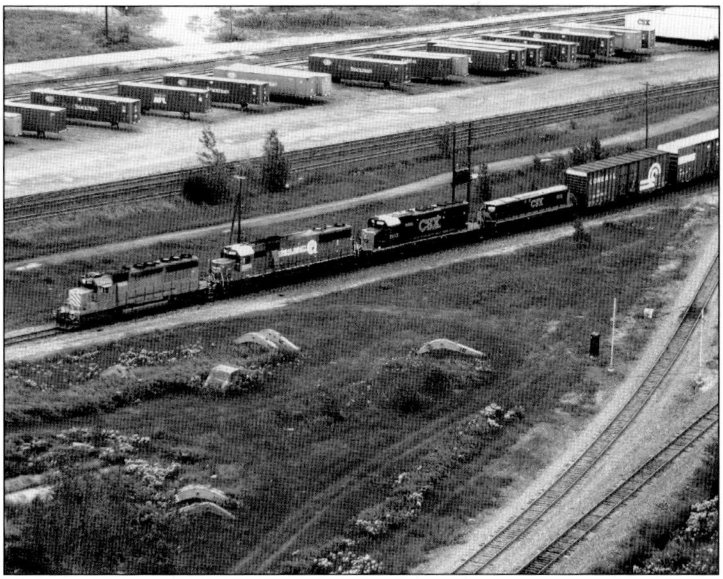

CSXT 2813, two units and a slug also known as a road mate unit lead a freight train east into Frontier Yard in this 2006 view from the office tower of the abandoned Buffalo Central Terminal. In the background intermodal trailers rest near the former Buffalo Stockyards adjacent to the Chicago Line. In the foreground are the tracks of the west leg of the Buffalo Belt Line. (Photograph by Stephan M. Koenig.)

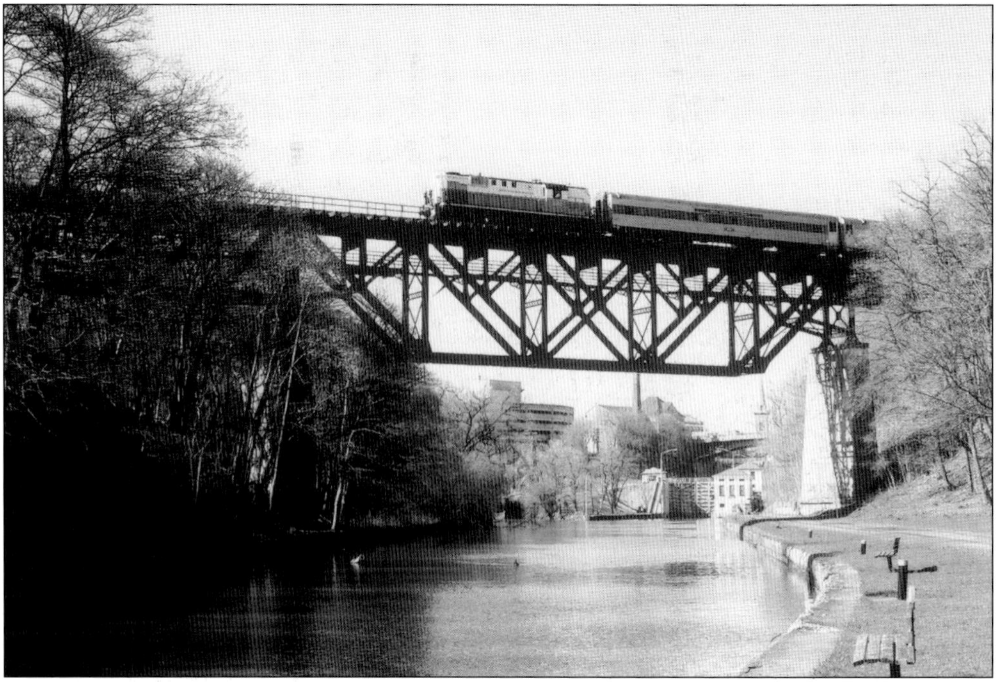

In 2007, a Falls Road Railroad excursion passenger train crosses the Erie Canal in Lockport on the famous "Upside Down" bridge. The Falls Road name derives from the Buffalo, Lockport, and Niagara Falls Railroad, or "Falls Road," opened in 1852. Conrail abandoned the east end from Brockport to Rochester in 1994 to prevent competitive access to Rochester. The Falls Road commenced operation in 1996. (Photograph by David Eagen.)

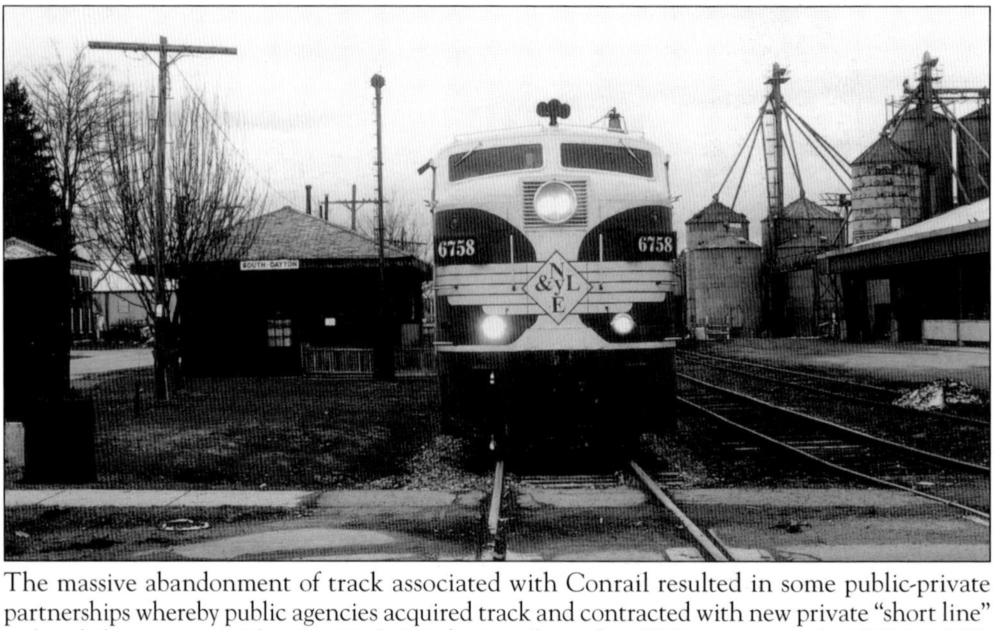


The massive abandonment of track associated with Conrail resulted in some public-private partnerships whereby public agencies acquired track and contracted with new private "short line" railroads for operation. The New York & Lake Erie, formed in 1978, is an example. NY&LE 6758, a former VIA Rail Canada FP-7, waits in South Dayton in 2003 with an excursion train. The depot was featured in the movie *The Natural*. (Photograph by David Eagen.)

Both CSXT and Norfolk Southern predecessors linked Detroit with Buffalo across southern Ontario but only NS still retains its route as demonstrated here in 2007 as NS 8365 brings its train into Black Rock over the International Bridge. From here the train's circuitous route puts it in conflict with Amtrak trains. Conrail abandoned the former Erie Lackawanna Railroad direct route. (Photograph by Stephen M. Koenig.)

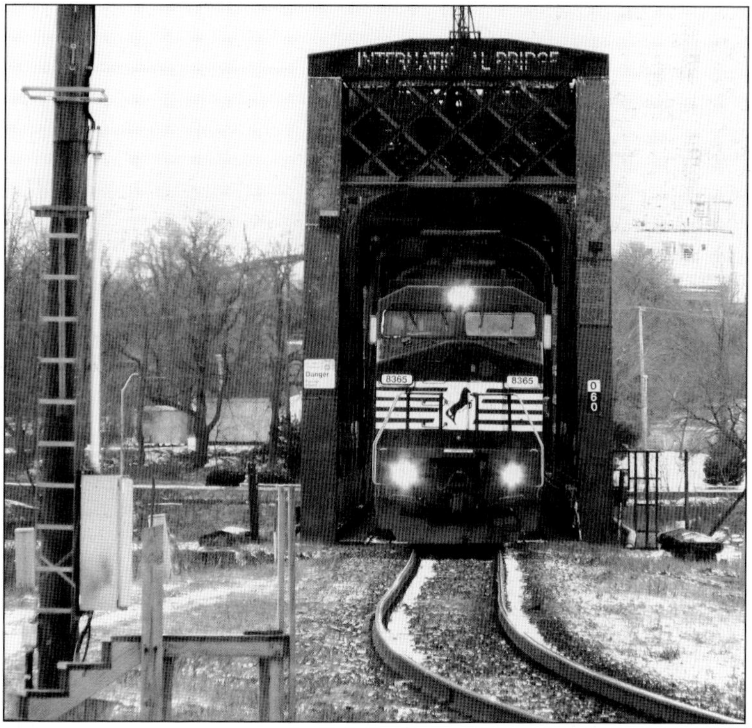

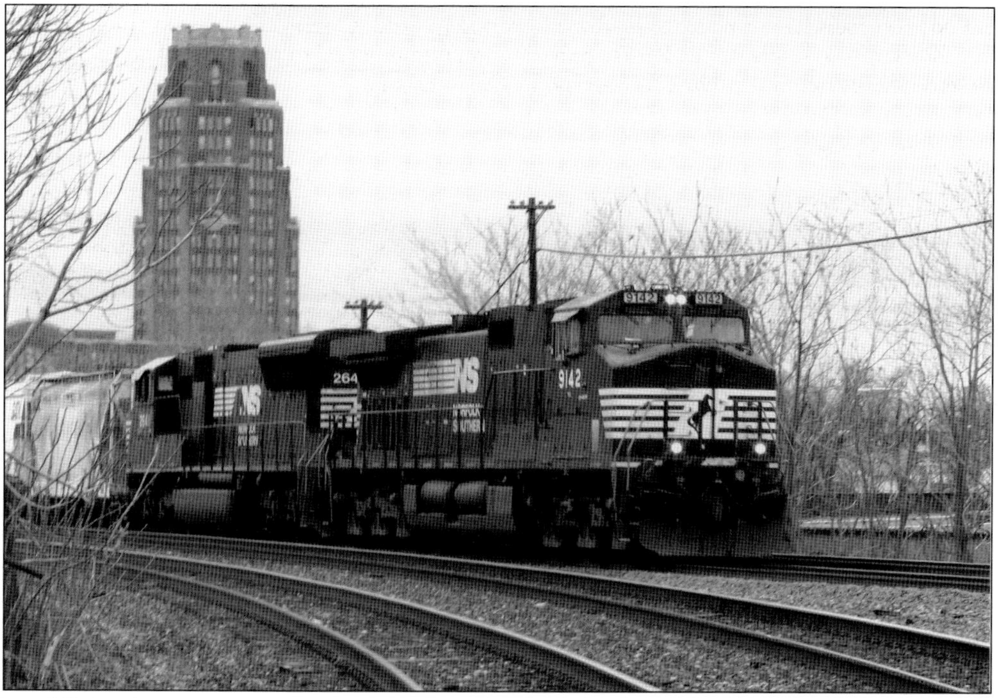

Norfolk Southern engines 9142 and 2641 are on the CSXT belt line track leading a train west of the derelict Buffalo Central Terminal in 2009. From here the train will travel on the former Pennsylvania Railroad to "FW" where it will reach the former Erie Railroad, now NS, for a short trip to the rebuilt Bison Yard in Sloan for classification and forwarding. (Photograph by Stephen M. Koenig.)

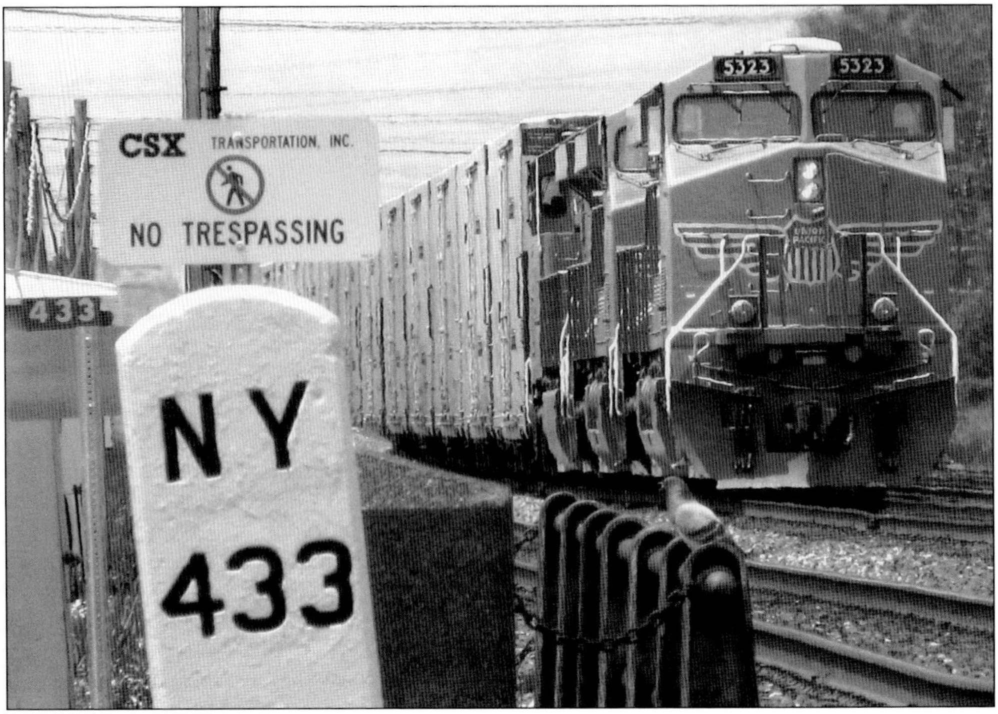


The "No Trespassing" sign says "CSX," the locomotives say "Union Pacific," and the milepost's "NY 433" hearkens to the former New York Central's Grand Central Terminal in the heart of Manhattan, 433 miles east, but this scene of contemporary 2007 railroading is illustrative of motive-power run-throughs and railroad consolidation. This is a CSX train of perishable fruits and vegetables for east coast markets and groceries. (Photograph by Stephan M. Koenig.)

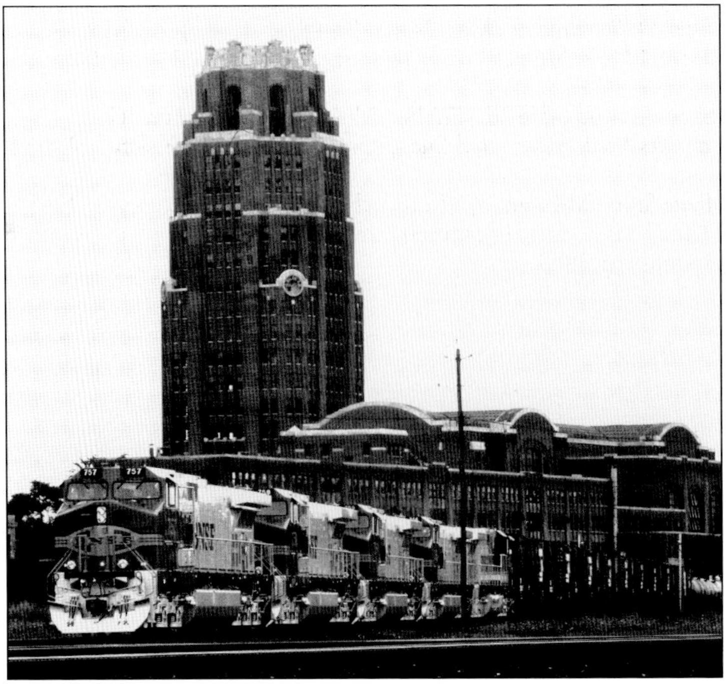


Burlington Northern Santa Fe Railway, like its western competitor, the Union Pacific Railroad, participates in many locomotive run-through agreements with other railroads. Here in 1997, BNSF 757 and three sisters lead a westbound CSXT freight train by the abandoned Buffalo Central Terminal. Buffalo railroading is still alive and well; they still employ many in the area and make an interesting hobby for the railroad enthusiasts. (Photograph by Stephan M. Koenig.)

# BIBLIOGRAPHY

Archer, Robert F. *The History of the Lehigh Valley Railroad.* Berkeley, CA: Howell North Books, 1977.

Dunn SJ, Rev. Edward T. *A History of Railroads in Western New York.* Buffalo, NY: The Heritage Press, 1996.

Edson, William D. *Keystone Steam & Electric.* New York: Wayner Publications, 1974.

Gordon, William R. *Buffalo & Lake Erie Traction Company 1906–1934.* Albion, NY; Eddy Printing Company, 1977.

Gordon, William R. *Ninety Years of Buffalo Railways.* Rochester, NY: self-published, 1970.

Koenig, Stephen M. *South Buffalo Railway.* David City, NE: South Platte Press/ Brueggenjohann/ Reese, Inc., 2004.

Leary, Thomas E., and Elizabeth C. Sholes. *From Fire to Rust: Business, Technology, and Work at the Lackawanna Steel Plant, 1899–1983.* Buffalo, NY: Buffalo and Erie County Historical Society, 1987.

Mott, Edward Harold. *The Story of Erie.* New York: Ticker Publishing Company, 1908.

Pietrak, Paul. *Buffalo, Rochester & Pittsburgh Railway.* North Boston, NY; self-published, 1979.

———. *The History of The Buffalo & Susquehanna.* Hamburg, NY: self-published, 1966, 5th printing 1995.

Pietrak, Paul V., Joseph G. Streamer and James A. Van Brocklin. *The History of the Western New York Railway Company and its Predecessors and Successors.* Hamburg, NY: self-published, 2000.

Rehor, John A. *The Nickel Plate Story.* Milwaukee, WI: Kalmbach Publishing Company, 1965.

Tabor, Thomas Townsend III. *The Delaware, Lackawanna & Western Railroad in the Twentieth Century.* Muncy, PA; self-published, 1980.